SUPER HOROSCOPE
VIRGO
2003
AUGUST 22–SEPTEMBER 22

BERKLEY BOOKS, NEW YORK

A Berkley Book
Published by The Berkley Publishing Group
A division of Penguin Putnam Inc.
375 Hudson Street
New York, New York 10014

2003 SUPER HOROSCOPE VIRGO

The publishers regret that they cannot answer
individual letters requesting personal horoscope information.

PRINTING HISTORY
Berkley trade paperback edition / July 2002

Berkley trade paperback ISBN: 0-425-18485-4

ISSN: 1535-9018

Visit our website at
www.penguinputnam.com

CONTENTS

THE CUSP-BORN VIRGO

Are you *really* a Virgo? If your birthday falls during the fourth week of August, at the beginning of Virgo, will you still retain the traits of Leo, the sign of the Zodiac before Virgo? And what if you were born late in September—are you more Libra than Virgo? Many people born at the edge, or cusp, of a sign have great difficulty determining exactly what sign they are. If you are one of these people, here's how you can figure it out, once and for all.

Consult the cusp table on the facing page, then locate the year of your birth. The table will tell you the precise days on which the Sun entered and left your sign for the year of your birth. In that way you can determine if you are a true Virgo—or whether you are a Leo or Libra—according to the variations in cusp dates from year to year (see also page 17).

If you were born either at the beginning or the end of Virgo, yours is a lifetime reflecting a process of subtle transformation. Your life on earth will symbolize a significant change in consciousness, for you are either about to enter a whole new way of living or are leaving one behind.

If you were born at the beginning of Virgo, you may want to read the horoscope book for Leo as well as Virgo, for Leo holds the key to much of your complexity of spirit, reflects certain hidden weaknesses and compulsions, and your unspoken wishes. Your tie to Leo symbolizes your romantic dilemma and your unusual—often timid—approach to love. You are afraid of taking a gamble and letting everything ride on your emotions. You may resist giving up the rational, logical, clear-minded approach to life, but you can never really flee from your need for love.

You symbolize the warmth and fullness of a late summer day, a natural ripeness and maturity that is mellow and comfortable to be near.

If you were born sometime after the third week of September, you may want to read the horoscope book for Libra as well as Virgo, for Libra is possibly your greatest asset. Though you are eager to get involved with another person and you crave warmth and companionship, you may hover between stiff mental analyzing and poetic romanticism. You have that Garboesque desire to be secluded, untouched—yet you want to share your life with another. You are a blend of monastic, spartan simplicity with grace,

4

harmony, and gentle beauty. You combine a profound power to sift, purify, and analyze with the sensibilities of recognizing what is right, beautiful, and just. You can be picky and faultfinding, inconsistent and small, needing someone desperately but rejecting the one you love most. Yet you are fundamentally a thoughtful, loving person with the sincere wish to serve and make someone happy.

Developing your capacity to share will aid you in joint financial ventures, bring your values into harmony, and create a balance in your life.

THE CUSPS OF VIRGO

DATES SUN ENTERS VIRGO (LEAVES LEO)

August 23 every year from 1900 to 2010, except for the following:

August 22				August 24	
1960	1980	1992	2001	1903	1919
64	84	93	2004	07	23
68	88	96	2005	11	27
72	89	97	2008	15	
76		2000	2009		

DATES SUN LEAVES VIRGO (ENTERS LIBRA)

September 23 every year from 1900 to 2010, except for the following:

September 22					September 24
1948	1968	1981	1992	2001	1903
52	72	84	93	2004	07
56	76	85	96	2005	
60	77	88	97	2008	
64	80	89	2000	2009	

THE ASCENDANT: VIRGO RISING

Could you be a "double" Virgo? That is, could you have Virgo as your Rising sign as well as your Sun sign? The tables on pages 8–9 will tell you Virgos what your Rising sign happens to be. Just find the hour of your birth, then find the day of your birth, and you will see which sign of the Zodiac is your Ascendant, as the Rising sign is called. The Ascendant is called that because it is the sign rising on the eastern horizon at the time of your birth. For a more detailed discussion of the Rising sign and the twelve houses of the Zodiac, see pages 17–20.

The Ascendant, or Rising sign, is placed on the 1st house in a horoscope, of which there are twelve houses. The first house represents your response to the environment—your unique response. Call it identity, personality, ego, self-image, facade, come-on, body-mind-spirit—whatever term best conveys to you the meaning of the you that acts and reacts in the world. It is a you that is always changing, discovering a new you. Your identity started with birth and early environment, over which you had little conscious control, and continues to experience, to adjust, to express itself. The 1st house also represents how others see you. Has anyone ever guessed your sign to be your Rising sign? People may respond to that personality, that facade, that body type governed by your Rising sign.

Your Ascendant, or Rising sign, modifies your basic Sun sign personality, and it affects the way you act out the daily predictions for your Sun sign. If your Rising sign is indeed Virgo, what follows is a description of its effects on your horoscope. If your Rising sign is not Virgo, but some other sign of the Zodiac, you may wish to read the horoscope book for that sign as well.

With Virgo on the Ascendant, that is, in the 1st house, your ruling planet Mercury is therefore in the 1st house. You are known for your inquiring mind, sharp verbal skills, love of learning. Your very appearance—fastidious, lean, efficient—gives the impression of a great openness to the environment; you seem to pick up clues from the most cursory observations, filing them away for future use. Mercury in the 1st house, however, can make you too self-absorbed with your own interests and thus lacking in sympathy for other people. And your quick wit and loquaciousness, if put into the service of petty gossip, could make you a tattletale who gets in trouble with people.

Your striving for perfection and your liking for details make many of you with Virgo Rising master craftspeople. That talent is not restricted to the arts of fashioning jewelry, fabric, metals, food, and other materials of the earth, though you are an earth sign. Mercury, your ruler, gives you a quicksilver mind, and you excel in the mathematical and scientific arts. Your memory is splendid, too. If you are not actually working in complex systems such as computer science or engineering, your talent for organizing details and structuring information certainly benefits your work life, as well as your social life.

Your love of learning has few boundaries, and no limits if you with Virgo Rising consistently apply yourself. You are equally attracted to medicine, art, science, literature. Your analytical mind, scalpel-sharp, can cut through a mass of confused information, selecting the wheat from the chaff, so to speak. Certainly you can distinguish theory from practice, and you know when and how to use the practice. Many of you, for that reason, and also because you like to help people, find yourselves in health and medical service careers.

Personally you are interested in the perfection of the body and the purity of the mind. Translated into everyday activities, you could be very fussy about your diet, your clothes, your living quarters, your spiritual beliefs, your exercise programs. It is not unlikely that you experiment often in these areas, and sometimes you're accused of being a faddist. If you cannot change where you live frequently, you'll be satisfied to take a few long trips and many short ones during your lifetime.

Basically you are patient, methodical, ambitious sometimes in a secretive way. Your caustic wit, which strips the facade from people, hides your true feelings and melancholy of spirit. As much as you like to quip in bright dialogue with others, you like to be alone. Even your travels can be solitary adventures; you commune with the nature around you. Some of these experiences may motivate an in-depth study of art and literature at some point in your lifetime. And you may well become a writer, merging a myriad of facts with personal data you are loathe to talk about.

For you with Virgo Rising, two key words are self-mastery and service. But while you are perfecting your knowledge and skills in serving others, don't forget your own needs. Develop compassion for yourself.

RISING SIGNS FOR VIRGO

Hour of Birth*	Day of Birth		
	August 22–26	August 27–31	September 1–5
Midnight	Gemini	Gemini	Cancer
1 AM	Cancer	Cancer	Cancer
2 AM	Cancer	Cancer	Cancer
3 AM	Leo	Leo	Leo
4 AM	Leo	Leo	Leo
5 AM	Leo	Leo; Virgo 8/31	Virgo
6 AM	Virgo	Virgo	Virgo
7 AM	Virgo	Virgo	Virgo
8 AM	Libra	Libra	Libra
9 AM	Libra	Libra	Libra
10 AM	Libra	Libra; Scorpio 8/29	Scorpio
11 AM	Scorpio	Scorpio	Scorpio
Noon	Scorpio	Scorpio	Scorpio
1 PM	Sagittarius	Sagittarius	Sagittarius
2 PM	Sagittarius	Sagittarius	Sagittarius
3 PM	Sagittarius	Capricorn	Capricorn
4 PM	Capricorn	Capricorn	Capricorn
5 PM	Capricorn; Aquarius 8/26	Aquarius	Aquarius
6 PM	Aquarius	Aquarius	Aquarius; Pisces 9/3
7 PM	Pisces	Pisces	Pisces
8 PM	Aries	Aries	Aries
9 PM	Aries; Taurus 8/26	Taurus	Taurus
10 PM	Taurus	Taurus	Taurus; Gemini 9/3
11 PM	Gemini	Gemini	Gemini

*Hour of birth given here is for Standard Time in any time zone. If your hour of birth was recorded in Daylight Saving Time, subtract one hour from it and consult that hour in the table above. For example, if you were born at 7 PM D.S.T., see 6 PM above.

Hour of Birth*	Day of Birth		
	September 6–10	September 11–15	September 16–24
Midnight	Cancer	Cancer	Cancer
1 AM	Cancer	Cancer	Cancer; Leo 9/21
2 AM	Leo	Leo	Leo
3 AM	Leo	Leo	Leo
4 AM	Leo	Leo; Virgo 9/14	Virgo
5 AM	Virgo	Virgo	Virgo
6 AM	Virgo	Virgo	Virgo; Libra 9/21
7 AM	Libra	Libra	Libra
8 AM	Libra	Libra	Libra
9 AM	Libra	Scorpio	Scorpio
10 AM	Scorpio	Scorpio	Scorpio
11 AM	Scorpio	Scorpio	Scorpio; Sagittarius 9/21
Noon	Sagittarius	Sagittarius	Sagittarius
1 PM	Sagittarius	Sagittarius	Sagittarius
2 PM	Sagittarius	Capricorn	Capricorn
3 PM	Capricorn	Capricorn	Capricorn
4 PM	Capricorn; Aquarius 9/10	Aquarius	Aquarius
5 PM	Aquarius	Aquarius	Pisces
6 PM	Pisces	Pisces	Pisces; Aries 9/21
7 PM	Aries	Aries	Aries
8 PM	Aries; Taurus 9/10	Taurus	Taurus
9 PM	Taurus	Taurus	Gemini
10 PM	Gemini	Gemini	Gemini
11 PM	Gemini	Gemini	Cancer

*See note on facing page.

THE PLACE OF ASTROLOGY IN TODAY'S WORLD

Does astrology have a place in the fast-moving, ultra-scientific world we live in today? Can it be justified in a sophisticated society whose outriders are already preparing to step off the moon into the deep space of the planets themselves? Or is it just a hangover of ancient superstition, a psychological dummy for neurotics and dreamers of every historical age?

These are the kind of questions that any inquiring person can be expected to ask when they approach a subject like astrology which goes beyond, but never excludes, the materialistic side of life.

The simple, single answer is that astrology works. It works for many millions of people in the western world alone. In the United States there are 10 million followers and in Europe, an estimated 25 million. America has more than 4000 practicing astrologers, Europe nearly three times as many. Even down-under Australia has its hundreds of thousands of adherents. In the eastern countries, astrology has enormous followings, again, because it has been proved to work. In India, for example, brides and grooms for centuries have been chosen on the basis of their astrological compatibility.

Astrology today is more vital than ever before, more practicable because all over the world the media devotes much space and time to it, more valid because science itself is confirming the precepts of astrological knowledge with every new exciting step. The ordinary person who daily applies astrology intelligently does not have to wonder whether it is true nor believe in it blindly. He can see it working for himself. And, if he can use it—and this book is designed to help the reader to do just that—he can make living a far richer experience, and become a more developed personality and a better person.

Astrology and Relationships

Astrology is the science of relationships. It is not just a study of planetary influences on man and his environment. It is the study of man himself.

We are at the center of our personal universe, of all our relationships. And our happiness or sadness depends on how we act, how we relate to the people and things that surround us. The emotions that we generate have a distinct effect—for better or worse—on the world around us. Our friends and our enemies will confirm this. Just look in the mirror the next time you are angry. In other words, each of us is a kind of sun or planet or star radiating our feelings on the environment around us. Our influence on our personal universe, whether loving, helpful, or destructive, varies with our changing moods, expressed through our individual character.

Our personal "radiations" are potent in the way they affect our moods and our ability to control them. But we usually are able to throw off our emotion in some sort of action—we have a good cry, walk it off, or tell someone our troubles—before it can build up too far and make us physically ill. Astrology helps us to understand the universal forces working on us, and through this understanding, we can become more properly adjusted to our surroundings so that we find ourselves coping where others may flounder.

The Challenge of Love

The challenge of love lies in recognizing the difference between infatuation, emotion, sex, and, sometimes, the intentional deceit of the other person. Mankind, with its record of broken marriages, despair, and disillusionment, is obviously not very good at making these distinctions.

Can astrology help?

Yes. In the same way that advance knowledge can usually help in any human situation. And there is probably no situation as human, as poignant, as pathetic and universal, as the failure of man's love.

Love, of course, is not just between man and woman. It involves love of children, parents, home, and friends. But the big problems usually involve the choice of partner.

Astrology has established degrees of compatibility that exist between people born under the various signs of the Zodiac. Because people are individuals, there are numerous variations and modifications. So the astrologer, when approached on mate and marriage matters, makes allowances for them. But the fact remains that some groups of people are suited for each other and some are not, and astrology has expressed this in terms of characteristics we all can study and use as a personal guide.

No matter how much enjoyment and pleasure we find in the different aspects of each other's character, if it is not an overall compatibility, the chances of our finding fulfillment or enduring happiness in each other are pretty hopeless. And astrology can help us to find someone compatible.

Astrology and Science

Closely related to our emotions is the "other side" of our personal universe, our physical welfare. Our body, of course, is largely influenced by things around us over which we have very little control. The phone rings, we hear it. The train runs late. We snag our stocking or cut our face shaving. Our body is under a constant bombardment of events that influence our daily lives to varying degrees.

The question that arises from all this is, what makes each of us act so that we have to involve other people and keep the ball of activity and evolution rolling? This is the question that both science and astrology are involved with. The scientists have attacked it from different angles: anthropology, the study of human evolution as body, mind and response to environment; anatomy, the study of bodily structure; psychology, the science of the human mind; and so on. These studies have produced very impressive classifications and valuable information, but because the approach to the problem is fragmented, so is the result. They remain "branches" of science. Science generally studies effects. It keeps turning up wonderful answers but no lasting solutions. Astrology, on the other hand, approaches the question from the broader viewpoint. Astrology began its inquiry with the totality of human experience and saw it as an effect. It then looked to find the cause, or at least the prime movers, and during thousands of years of observation of man and his *universal* environment came up with the extraordinary principle of planetary influence—or astrology, which, from the Greek, means the science of the stars.

Modern science, as we shall see, has confirmed much of astrology's foundations—most of it unintentionally, some of it reluctantly, but still, indisputably.

It is not difficult to imagine that there must be a connection between outer space and Earth. Even today, scientists are not too sure how our Earth was created, but it is generally agreed that it is only a tiny part of the universe. And as a part of the universe, people on Earth see and feel the influence of heavenly bodies in almost every aspect of our existence. There is no doubt that the Sun has the greatest influence on life on this planet. Without it there would be no life, for without it there would be no warmth, no division into day and night, no cycles of time or season at all. This is clear and easy to see. The influence of the Moon, on the other hand, is more subtle, though no less definite.

There are many ways in which the influence of the Moon manifests itself here on Earth, both on human and animal life. It is a well-known fact, for instance, that the large movements of water on our planet—that is the ebb and flow of the tides—are caused by the Moon's gravitational pull. Since this is so, it follows that these water movements do not occur only in the oceans, but that all bodies of water are affected, even down to the tiniest puddle.

The human body, too, which consists of about 70 percent water, falls within the scope of this lunar influence. For example the menstrual cycle of most women corresponds to the 28-day lunar month; the period of pregnancy in humans is 273 days, or equal to nine lunar months. Similarly, many illnesses reach a crisis at the change of the Moon, and statistics in many countries have shown that the crime rate is highest at the time of the Full Moon. Even human sexual desire has been associated with the phases of the Moon. But it is in the movement of the tides that we get the clearest demonstration of planetary influence, which leads to the irresistible correspondence between the so-called metaphysical and the physical.

Tide tables are prepared years in advance by calculating the future positions of the Moon. Science has known for a long time that the Moon is the main cause of tidal action. But only in the last few years has it begun to realize the possible extent of this influence on mankind. To begin with, the ocean tides do not rise and fall as we might imagine from our personal observations of them. The Moon as it orbits around Earth sets up a circular wave of attraction which pulls the oceans of the world after it, broadly in an east to west direction. This influence is like a phantom wave crest, a loop of power stretching from pole to pole which passes over and around the Earth like an invisible shadow. It travels with equal effect across the land masses and, as scientists were recently amazed to observe, caused oysters placed in the dark in the middle of the United States where there is no sea to open their shells to receive the nonexistent tide. If the land-locked oysters react to this invisible signal, what effect does it have on us who not so long ago in evolutionary time came out of the sea and still have its salt in our blood and sweat?

Less well known is the fact that the Moon is also the primary force behind the circulation of blood in human beings and animals, and the movement of sap in trees and plants. Agriculturists have established that the Moon has a distinct influence on crops, which explains why for centuries people have planted according to Moon cycles. The habits of many animals, too, are directed by the movement of the Moon. Migratory birds, for instance, depart only at or near the time of the Full Moon. And certain sea creatures, eels in particular, move only in accordance with certain phases of the Moon.

Know Thyself—Why?

In today's fast-changing world, everyone still longs to know what the future holds. It is the one thing that everyone has in common: rich and poor, famous and infamous, all are deeply concerned about tomorrow.

But the key to the future, as every historian knows, lies in the past. This is as true of individual people as it is of nations. You cannot understand your future without first understanding your past, which is simply another way of saying that you must first of all know yourself.

The motto "know thyself" seems obvious enough nowadays, but it was originally put forward as the foundation of wisdom by the ancient Greek philosophers. It was then adopted by the "mystery religions" of the ancient Middle East, Greece, Rome, and is still used in all genuine schools of mind training or mystical discipline, both in those of the East, based on yoga, and those of the West. So it is universally accepted now, and has been through the ages.

But how do you go about discovering what sort of person you are? The first step is usually classification into some sort of system of types. Astrology did this long before the birth of Christ. Psychology has also done it. So has modern medicine, in its way.

One system classifies people according to the source of the impulses they respond to most readily: the muscles, leading to direct bodily action; the digestive organs, resulting in emotion; or the brain and nerves, giving rise to thinking. Another such system says that character is determined by the endocrine glands, and gives us such labels as "pituitary," "thyroid," and "hyperthyroid" types. These different systems are neither contradictory nor mutually exclusive. In fact, they are very often different ways of saying the same thing.

Very popular, useful classifications were devised by Carl Jung, the eminent disciple of Freud. Jung observed among the different faculties of the mind, four which have a predominant influence on character. These four faculties exist in all of us without exception, but not in perfect balance. So when we say, for instance, that someone is a "thinking type," it means that in any situation he or she tries to be rational. Emotion, which may be the opposite of thinking, will be his or her weakest function. This thinking type can be sensible and reasonable, or calculating and unsympathetic. The emotional type, on the other hand, can often be recognized by exaggerated language—everything is either marvelous or terrible—and in extreme cases they even invent dramas and quarrels out of nothing just to make life more interesting.

The other two faculties are intuition and physical sensation. The sensation type does not only care for food and drink, nice clothes and furniture; he or she is also interested in all forms of physical experience. Many scientists are sensation types as are athletes and nature-lovers. Like sensation, intuition is a form of perception and we all possess it. But it works through that part of the mind which is not under conscious control—consequently it sees meanings and connections which are not obvious to thought or emotion. Inventors and original thinkers are always intuitive, but so, too, are superstitious people who see meanings where none exist.

Thus, sensation tells us what is going on in the world, feeling (that is, emotion) tells us how important it is to ourselves, thinking enables us to interpret it and work out what we should do about it, and intuition tells us what it means to ourselves and others. All four faculties are essential, and all are present in every one of us. But some people are guided chiefly by one, others by another. In addition, Jung also observed a division of the human personality into the extrovert and the introvert, which cuts across these four types.

A disadvantage of all these systems of classification is that one cannot tell very easily where to place oneself. Some people are reluctant to admit that they act to please their emotions. So they deceive themselves for years by trying to belong to whichever type they think is the "best." Of course, there is no best; each has its faults and each has its good points.

The advantage of the signs of the Zodiac is that they simplify classification. Not only that, but your date of birth is personal—it is unarguably yours. What better way to know yourself than by going back as far as possible to the very moment of your birth? And this is precisely what your horoscope is all about, as we shall see in the next section.

WHAT IS A HOROSCOPE?

If you had been able to take a picture of the skies at the moment of your birth, that photograph would be your horoscope. Lacking such a snapshot, it is still possible to recreate the picture—and this is at the basis of the astrologer's art. In other words, your horoscope is a representation of the skies with the planets in the exact positions they occupied at the time you were born.

The year of birth tells an astrologer the positions of the distant, slow-moving planets Jupiter, Saturn, Uranus, Neptune, and Pluto. The month of birth indicates the Sun sign, or birth sign as it is commonly called, as well as indicating the positions of the rapidly moving planets Venus, Mercury, and Mars. The day and time of birth will locate the position of our Moon. And the moment—the exact hour and minute—of birth determines the houses through what is called the Ascendant, or Rising sign.

With this information the astrologer consults various tables to calculate the specific positions of the Sun, Moon, and other planets relative to your birthplace at the moment you were born. Then he or she locates them by means of the Zodiac.

The Zodiac

The Zodiac is a band of stars (constellations) in the skies, centered on the Sun's apparent path around the Earth, and is divided into twelve equal segments, or signs. What we are actually dividing up is the Earth's path around the Sun. But from our point of view here on Earth, it seems as if the Sun is making a great circle around our planet in the sky, so we say it is the Sun's apparent path. This twelvefold division, the Zodiac, is a reference system for the astrologer. At any given moment the planets—and in astrology both the Sun and Moon are considered to be planets—can all be located at a specific point along this path.

Now where in all this are you, the subject of the horoscope? Your character is largely determined by the sign the Sun is in. So that is where the astrologer looks first in your horoscope, at your Sun sign.

The Sun Sign and the Cusp

There are twelve signs in the Zodiac, and the Sun spends approximately one month in each sign. But because of the motion of the Earth around the Sun—the Sun's apparent motion—the dates when the Sun enters and leaves each sign may change from year to year. Some people born near the cusp, or edge, of a sign have difficulty determining which is their Sun sign. But in this book a Table of Cusps is provided for the years 1900 to 2010 (page 5) so you can find out what your true Sun sign is.

Here are the twelve signs of the Zodiac, their ancient zodiacal symbol, and the dates when the Sun enters and leaves each sign for the year 2003. Remember, these dates may change from year to year.

ARIES	Ram	March 20–April 20
TAURUS	Bull	April 20–May 21
GEMINI	Twins	May 21–June 21
CANCER	Crab	June 21–July 23
LEO	Lion	July 23–August 23
VIRGO	Virgin	August 23–September 23
LIBRA	Scales	September 23–October 23
SCORPIO	Scorpion	October 23–November 22
SAGITTARIUS	Archer	November 22–December 22
CAPRICORN	Sea Goat	December 22–January 20
AQUARIUS	Water Bearer	January 20–February 18
PISCES	Fish	February 18–March 20

It is possible to draw significant conclusions and make meaningful predictions based simply on the Sun sign of a person. There are many people who have been amazed at the accuracy of the description of their own character based only on the Sun sign. But an astrologer needs more information than just your Sun sign to interpret the photograph that is your horoscope.

The Rising Sign and the Zodiacal Houses

An astrologer needs the exact time and place of your birth in order to construct and interpret your horoscope. The illustration on the next page shows the flat chart, or natural wheel, an astrologer uses. Note the inner circle of the wheel labeled 1 through 12. These 12 divisions are known as the houses of the Zodiac.

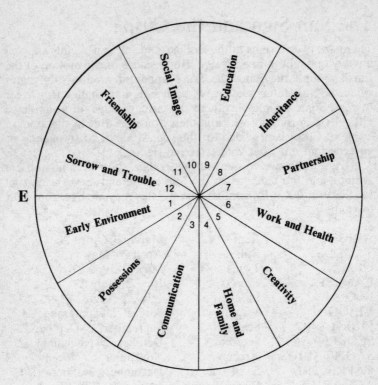

The 1st house always starts from the position marked E, which corresponds to the eastern horizon. The rest of the houses 2 through 12 follow around in a "counterclockwise" direction. The point where each house starts is known as a cusp, or edge.

The cusp, or edge, of the 1st house (point E) is where an astrologer would place your Rising sign, the Ascendant. And, as already noted, the exact time of your birth determines your Rising sign. Let's see how this works.

As the Earth rotates on its axis once every 24 hours, each one of the twelve signs of the Zodiac appears to be "rising" on the horizon, with a new one appearing about every 2 hours. Actually it is the turning of the Earth that exposes each sign to view, but in our astrological work we are discussing apparent motion. This Rising sign marks the Ascendant, and it colors the whole orientation of a horoscope. It indicates the sign governing the 1st house of the chart, and will thus determine which signs will govern all the other houses.

To visualize this idea, imagine two color wheels with twelve divisions superimposed upon each other. For just as the Zodiac is divided into twelve constellations that we identify as the signs, another twelvefold division is used to denote the houses. Now imagine one wheel (the signs) moving slowly while the other wheel (the houses) remains still. This analogy may help you see how the signs keep shifting the "color" of the houses as the Rising sign continues to change every two hours. To simplify things, a Table of Rising Signs has been provided (pages 8–9) for your specific Sun sign.

Once your Rising sign has been placed on the cusp of the 1st house, the signs that govern the rest of the 11 houses can be placed on the chart. In any individual's horoscope the signs do not necessarily correspond with the houses. For example, it could be that a sign covers part of two adjacent houses. It is the interpretation of such variations in an individual's horoscope that marks the professional astrologer.

But to gain a workable understanding of astrology, it is not necessary to go into great detail. In fact, we just need a description of the houses and their meanings, as is shown in the illustration above and in the table below.

THE 12 HOUSES OF THE ZODIAC

1st	Individuality, body appearance, general outlook on life	Personality house
2nd	Finance, possessions, ethical principles, gain or loss	Money house
3rd	Relatives, communication, short journeys, writing, education	Relatives house
4th	Family and home, parental ties, land and property, security	Home house
5th	Pleasure, children, creativity, entertainment, risk	Pleasure house
6th	Health, harvest, hygiene, work and service, employees	Health house
7th	Marriage and divorce, the law, partnerships and alliances	Marriage house
8th	Inheritance, secret deals, sex, death, regeneration	Inheritance house
9th	Travel, sports, study, philosophy and religion	Travel house
10th	Career, social standing, success and honor	Business house
11th	Friendship, social life, hopes and wishes	Friends house
12th	Troubles, illness, secret enemies, hidden agendas	Trouble house

The Planets in the Houses

An astrologer, knowing the exact time and place of your birth, will use tables of planetary motion in order to locate the planets in your horoscope chart. He or she will determine which planet or planets are in which sign and in which house. It is not uncommon, in an individual's horoscope, for there to be two or more planets in the same sign and in the same house.

The characteristics of the planets modify the influence of the Sun according to their natures and strengths.

Sun: Source of life. Basic temperament according to the Sun sign. The conscious will. Human potential.
Moon: Emotions. Moods. Customs. Habits. Changeable. Adaptive. Nurturing.
Mercury: Communication. Intellect. Reasoning power. Curiosity. Short travels.
Venus: Love. Delight. Charm. Harmony. Balance. Art. Beautiful possessions.
Mars: Energy. Initiative. War. Anger. Adventure. Courage. Daring. Impulse.
Jupiter: Luck. Optimism. Generous. Expansive. Opportunities. Protection.
Saturn: Pessimism. Privation. Obstacles. Delay. Hard work. Research. Lasting rewards after long struggle.
Uranus: Fashion. Electricity. Revolution. Independence. Freedom. Sudden changes. Modern science.
Neptune: Sensationalism. Theater. Dreams. Inspiration. Illusion. Deception.
Pluto: Creation and destruction. Total transformation. Lust for power. Strong obsessions.

Superimpose the characteristics of the planets on the functions of the house in which they appear. Express the result through the character of the Sun sign, and you will get the basic idea.

Of course, many other considerations have been taken into account in producing the carefully worked out predictions in this book: the aspects of the planets to each other; their strength according to position and sign; whether they are in a house of exaltation or decline; whether they are natural enemies or not; whether a planet occupies its own sign; the position of a planet in relation to its own house or sign; whether the sign is male or female; whether the sign is a fire, earth, water, or air sign. These are only a few of the colors on the astrologer's pallet which he or she must mix with the inspiration of the artist and the accuracy of the mathematician.

How To Use These Predictions

A person reading the predictions in this book should understand that they are produced from the daily position of the planets for a group of people and are not, of course, individually specialized. To get the full benefit of them our readers should relate the predictions to their own character and circumstances, coordinate them, and draw their own conclusions from them.

If you are a serious observer of your own life, you should find a definite pattern emerging that will be a helpful and reliable guide.

The point is that we always retain our free will. The stars indicate certain directional tendencies but we are not compelled to follow. We can do or not do, and wisdom must make the choice.

We all have our good and bad days. Sometimes they extend into cycles of weeks. It is therefore advisable to study daily predictions in a span ranging from the day before to several days ahead.

Daily predictions should be taken very generally. The word "difficult" does not necessarily indicate a whole day of obstruction or inconvenience. It is a warning to you to be cautious. Your caution will often see you around the difficulty before you are involved. This is the correct use of astrology.

In another section (pages 78–84), detailed information is given about the influence of the Moon as it passes through each of the twelve signs of the Zodiac. There are instructions on how to use the Moon Tables (pages 85–92), which provide Moon Sign Dates throughout the year as well as the Moon's role in health and daily affairs. This information should be used in conjunction with the daily forecasts to give a fuller picture of the astrological trends.

HISTORY OF ASTROLOGY

The origins of astrology have been lost far back in history, but we do know that reference is made to it as far back as the first written records of the human race. It is not hard to see why. Even in primitive times, people must have looked for an explanation for the various happenings in their lives. They must have wanted to know why people were different from one another. And in their search they turned to the regular movements of the Sun, Moon, and stars to see if they could provide an answer.

It is interesting to note that as soon as man learned to use his tools in any type of design, or his mind in any kind of calculation, he turned his attention to the heavens. Ancient cave dwellings reveal dim crescents and circles representative of the Sun and Moon, rulers of day and night. Mesopotamia and the civilization of Chaldea, in itself the foundation of those of Babylonia and Assyria, show a complete picture of astronomical observation and well-developed astrological interpretation.

Humanity has a natural instinct for order. The study of anthropology reveals that primitive people—even as far back as prehistoric times—were striving to achieve a certain order in their lives. They tried to organize the apparent chaos of the universe. They had the desire to attach meaning to things. This demand for order has persisted throughout the history of man. So that observing the regularity of the heavenly bodies made it logical that primitive peoples should turn heavenward in their search for an understanding of the world in which they found themselves so random and alone.

And they did find a significance in the movements of the stars. Shepherds tending their flocks, for instance, observed that when the cluster of stars now known as the constellation Aries was in sight, it was the time of fertility and they associated it with the Ram. And they noticed that the growth of plants and plant life corresponded with different phases of the Moon, so that certain times were favorable for the planting of crops, and other times were not. In this way, there grew up a tradition of seasons and causes connected with the passage of the Sun through the twelve signs of the Zodiac.

Astrology was valued so highly that the king was kept informed of the daily and monthly changes in the heavenly bodies, and the results of astrological studies regarding events of the future. Head astrologers were clearly men of great rank and position, and the office was said to be a hereditary one.

Omens were taken, not only from eclipses and conjunctions of the Moon or Sun with one of the planets, but also from storms and earthquakes. In the eastern civilizations, particularly, the reverence inspired by astrology appears to have remained unbroken since the very earliest days. In ancient China, astrology, astronomy, and religion went hand in hand. The astrologer, who was also an astronomer, was part of the official government service and had his own corner in the Imperial Palace. The duties of the Imperial astrologer, whose office was one of the most important in the land, were clearly defined, as this extract from early records shows:

> This exalted gentleman must concern himself with the stars in the heavens, keeping a record of the changes and movements of the Planets, the Sun and the Moon, in order to examine the movements of the terrestrial world with the object of prognosticating good and bad fortune. He divides the territories of the nine regions of the empire in accordance with their dependence on particular celestial bodies. All the fiefs and principalities are connected with the stars and from this their prosperity or misfortune should be ascertained. He makes prognostications according to the twelve years of the Jupiter cycle of good and evil of the terrestrial world. From the colors of the five kinds of clouds, he determines the coming of floods or droughts, abundance or famine. From the twelve winds, he draws conclusions about the state of harmony of heaven and earth, and takes note of good and bad signs that result from their accord or disaccord. In general, he concerns himself with five kinds of phenomena so as to warn the Emperor to come to the aid of the government and to allow for variations in the ceremonies according to their circumstances.

The Chinese were also keen observers of the fixed stars, giving them such unusual names as Ghost Vehicle, Sun of Imperial Concubine, Imperial Prince, Pivot of Heaven, Twinkling Brilliance, Weaving Girl. But, great astrologers though they may have been, the Chinese lacked one aspect of mathematics that the Greeks applied to astrology—deductive geometry. Deductive geometry was the basis of much classical astrology in and after the time of the Greeks, and this explains the different methods of prognostication used in the East and West.

Down through the ages the astrologer's art has depended, not so much on the uncovering of new facts, though this is important, as on the interpretation of the facts already known. This is the essence of the astrologer's skill.

But why should the signs of the Zodiac have any effect at all on the formation of human character? It is easy to see why people thought they did, and even now we constantly use astrological expressions in our everyday speech. The thoughts of "lucky star," "ill-fated," "star-crossed," "mooning around," are interwoven into the very structure of our language.

Wherever the concept of the Zodiac is understood and used, it could well appear to have an influence on the human character. Does this mean, then, that the human race, in whose civilization the idea of the twelve signs of the Zodiac has long been embedded, is divided into only twelve types? Can we honestly believe that it is really as simple as that? If so, there must be pretty wide ranges of variation within each type. And if, to explain the variation, we call in heredity and environment, experiences in early childhood, the thyroid and other glands, and also the four functions of the mind together with extroversion and introversion, then one begins to wonder if the original classification was worth making at all. No sensible person believes that his favorite system explains everything. But even so, he will not find the system much use at all if it does not even save him the trouble of bothering with the others.

In the same way, if we were to put every person under only one sign of the Zodiac, the system becomes too rigid and unlike life. Besides, it was never intended to be used like that. It may be convenient to have only twelve types, but we know that in practice there is every possible gradation between aggressiveness and timidity, or between conscientiousness and laziness. How, then, do we account for this?

A person born under any given Sun sign can be mainly influenced by one or two of the other signs that appear in their individual horoscope. For instance, famous persons born under the sign of Gemini include Henry VIII, whom nothing and no one could have induced to abdicate, and Edward VIII, who did just that. Obviously, then, the sign Gemini does not fully explain the complete character of either of them.

Again, under the opposite sign, Sagittarius, were both Stalin, who was totally consumed with the notion of power, and Charles V, who freely gave up an empire because he preferred to go into a monastery. And we find under Scorpio many uncompromising characters such as Luther, de Gaulle, Indira Gandhi, and Montgomery, but also Petain, a successful commander whose name later became synonymous with collaboration.

A single sign is therefore obviously inadequate to explain the differences between people; it can only explain resemblances, such as the combativeness of the Scorpio group, or the far-reaching devotion of Charles V and Stalin to their respective ideals—the Christian heaven and the Communist utopia.

But very few people have only one sign in their horoscope chart. In addition to the month of birth, the day and, even more, the hour to the nearest minute if possible, ought to be considered. Without this, it is impossible to have an actual horoscope, for the word horoscope literally means "a consideration of the hour."

The month of birth tells you only which sign of the Zodiac was occupied by the Sun. The day and hour tell you what sign was occupied by the Moon. And the minute tells you which sign was rising on the eastern horizon. This is called the Ascendant, and, as some astrologers believe, it is supposed to be the most important thing in the whole horoscope.

The Sun is said to signify one's heart, that is to say, one's deepest desires and inmost nature. This is quite different from the Moon, which signifies one's superficial way of behaving. When the ancient Romans referred to the Emperor Augustus as a Capricorn, they meant that he had the Moon in Capricorn. Or, to take another example, a modern astrologer would call Disraeli a Scorpion because he had Scorpio Rising, but most people would call him Sagittarius because he had the Sun there. The Romans would have called him Leo because his Moon was in Leo.

So if one does not seem to fit one's birth month, it is always worthwhile reading the other signs, for one may have been born at a time when any of them were rising or occupied by the Moon. It also seems to be the case that the influence of the Sun develops as life goes on, so that the month of birth is easier to guess in people over the age of forty. The young are supposed to be influenced mainly by their Ascendant, the Rising sign, which characterizes the body and physical personality as a whole.

It is nonsense to assume that all people born at a certain time will exhibit the same characteristics, or that they will even behave in the same manner. It is quite obvious that, from the very moment of its birth, a child is subject to the effects of its environment, and that this in turn will influence its character and heritage to a decisive extent. Also to be taken into account are education and economic conditions, which play a very important part in the formation of one's character as well.

People have, in general, certain character traits and qualities which, according to their environment, develop in either a positive or a negative manner. Therefore, selfishness (inherent selfishness, that is) might emerge as unselfishness; kindness and consideration as cruelty and lack of consideration toward others. In the same way, a naturally constructive person may, through frustration, become destructive, and so on. The latent characteristics with which people are born can, therefore, through environment and good or bad training, become something that would appear to be its opposite, and so give the lie to the astrologer's description of their character. But this is not the case. The true character is still there, but it is buried deep beneath these external superficialities.

Careful study of the character traits of various signs of the Zodiac are of immeasurable help, and can render beneficial service to the intelligent person. Undoubtedly, the reader will already have discovered that, while he is able to get on very well with some people, he just "cannot stand" others. The causes sometimes seem inexplicable. At times there is intense dislike, at other times immediate sympathy. And there is, too, the phenomenon of love at first sight, which is also apparently inexplicable. People appear to be either sympathetic or unsympathetic toward each other for no apparent reason.

Now if we look at this in the light of the Zodiac, we find that people born under different signs are either compatible or incompatible with each other. In other words, there are good and bad interrelating factors among the various signs. This does not, of course, mean that humanity can be divided into groups of hostile camps. It would be quite wrong to be hostile or indifferent toward people who happen to be born under an incompatible sign. There is no reason why everybody should not, or cannot, learn to control and adjust their feelings and actions, especially after they are aware of the positive qualities of other people by studying their character analyses, among other things.

Every person born under a certain sign has both positive and negative qualities, which are developed more or less according to our free will. Nobody is entirely good or entirely bad, and it is up to each of us to learn to control ourselves on the one hand and at the same time to endeavor to learn about ourselves and others.

It cannot be emphasized often enough that it is free will that determines whether we will make really good use of our talents and abilities. Using our free will, we can either overcome our failings or allow them to rule us. Our free will enables us to exert sufficient willpower to control our failings so that they do not harm ourselves or others.

Astrology can reveal our inclinations and tendencies. Astrology can tell us about ourselves so that we are able to use our free will to overcome our shortcomings. In this way astrology helps us do our best to become needed and valuable members of society as well as helpmates to our family and our friends. Astrology also can save us a great deal of unhappiness and remorse.

Yet it may seem absurd that an ancient philosophy could be a prop to modern men and women. But below the materialistic surface of modern life, there are hidden streams of feeling and thought. Symbology is reappearing as a study worthy of the scholar; the psychosomatic factor in illness has passed from the writings of the crank to those of the specialist; spiritual healing in all its forms is no longer a pious hope but an accepted phenomenon. And it is into this context that we consider astrology, in the sense that it is an analysis of human types.

Astrology and medicine had a long journey together, and only parted company a couple of centuries ago. There still remain in medical language such astrological terms as "saturnine," "choleric," and "mercurial," used in the diagnosis of physical tendencies. The herbalist, for long the handyman of the medical profession, has been dominated by astrology since the days of the Greeks. Certain herbs traditionally respond to certain planetary influences, and diseases must therefore be treated to ensure harmony between the medicine and the disease.

But the stars are expected to foretell and not only to diagnose.

Astrological forecasting has been remarkably accurate, but often it is wide of the mark. The brave person who cares to predict world events takes dangerous chances. Individual forecasting is less clear cut; it can be a help or a disillusionment. Then we come to the nagging question: if it is possible to foreknow, is it right to foretell? This is a point of ethics on which it is hard to pronounce judgment. The doctor faces the same dilemma if he finds that symptoms of a mortal disease are present in his patient and that he can only prognosticate a steady decline. How much to tell an individual in a crisis is a problem that has perplexed many distinguished scholars. Honest and conscientious astrologers in this modern world, where so many people are seeking guidance, face the same problem.

Five hundred years ago it was customary to call in a learned man who was an astrologer who was probably also a doctor and a philosopher. By his knowledge of astrology, his study of planetary influences, he felt himself qualified to guide those in distress. The world has moved forward at a fantastic rate since then, and yet people are still uncertain of themselves. At first sight it seems fantastic in the light of modern thinking that they turn to the most ancient of all studies, and get someone to calculate a horoscope for them. But is it *really* so fantastic if you take a second look? For astrology is concerned with tomorrow, with survival. And in a world such as ours, tomorrow and survival are the keywords for the twenty-first century.

ASTROLOGICAL BRIDGE TO THE 21st CENTURY

As the decade opens on a new century, indeed on a new millennium, the planets set the stage for change and challenge. Themes connecting past, present, and future are in play as new planetary cycles form the bridge to the twenty-first century and its broad horizons. The first few years of the new decade reveal hidden paths and personal hints for achieving your potential, for making the most of your message from the planets.

With the dawning of the twenty-first century look first to Jupiter, the planet of good fortune. Each new yearly Jupiter cycle follows the natural progression of the Zodiac. First is Jupiter in Aries and in Taurus through spring 2000, next Jupiter is in Gemini to summer 2001, then in Cancer to midsummer 2002, in Leo to late summer 2003, in Virgo to early autumn 2004, and so on through Jupiter in Pisces through June 2010. The beneficent planet Jupiter promotes your professional and educational goals while urging informed choice and deliberation. Jupiter sharpens your focus and hones your skills, providing a rich medium for creativity. Planet Jupiter's influence is protective, the generous helper that comes to the rescue just in the nick of time. And while safeguarding good luck, Jupiter can turn unusual risks into achievable aims.

In order to take advantage of luck and opportunity, to gain wisdom from experience, to persevere against adversity, look to beautiful planet Saturn. Saturn, planet of reason and responsibility, began a new cycle in earthy Taurus at the turn of the century. Saturn in Taurus until spring 2001 inspires industry and affection, blends practicality and imagination, all the while inviting caution and care. Persistence and planning can reverse setbacks and minimize risk. Saturn in Taurus lends beauty, order, and structure to your life. Then Saturn is in Gemini, the sign of mind and communication, until June 2003. Saturn in Gemini gives depth and inspiration to thought and feeling. Here, because of a lively intellectual capacity, the limits of creativity can be stretched and boundaries broken. Saturn in Gemini holds the promise of fruitful endeavor through sustained study, learning, and application. Saturn in Cancer from early June 2003 to mid-July 2005 poses issues of long-term security versus immediate gratification. Rely on deliberation and choice to make sense out of diversity and change. Saturn in Cancer can be a revealing cycle, leading to the desired outcomes of growth and maturity.

Uranus, planet of innovation and surprise, started an important new cycle in January of 1996. At that time Uranus entered its natural home in airy Aquarius. Uranus in Aquarius into the year 2003 has a profound effect on your personality and the lens through which you see the world. A basic change in the way you project yourself is just one impact of Uranus in Aquarius. More significantly, a whole new consciousness is evolving. Winds of change blowing your way emphasize movement and freedom. Uranus in Aquarius poses involvement in the larger community beyond self, family, friends, lovers, associates. Radical ideas and progressive thought signal a journey of liberation. As the new century begins, follow Uranus on the path of humanitarianism. A new Uranus cycle begins March 2003 when Uranus visits Pisces, briefly revisits Aquarius, then returns late in 2003 to Pisces where it will stay into May 2010. Uranus in Pisces, a strongly intuitive force, urges work and service for the good of humankind to make the world a better place for all people.

Neptune, planet of vision and mystery, is enjoying a long cycle that excites creativity and imaginative thinking. Neptune is in airy Aquarius from November 1998 to February of 2012. Neptune in Aquarius, the sign of the Water Bearer, represents two sides of the coin of wisdom: inspiration and reason. Here Neptune stirs powerful currents bearing a rich and varied harvest, the fertile breeding ground for idealistic aims and practical considerations. Neptune's fine intuition tunes in to your dreams, your imagination, your spirituality. You can never turn your back on the mysteries of life. Uranus and Neptune, the planets of enlightenment and idealism, give you glimpses into the future, letting you peek through secret doorways into the twenty-first century.

Pluto, planet of beginnings and endings, began a new cycle of growth and learning late in 1995. Pluto entered fiery Sagittarius and remains there into the year 2008. Pluto in Sagittarius during its long stay over twelve years can create significant change. The great power of Pluto in Sagittarius is already starting its transformation of your character and lifestyle. Pluto in Sagittarius takes you on a new journey of exploration and learning. The awakening you experience on intellectual and artistic levels heralds a new cycle of growth. Uncompromising Pluto, seeker of truth, challenges your identity, persona, and self-expression. Uncovering the real you, Pluto holds the key to understanding and meaningful communication. Pluto in Sagittarius can be the guiding light illuminating the first decade of the twenty-first century. Good luck is riding on the waves of change.

THE SIGNS OF THE ZODIAC

Dominant Characteristics

Aries: March 21–April 20

The Positive Side of Aries

The Aries has many positive points to his character. People born under this first sign of the Zodiac are often quite strong and enthusiastic. On the whole, they are forward-looking people who are not easily discouraged by temporary setbacks. They know what they want out of life and they go out after it. Their personalities are strong. Others are usually quite impressed by the Ram's way of doing things. Quite often they are sources of inspiration for others traveling the same route. Aries men and women have a special zest for life that can be contagious; for others, they are a fine example of how life should be lived.

The Aries person usually has a quick and active mind. He is imaginative and inventive. He enjoys keeping busy and active. He generally gets along well with all kinds of people. He is interested in mankind, as a whole. He likes to be challenged. Some would say he thrives on opposition, for it is when he is set against that he often does his best. Getting over or around obstacles is a challenge he generally enjoys. All in all, Aries is quite positive and young-thinking. He likes to keep abreast of new things that are happening in the world. Aries are often fond of speed. They like things to be done quickly, and this sometimes aggravates their slower colleagues and associates.

The Aries man or woman always seems to remain young. Their whole approach to life is youthful and optimistic. They never say die, no matter what the odds. They may have an occasional setback, but it is not long before they are back on their feet again.

The Negative Side of Aries

Everybody has his less positive qualities—and Aries is no exception. Sometimes the Aries man or woman is not very tactful in communicating with others; in his hurry to get things done he is apt to be a little callous or inconsiderate. Sensitive people are likely to find him somewhat sharp-tongued in some situations. Often in his eagerness to get the show on the road, he misses the mark altogether and cannot achieve his aims.

At times Aries can be too impulsive. He can occasionally be stubborn and refuse to listen to reason. If things do not move quickly enough to suit the Aries man or woman, he or she is apt to become rather nervous or irritable. The uncultivated Aries is not unfamiliar with moments of doubt and fear. He is capable of being destructive if he does not get his way. He can overcome some of his emotional problems by steadily trying to express himself as he really is, but this requires effort.

Taurus: April 21–May 20

The Positive Side of Taurus

The Taurus person is known for his ability to concentrate and for his tenacity. These are perhaps his strongest qualities. The Taurus man or woman generally has very little trouble in getting along with others; it's his nature to be helpful toward people in need. He can always be depended on by his friends, especially those in trouble.

Taurus generally achieves what he wants through his ability to persevere. He never leaves anything unfinished but works on something until it has been completed. People can usually take him at his word; he is honest and forthright in most of his dealings. The Taurus person has a good chance to make a success of his life because of his many positive qualities. The Taurus who aims high seldom falls short of his mark. He learns well by experience. He is thorough and does not believe in shortcuts of any kind. The Bull's thoroughness pays off in the end, for through his deliberateness he learns how to rely on himself and what he has learned. The Taurus person tries to get along with others, as a rule. He is not overly critical and likes people to be themselves. He is a tolerant person and enjoys peace and harmony—especially in his home life.

Taurus is usually cautious in all that he does. He is not a person who believes in taking unnecessary risks. Before adopting any one line of action, he will weigh all of the pros and cons. The Taurus person is steadfast. Once his mind is made up it seldom changes. The person born under this sign usually is a good family person—reliable and loving.

The Negative Side of Taurus

Sometimes the Taurus man or woman is a bit too stubborn. He won't listen to other points of view if his mind is set on something. To others, this can be quite annoying. Taurus also does not like to be told what to do. He becomes rather angry if others think him not too bright. He does not like to be told he is wrong, even when he is. He dislikes being contradicted.

Some people who are born under this sign are very suspicious of others—even of those persons close to them. They find it difficult to trust people fully. They are often afraid of being deceived or taken advantage of. The Bull often finds it difficult to forget or forgive. His love of material things sometimes makes him rather avaricious and petty.

Gemini: May 21–June 20

The Positive Side of Gemini

The person born under this sign of the Heavenly Twins is usually quite bright and quick-witted. Some of them are capable of doing many different things. The Gemini person very often has many different interests. He keeps an open mind and is always anxious to learn new things.

Gemini is often an analytical person. He is a person who enjoys making use of his intellect. He is governed more by his mind than by his emotions. He is a person who is not confined to one view; he can often understand both sides to a problem or question. He knows how to reason, how to make rapid decisions if need be.

He is an adaptable person and can make himself at home almost anywhere. There are all kinds of situations he can adapt to. He is a person who seldom doubts himself; he is sure of his talents and his ability to think and reason. Gemini is generally most satisfied

when he is in a situation where he can make use of his intellect. Never short of imagination, he often has strong talents for invention. He is rather a modern person when it comes to life; Gemini almost always moves along with the times—perhaps that is why he remains so youthful throughout most of his life.

Literature and art appeal to the person born under this sign. Creativity in almost any form will interest and intrigue the Gemini man or woman.

The Gemini is often quite charming. A good talker, he often is the center of attraction at any gathering. People find it easy to like a person born under this sign because he can appear easygoing and usually has a good sense of humor.

The Negative Side of Gemini

Sometimes the Gemini person tries to do too many things at one time—and as a result, winds up finishing nothing. Some Twins are easily distracted and find it rather difficult to concentrate on one thing for too long a time. Sometimes they give in to trifling fancies and find it rather boring to become too serious about any one thing. Some of them are never dependable, no matter what they promise.

Although the Gemini man or woman often appears to be well-versed on many subjects, this is sometimes just a veneer. His knowledge may be only superficial, but because he speaks so well he gives people the impression of erudition. Some Geminis are sharp-tongued and inconsiderate; they think only of themselves and their own pleasure.

Cancer: June 21–July 20

The Positive Side of Cancer

The Moon Child's most positive point is his understanding nature. On the whole, he is a loving and sympathetic person. He would never go out of his way to hurt anyone. The Cancer man or woman is often very kind and tender; they give what they can to others. They hate to see others suffering and will do what they can to help someone in less fortunate circumstances than themselves. They are often very concerned about the world. Their interest in people generally goes beyond that of just their own families and close friends; they have a deep sense of community and respect humanitarian values. The Moon Child means what he says, as a rule; he is honest about his feelings.

The Cancer man or woman is a person who knows the art of patience. When something seems difficult, he is willing to wait until the situation becomes manageable again. He is a person who knows how to bide his time. Cancer knows how to concentrate on one thing at a time. When he has made his mind up he generally sticks with what he does, seeing it through to the end.

Cancer is a person who loves his home. He enjoys being surrounded by familiar things and the people he loves. Of all the signs, Cancer is the most maternal. Even the men born under this sign often have a motherly or protective quality about them. They like to take care of people in their family—to see that they are well loved and well provided for. They are usually loyal and faithful. Family ties mean a lot to the Cancer man or woman. Parents and in-laws are respected and loved. Young Cancer responds very well to adults who show faith in him. The Moon Child has a strong sense of tradition. He is very sensitive to the moods of others.

The Negative Side of Cancer

Sometimes Cancer finds it rather hard to face life. It becomes too much for him. He can be a little timid and retiring, when things don't go too well. When unfortunate things happen, he is apt to just shrug and say, "Whatever will be will be." He can be fatalistic to a fault. The uncultivated Cancer is a bit lazy. He doesn't have very much ambition. Anything that seems a bit difficult he'll gladly leave to others. He may be lacking in initiative. Too sensitive, when he feels he's been injured, he'll crawl back into his shell and nurse his imaginary wounds. The immature Moon Child often is given to crying when the smallest thing goes wrong.

Some Cancers find it difficult to enjoy themselves in environments outside their homes. They make heavy demands on others, and need to be constantly reassured that they are loved. Lacking such reassurance, they may resort to sulking in silence.

Leo: July 21–August 21

The Positive Side of Leo

Often Leos make good leaders. They seem to be good organizers and administrators. Usually they are quite popular with others. Whatever group it is that they belong to, the Leo man or woman is almost sure to be or become the leader. Loyalty, one of the Lion's noblest traits, enables him or her to maintain this leadership position.

Leo is generous most of the time. It is his best characteristic. He or she likes to give gifts and presents. In making others happy, the Leo person becomes happy himself. He likes to splurge when spending money on others. In some instances it may seem that the Lion's generosity knows no boundaries. A hospitable person, the Leo man or woman is very fond of welcoming people to his house and entertaining them. He is never short of company.

Leo has plenty of energy and drive. He enjoys working toward some specific goal. When he applies himself correctly, he gets what he wants most often. The Leo person is almost never unsure of himself. He has plenty of confidence and aplomb. He is a person who is direct in almost everything he does. He has a quick mind and can make a decision in a very short time.

He usually sets a good example for others because of his ambitious manner and positive ways. He knows how to stick to something once he's started. Although Leo may be good at making a joke, he is not superficial or glib. He is a loving person, kind and thoughtful.

There is generally nothing small or petty about the Leo man or woman. He does what he can for those who are deserving. He is a person others can rely upon at all times. He means what he says. An honest person, generally speaking, he is a friend who is valued and sought out.

The Negative Side of Leo

Leo, however, does have his faults. At times, he can be just a bit too arrogant. He thinks that no one deserves a leadership position except him. Only he is capable of doing things well. His opinion of himself is often much too high. Because of his conceit, he is

sometimes rather unpopular with a good many people. Some Leos are too materialistic; they can only think in terms of money and profit.

Some Leos enjoy lording it over others—at home or at their place of business. What is more, they feel they have the right to. Egocentric to an impossible degree, this sort of Leo cares little about how others think or feel. He can be rude and cutting.

Virgo: August 22–September 22

The Positive Side of Virgo

The person born under the sign of Virgo is generally a busy person. He knows how to arrange and organize things. He is a good planner. Above all, he is practical and is not afraid of hard work.

Often called the sign of the Harvester, Virgo knows how to attain what he desires. He sticks with something until it is finished. He never shirks his duties, and can always be depended upon. The Virgo person can be thoroughly trusted at all times.

The man or woman born under this sign tries to do everything to perfection. He doesn't believe in doing anything halfway. He always aims for the top. He is the sort of a person who is always learning and constantly striving to better himself—not because he wants more money or glory, but because it gives him a feeling of accomplishment.

The Virgo man or woman is a very observant person. He is sensitive to how others feel, and can see things below the surface of a situation. He usually puts this talent to constructive use.

It is not difficult for the Virgo to be open and earnest. He believes in putting his cards on the table. He is never secretive or underhanded. He's as good as his word. The Virgo person is generally plainspoken and down to earth. He has no trouble in expressing himself.

The Virgo person likes to keep up to date on new developments in his particular field. Well-informed, generally, he sometimes has a keen interest in the arts or literature. What he knows, he knows well. His ability to use his critical faculties is well-developed and sometimes startles others because of its accuracy.

Virgos adhere to a moderate way of life; they avoid excesses. Virgo is a responsible person and enjoys being of service.

The Negative Side of Virgo

Sometimes a Virgo person is too critical. He thinks that only he can do something the way it should be done. Whatever anyone else does is inferior. He can be rather annoying in the way he quibbles over insignificant details. In telling others how things should be done, he can be rather tactless and mean.

Some Virgos seem rather emotionless and cool. They feel emotional involvement is beneath them. They are sometimes too tidy, too neat. With money they can be rather miserly. Some Virgos try to force their opinions and ideas on others.

Libra: September 23–October 22

The Positive Side of Libra

Libras love harmony. It is one of their most outstanding character traits. They are interested in achieving balance; they admire beauty and grace in things as well as in people. Generally speaking, they are kind and considerate people. Libras are usually very sympathetic. They go out of their way not to hurt another person's feelings. They are outgoing and do what they can to help those in need.

People born under the sign of Libra almost always make good friends. They are loyal and amiable. They enjoy the company of others. Many of them are rather moderate in their views; they believe in keeping an open mind, however, and weighing both sides of an issue fairly before making a decision.

Alert and intelligent, Libra, often known as the Lawgiver, is always fair-minded and tries to put himself in the position of the other person. They are against injustice; quite often they take up for the underdog. In most of their social dealings, they try to be tactful and kind. They dislike discord and bickering, and most Libras strive for peace and harmony in all their relationships.

The Libra man or woman has a keen sense of beauty. They appreciate handsome furnishings and clothes. Many of them are artistically inclined. Their taste is usually impeccable. They know how to use color. Their homes are almost always attractively arranged and inviting. They enjoy entertaining people and see to it that their guests always feel at home and welcome.

Libra gets along with almost everyone. He is well-liked and socially much in demand.

The Negative Side of Libra

Some people born under this sign tend to be rather insincere. So eager are they to achieve harmony in all relationships that they will even go so far as to lie. Many of them are escapists. They find facing the truth an ordeal and prefer living in a world of make-believe.

In a serious argument, some Libras give in rather easily even when they know they are right. Arguing, even about something they believe in, is too unsettling for some of them.

Libras sometimes care too much for material things. They enjoy possessions and luxuries. Some are vain and tend to be jealous.

Scorpio: October 23–November 22

The Positive Side of Scorpio

The Scorpio man or woman generally knows what he or she wants out of life. He is a determined person. He sees something through to the end. Scorpio is quite sincere, and seldom says anything he doesn't mean. When he sets a goal for himself he tries to go about achieving it in a very direct way.

The Scorpion is brave and courageous. They are not afraid of hard work. Obstacles do not frighten them. They forge ahead until they achieve what they set out for. The Scorpio man or woman has a strong will.

Although Scorpio may seem rather fixed and determined, inside he is often quite tender and loving. He can care very much for others. He believes in sincerity in all relationships. His feelings about someone tend to last; they are profound and not superficial.

The Scorpio person is someone who adheres to his principles no matter what happens. He will not be deterred from a path he believes to be right.

Because of his many positive strengths, the Scorpion can often achieve happiness for himself and for those that he loves.

He is a constructive person by nature. He often has a deep understanding of people and of life, in general. He is perceptive and unafraid. Obstacles often seem to spur him on. He is a positive person who enjoys winning. He has many strengths and resources; challenge of any sort often brings out the best in him.

The Negative Side of Scorpio

The Scorpio person is sometimes hypersensitive. Often he imagines injury when there is none. He feels that others do not bother to recognize him for his true worth. Sometimes he is given to excessive boasting in order to compensate for what he feels is neglect.

Scorpio can be proud, arrogant, and competitive. They can be sly when they put their minds to it and they enjoy outwitting persons or institutions noted for their cleverness.

Their tactics for getting what they want are sometimes devious and ruthless. They don't care too much about what others may think. If they feel others have done them an injustice, they will do their best to seek revenge. The Scorpion often has a sudden, violent temper; and this person's interest in sex is sometimes quite unbalanced or excessive.

Sagittarius: November 23–December 20

The Positive Side of Sagittarius

People born under this sign are honest and forthright. Their approach to life is earnest and open. Sagittarius is often quite adult in his way of seeing things. They are broad-minded and tolerant people. When dealing with others the person born under the sign of the Archer is almost always open and forthright. He doesn't believe in deceit or pretension. His standards are high. People who associate with Sagittarius generally admire and respect his tolerant viewpoint.

The Archer trusts others easily and expects them to trust him. He is never suspicious or envious and almost always thinks well of others. People always enjoy his company because he is so friendly and easygoing. The Sagittarius man or woman is often good-humored. He can always be depended upon by his friends, family, and co-workers.

The person born under this sign of the Zodiac likes a good joke every now and then. Sagittarius is eager for fun and laughs, which makes him very popular with others.

A lively person, he enjoys sports and outdoor life. The Archer is fond of animals. Intelligent and interesting, he can begin an

animated conversation with ease. He likes exchanging ideas and discussing various views.

He is not selfish or proud. If someone proposes an idea or plan that is better than his, he will immediately adopt it. Imaginative yet practical, he knows how to put ideas into practice.

The Archer enjoys sport and games, and it doesn't matter if he wins or loses. He is a forgiving person, and never sulks over something that has not worked out in his favor.

He is seldom critical, and is almost always generous.

The Negative Side of Sagittarius

Some Sagittarius are restless. They take foolish risks and seldom learn from the mistakes they make. They don't have heads for money and are often mismanaging their finances. Some of them devote much of their time to gambling.

Some are too outspoken and tactless, always putting their feet in their mouths. They hurt others carelessly by being honest at the wrong time. Sometimes they make promises which they don't keep. They don't stick close enough to their plans and go from one failure to another. They are undisciplined and waste a lot of energy.

Capricorn: December 21–January 19

The Positive Side of Capricorn

The person born under the sign of Capricorn, known variously as the Mountain Goat or Sea Goat, is usually very stable and patient. He sticks to whatever tasks he has and sees them through. He can always be relied upon and he is not averse to work.

An honest person, Capricorn is generally serious about whatever he does. He does not take his duties lightly. He is a practical person and believes in keeping his feet on the ground.

Quite often the person born under this sign is ambitious and knows how to get what he wants out of life. The Goat forges ahead and never gives up his goal. When he is determined about something, he almost always wins. He is a good worker—a hard worker. Although things may not come easy to him, he will not complain, but continue working until his chores are finished.

He is usually good at business matters and knows the value of money. He is not a spendthrift and knows how to put something away for a rainy day; he dislikes waste and unnecessary loss.

Capricorn knows how to make use of his self-control. He can apply himself to almost anything once he puts his mind to it. His ability to concentrate sometimes astounds others. He is diligent and does well when involved in detail work.

The Capricorn man or woman is charitable, generally speaking, and will do what is possible to help others less fortunate. As a friend, he is loyal and trustworthy. He never shirks his duties or responsibilities. He is self-reliant and never expects too much of the other fellow. He does what he can on his own. If someone does him a good turn, then he will do his best to return the favor.

The Negative Side of Capricorn

Like everyone, Capricorn, too, has faults. At times, the Goat can be overcritical of others. He expects others to live up to his own high standards. He thinks highly of himself and tends to look down on others.

His interest in material things may be exaggerated. The Capricorn man or woman thinks too much about getting on in the world and having something to show for it. He may even be a little greedy.

He sometimes thinks he knows what's best for everyone. He is too bossy. He is always trying to organize and correct others. He may be a little narrow in his thinking.

Aquarius: January 20–February 18

The Positive Side of Aquarius

The Aquarius man or woman is usually very honest and forthright. These are his two greatest qualities. His standards for himself are generally very high. He can always be relied upon by others. His word is his bond.

Aquarius is perhaps the most tolerant of all the Zodiac personalities. He respects other people's beliefs and feels that everyone is entitled to his own approach to life.

He would never do anything to injure another's feelings. He is never unkind or cruel. Always considerate of others, the Water

Bearer is always willing to help a person in need. He feels a very strong tie between himself and all the other members of mankind.

The person born under this sign, called the Water Bearer, is almost always an individualist. He does not believe in teaming up with the masses, but prefers going his own way. His ideas about life and mankind are often quite advanced. There is a saying to the effect that the average Aquarius is fifty years ahead of his time.

Aquarius is community-minded. The problems of the world concern him greatly. He is interested in helping others no matter what part of the globe they live in. He is truly a humanitarian sort. He likes to be of service to others.

Giving, considerate, and without prejudice, Aquarius have no trouble getting along with others.

The Negative Side of Aquarius

Aquarius may be too much of a dreamer. He makes plans but seldom carries them out. He is rather unrealistic. His imagination has a tendency to run away with him. Because many of his plans are impractical, he is always in some sort of a dither.

Others may not approve of him at all times because of his unconventional behavior. He may be a bit eccentric. Sometimes he is so busy with his own thoughts that he loses touch with the realities of existence.

Some Aquarius feel they are more clever and intelligent than others. They seldom admit to their own faults, even when they are quite apparent. Some become rather fanatic in their views. Their criticism of others is sometimes destructive and negative.

Pisces: February 19–March 20

The Positive Side of Pisces

Known as the sign of the Fishes, Pisces has a sympathetic nature. Kindly, he is often dedicated in the way he goes about helping others. The sick and the troubled often turn to him for advice and assistance. Possessing keen intuition, Pisces can easily understand people's deepest problems.

He is very broad-minded and does not criticize others for their faults. He knows how to accept people for what they are. On the whole, he is a trustworthy and earnest person. He is loyal to his friends and will do what he can to help them in time of need. Generous and good-natured, he is a lover of peace; he is often willing to help others solve their differences. People who have taken a wrong turn in life often interest him and he will do what he can to persuade them to rehabilitate themselves.

He has a strong intuitive sense and most of the time he knows how to make it work for him. Pisces is unusually perceptive and often knows what is bothering someone before that person, himself, is aware of it. The Pisces man or woman is an idealistic person, basically, and is interested in making the world a better place in which to live. Pisces believes that everyone should help each other. He is willing to do more than his share in order to achieve cooperation with others.

The person born under this sign often is talented in music or art. He is a receptive person; he is able to take the ups and downs of life with philosophic calm.

The Negative Side of Pisces

Some Pisces are often depressed; their outlook on life is rather glum. They may feel that they have been given a bad deal in life and that others are always taking unfair advantage of them. Pisces sometimes feel that the world is a cold and cruel place. The Fishes can be easily discouraged. The Pisces man or woman may even withdraw from the harshness of reality into a secret shell of his own where he dreams and idles away a good deal of his time.

Pisces can be lazy. He lets things happen without giving the least bit of resistance. He drifts along, whether on the high road or on the low. He can be lacking in willpower.

Some Pisces people seek escape through drugs or alcohol. When temptation comes along they find it hard to resist. In matters of sex, they can be rather permissive.

Sun Sign Personalities

ARIES: Hans Christian Andersen, Pearl Bailey, Marlon Brando, Wernher Von Braun, Charlie Chaplin, Joan Crawford, Da Vinci, Bette Davis, Doris Day, W. C. Fields, Alec Guinness, Adolf Hitler, William Holden, Thomas Jefferson, Nikita Khrushchev, Elton John, Arturo Toscanini, J. P. Morgan, Paul Robeson, Gloria Steinem, Sarah Vaughn, Vincent van Gogh, Tennessee Williams

TAURUS: Fred Astaire, Charlotte Brontë, Carol Burnett, Irving Berlin, Bing Crosby, Salvador Dali, Tchaikovsky, Queen Elizabeth II, Duke Ellington, Ella Fitzgerald, Henry Fonda, Sigmund Freud, Orson Welles, Joe Louis, Lenin, Karl Marx, Golda Meir, Eva Peron, Bertrand Russell, Shakespeare, Kate Smith, Benjamin Spock, Barbra Streisand, Shirley Temple, Harry Truman

GEMINI: Ruth Benedict, Josephine Baker, Rachel Carson, Carlos Chavez, Walt Whitman, Bob Dylan, Ralph Waldo Emerson, Judy Garland, Paul Gauguin, Allen Ginsberg, Benny Goodman, Bob Hope, Burl Ives, John F. Kennedy, Peggy Lee, Marilyn Monroe, Joe Namath, Cole Porter, Laurence Olivier, Harriet Beecher Stowe, Queen Victoria, John Wayne, Frank Lloyd Wright

CANCER: "Dear Abby," Lizzie Borden, David Brinkley, Yul Brynner, Pearl Buck, Marc Chagall, Princess Diana, Babe Didrikson, Mary Baker Eddy, Henry VIII, John Glenn, Ernest Hemingway, Lena Horne, Oscar Hammerstein, Helen Keller, Ann Landers, George Orwell, Nancy Reagan, Rembrandt, Richard Rodgers, Ginger Rogers, Rubens, Jean-Paul Sartre, O. J. Simpson

LEO: Neil Armstrong, James Baldwin, Lucille Ball, Emily Brontë, Wilt Chamberlain, Julia Child, William J. Clinton, Cecil B. De Mille, Ogden Nash, Amelia Earhart, Edna Ferber, Arthur Goldberg, Alfred Hitchcock, Mick Jagger, George Meany, Annie Oakley, George Bernard Shaw, Napoleon, Jacqueline Onassis, Henry Ford, Francis Scott Key, Andy Warhol, Mae West, Orville Wright

VIRGO: Ingrid Bergman, Warren Burger, Maurice Chevalier, Agatha Christie, Sean Connery, Lafayette, Peter Falk, Greta Garbo, Althea Gibson, Arthur Godfrey, Goethe, Buddy Hackett, Michael Jackson, Lyndon Johnson, D. H. Lawrence, Sophia Loren, Grandma Moses, Arnold Palmer, Queen Elizabeth I, Walter Reuther, Peter Sellers, Lily Tomlin, George Wallace

LIBRA: Brigitte Bardot, Art Buchwald, Truman Capote, Dwight D. Eisenhower, William Faulkner, F. Scott Fitzgerald, Gandhi, George Gershwin, Micky Mantle, Helen Hayes, Vladimir Horowitz, Doris Lessing, Martina Navratalova, Eugene O'Neill, Luciano Pavarotti, Emily Post, Eleanor Roosevelt, Bruce Springsteen, Margaret Thatcher, Gore Vidal, Barbara Walters, Oscar Wilde

SCORPIO: Vivien Leigh, Richard Burton, Art Carney, Johnny Carson, Billy Graham, Grace Kelly, Walter Cronkite, Marie Curie, Charles de Gaulle, Linda Evans, Indira Gandhi, Theodore Roosevelt, Rock Hudson, Katherine Hepburn, Robert F. Kennedy, Billie Jean King, Martin Luther, Georgia O'Keeffe, Pablo Picasso, Jonas Salk, Alan Shepard, Robert Louis Stevenson

SAGITTARIUS: Jane Austen, Louisa May Alcott, Woody Allen, Beethoven, Willy Brandt, Mary Martin, William F. Buckley, Maria Callas, Winston Churchill, Noel Coward, Emily Dickinson, Walt Disney, Benjamin Disraeli, James Doolittle, Kirk Douglas, Chet Huntley, Jane Fonda, Chris Evert Lloyd, Margaret Mead, Charles Schulz, John Milton, Frank Sinatra, Steven Spielberg

CAPRICORN: Muhammad Ali, Isaac Asimov, Pablo Casals, Dizzy Dean, Marlene Dietrich, James Farmer, Ava Gardner, Barry Goldwater, Cary Grant, J. Edgar Hoover, Howard Hughes, Joan of Arc, Gypsy Rose Lee, Martin Luther King, Jr., Rudyard Kipling, Mao Tse-tung, Richard Nixon, Gamal Nasser, Louis Pasteur, Albert Schweitzer, Stalin, Benjamin Franklin, Elvis Presley

AQUARIUS: Marian Anderson, Susan B. Anthony, Jack Benny, John Barrymore, Mikhail Baryshnikov, Charles Darwin, Charles Dickens, Thomas Edison, , Clark Gable, Jascha Heifetz, Abraham Lincoln, Yehudi Menuhin, Mozart, Jack Nicklaus, Ronald Reagan, Jackie Robinson, Norman Rockwell, Franklin D. Roosevelt, Gertrude Stein, Charles Lindbergh, Margaret Truman

PISCES: Edward Albee, Harry Belafonte, Alexander Graham Bell, Chopin, Adelle Davis, Albert Einstein, Golda Meir, Jackie Gleason, Winslow Homer, Edward M. Kennedy, Victor Hugo, Mike Mansfield, Michelangelo, Edna St. Vincent Millay, Liza Minelli, John Steinbeck, Linus Pauling, Ravel, Renoir, Diana Ross, William Shirer, Elizabeth Taylor, George Washington

The Signs and Their Key Words

		POSITIVE	NEGATIVE
ARIES	self	courage, initiative, pioneer instinct	brash rudeness, selfish impetuosity
TAURUS	money	endurance, loyalty, wealth	obstinacy, gluttony
GEMINI	mind	versatility	capriciousness, unreliability
CANCER	family	sympathy, homing instinct	clannishness, childishness
LEO	children	love, authority, integrity	egotism, force
VIRGO	work	purity, industry, analysis	faultfinding, cynicism
LIBRA	marriage	harmony, justice	vacillation, superficiality
SCORPIO	sex	survival, regeneration	vengeance, discord
SAGITTARIUS	travel	optimism, higher learning	lawlessness
CAPRICORN	career	depth	narrowness, gloom
AQUARIUS	friends	human fellowship, genius	perverse unpredictability
PISCES	confinement	spiritual love, universality	diffusion, escapism

The Elements and Qualities of The Signs

Every sign has both an *element* and a *quality* associated with it. The element indicates the basic makeup of the sign, and the quality describes the kind of activity associated with each.

Element	Sign	Quality	Sign
FIRE	ARIES	CARDINAL	ARIES
	LEO		LIBRA
	SAGITTARIUS		CANCER
			CAPRICORN
EARTH	TAURUS		
	VIRGO		
	CAPRICORN	FIXED	TAURUS
			LEO
			SCORPIO
AIR	GEMINI		AQUARIUS
	LIBRA		
	AQUARIUS		
		MUTABLE	GEMINI
WATER	CANCER		VIRGO
	SCORPIO		SAGITTARIUS
	PISCES		PISCES

Signs can be grouped together according to their element and quality. Signs of the same element share many basic traits in common. They tend to form stable configurations and ultimately harmonious relationships. Signs of the same quality are often less harmonious, but they share many dynamic potentials for growth as well as profound fulfillment.

Further discussion of each of these sign groupings is provided on the following pages.

The Fire Signs

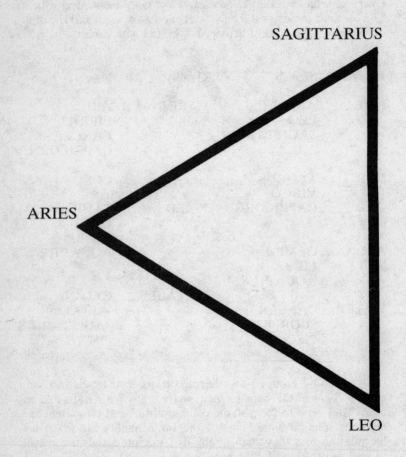

This is the fire group. On the whole these are emotional, volatile types, quick to anger, quick to forgive. They are adventurous, powerful people and act as a source of inspiration for everyone. They spark into action with immediate exuberant impulses. They are intelligent, self-involved, creative, and idealistic. They all share a certain vibrancy and glow that outwardly reflects an inner flame and passion for living.

The Earth Signs

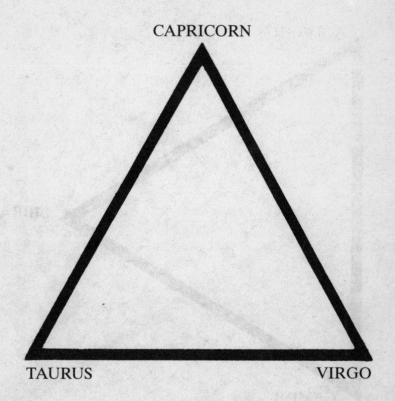

CAPRICORN

TAURUS

VIRGO

This is the earth group. They are in constant touch with the material world and tend to be conservative. Although they are all capable of spartan self-discipline, they are earthy, sensual people who are stimulated by the tangible, elegant, and luxurious. The thread of their lives is always practical, but they do fantasize and are often attracted to dark, mysterious, emotional people. They are like great cliffs overhanging the sea, forever married to the ocean but always resisting erosion from the dark, emotional forces that thunder at their feet.

The Air Signs

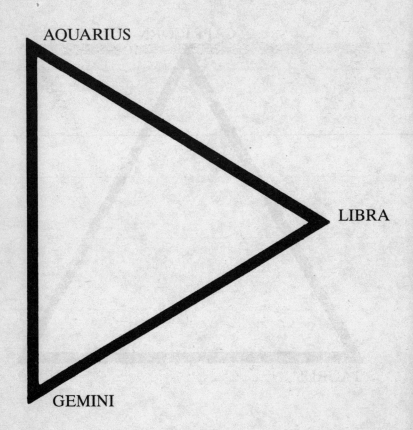

AQUARIUS

LIBRA

GEMINI

This is the air group. They are light, mental creatures desirous of contact, communication, and relationship. They are involved with people and the forming of ties on many levels. Original thinkers, they are the bearers of human news. Their language is their sense of word, color, style, and beauty. They provide an atmosphere suitable and pleasant for living. They add change and versatility to the scene, and it is through them that we can explore new territory of human intelligence and experience.

The Water Signs

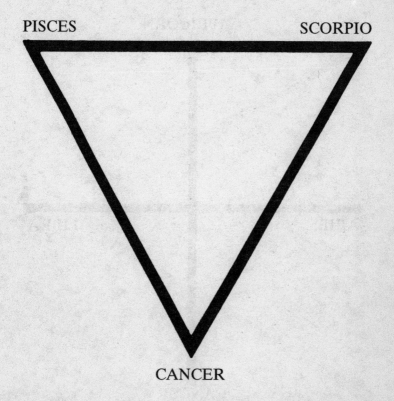

PISCES

SCORPIO

CANCER

This is the water group. Through the water people, we are all joined together on emotional, nonverbal levels. They are silent, mysterious types whose magic hypnotizes even the most determined realist. They have uncanny perceptions about people and are as rich as the oceans when it comes to feeling, emotion, or imagination. They are sensitive, mystical creatures with memories that go back beyond time. Through water, life is sustained. These people have the potential for the depths of darkness or the heights of mysticism and art.

The Cardinal Signs

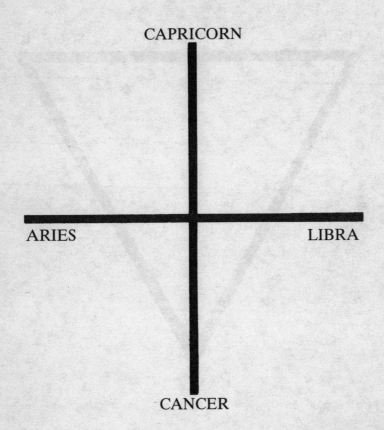

CAPRICORN

ARIES   LIBRA

CANCER

Put together, this is a clear-cut picture of dynamism, activity, tremendous stress, and remarkable achievement. These people know the meaning of great change since their lives are often characterized by significant crises and major successes. This combination is like a simultaneous storm of summer, fall, winter, and spring. The danger is chaotic diffusion of energy; the potential is irrepressible growth and victory.

The Fixed Signs

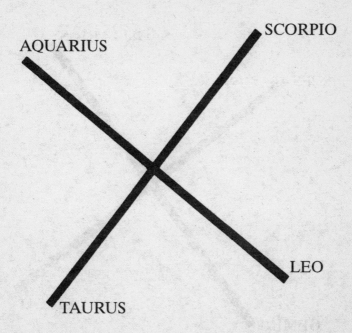

AQUARIUS

SCORPIO

TAURUS

LEO

Fixed signs are always establishing themselves in a given place or area of experience. Like explorers who arrive and plant a flag, these people claim a position from which they do not enjoy being deposed. They are staunch, stalwart, upright, trusty, honorable people, although their obstinacy is well-known. Their contribution is fixity, and they are the angels who support our visible world.

The Mutable Signs

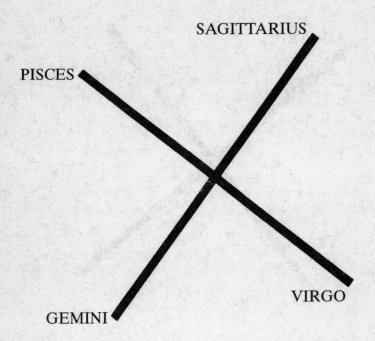

Mutable people are versatile, sensitive, intelligent, nervous, and deeply curious about life. They are the translators of all energy. They often carry out or complete tasks initiated by others. Combinations of these signs have highly developed minds; they are imaginative and jumpy and think and talk a lot. At worst their lives are a Tower of Babel. At best they are adaptable and ready creatures who can assimilate one kind of experience and enjoy it while anticipating coming changes.

THE PLANETS
OF THE SOLAR SYSTEM

This section describes the planets of the solar system. In astrology, both the Sun and the Moon are considered to be planets. Because of the Moon's influence in our day-to-day lives, the Moon is described in a separate section following this one.

The Planets and the Signs They Rule

The signs of the Zodiac are linked to the planets in the following way. Each sign is governed or ruled by one or more planets. No matter where the planets are located in the sky at any given moment, they still rule their respective signs, and when they travel through the signs they rule, they have special dignity and their effects are stronger.

Following is a list of the planets and the signs they rule. After looking at the list, read the definitions of the planets and see if you can determine how the planet ruling *your* Sun sign has affected your life.

SIGNS	RULING PLANETS
Aries	Mars, Pluto
Taurus	Venus
Gemini	Mercury
Cancer	Moon
Leo	Sun
Virgo	Mercury
Libra	Venus
Scorpio	Mars, Pluto
Sagittarius	Jupiter
Capricorn	Saturn
Aquarius	Saturn, Uranus
Pisces	Jupiter, Neptune

Characteristics of the Planets

The following pages give the meaning and characteristics of the planets of the solar system. They all travel around the Sun at different speeds and different distances. Taken with the Sun, they all distribute individual intelligence and ability throughout the entire chart.

The planets modify the influence of the Sun in a chart according to their own particular natures, strengths, and positions. Their positions must be calculated for each year and day, and their function and expression in a horoscope will change as they move from one area of the Zodiac to another.

We start with a description of the sun.

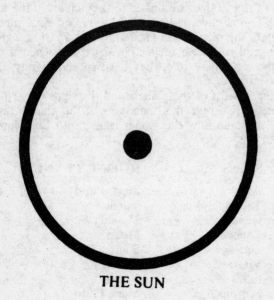

THE SUN

SUN

This is the center of existence. Around this flaming sphere all the planets revolve in endless orbits. Our star is constantly sending out its beams of light and energy without which no life on Earth would be possible. In astrology it symbolizes everything we are trying to become, the center around which all of our activity in life will always revolve. It is the symbol of our basic nature and describes the natural and constant thread that runs through everything that we do from birth to death on this planet.

To early astrologers, the Sun seemed to be another planet because it crossed the heavens every day, just like the rest of the bodies in the sky.

It is the only star near enough to be seen well—it is, in fact, a dwarf star. Approximately 860,000 miles in diameter, it is about ten times as wide as the giant planet Jupiter. The next nearest star is nearly 300,000 times as far away, and if the Sun were located as far away as most of the bright stars, it would be too faint to be seen without a telescope.

Everything in the horoscope ultimately revolves around this singular body. Although other forces may be prominent in the charts of some individuals, still the Sun is the total nucleus of being and symbolizes the complete potential of every human being alive. It is vitality and the life force. Your whole essence comes from the position of the Sun.

You are always trying to express the Sun according to its position by house and sign. Possibility for all development is found in the Sun, and it marks the fundamental character of your personal radiations all around you.

It is the symbol of strength, vigor, wisdom, dignity, ardor, and generosity, and the ability for a person to function as a mature individual. It is also a creative force in society. It is consciousness of the gift of life.

The underdeveloped solar nature is arrogant, pushy, undependable, and proud, and is constantly using force.

MERCURY

Mercury is the planet closest to the Sun. It races around our star, gathering information and translating it to the rest of the system. Mercury represents your capacity to understand the desires of your own will and to translate those desires into action.

In other words it is the planet of mind and the power of communication. Through Mercury we develop an ability to think, write, speak, and observe—to become aware of the world around us. It colors our attitudes and vision of the world, as well as our capacity to communicate our inner responses to the outside world. Some people who have serious disabilities in their power of verbal communication have often wrongly been described as people lacking intelligence.

Although this planet (and its position in the horoscope) indicates your power to communicate your thoughts and perceptions to the world, intelligence is something deeper. Intelligence is distributed throughout all the planets. It is the relationship of the planets to each other that truly describes what we call intelligence. Mercury rules speaking, language, mathematics, draft and design, students, messengers, young people, offices, teachers, and any pursuits where the mind of man has wings.

VENUS

Venus is beauty. It symbolizes the harmony and radiance of a rare
and elusive quality: beauty itself. It is refinement and delicacy,
softness and charm. In astrology it indicates grace, balance, and
the aesthetic sense. Where Venus is we see beauty, a gentle draw-
ing in of energy and the need for satisfaction and completion. It
is a special touch that finishes off rough edges. It is sensitivity, and
affection, and it is always the place for that other elusive phenomenon: love. Venus describes our sense of what is beautiful and
loving. Poorly developed, it is vulgar, tasteless, and self-indulgent.
But its ideal is the flame of spiritual love—Aphrodite, goddess of
love, and the sweetness and power of personal beauty.

MARS

Mars is raw, crude energy. The planet next to Earth but outward from the Sun is a fiery red sphere that charges through the horoscope with force and fury. It represents the way you reach out for new adventure and new experience. It is energy and drive, initiative, courage, and daring. It is the power to start something and see it through. It can be thoughtless, cruel and wild, angry and hostile, causing cuts, burns, scalds, and wounds. It can stab its way through a chart, or it can be the symbol of healthy spirited adventure, well-channeled constructive power to begin and keep up the drive. If you have trouble starting things, if you lack the get-up-and-go to start the ball rolling, if you lack aggressiveness and self-confidence, chances are there's another planet influencing your Mars. Mars rules soldiers, butchers, surgeons, salesmen—any field that requires daring, bold skill, operational technique, or self-promotion.

JUPITER

This is the largest planet of the solar system. Scientists have recently learned that Jupiter reflects more light than it receives from the Sun. In a sense it is like a star itself. In astrology it rules good luck and good cheer, health, wealth, optimism, happiness, success, and joy. It is the symbol of opportunity and always opens the way for new possibilities in your life. It rules exuberance, enthusiasm, wisdom, knowledge, generosity, and all forms of expansion in general. It rules actors, statesmen, clerics, professional people, religion, publishing, and the distribution of many people over large areas.

Sometimes Jupiter makes you think you deserve everything, and you become sloppy, wasteful, careless and rude, prodigal and lawless, in the illusion that nothing can ever go wrong. Then there is the danger of overconfidence, exaggeration, undependability, and overindulgence.

Jupiter is the minimization of limitation and the emphasis on spirituality and potential. It is the thirst for knowledge and higher learning.

SATURN

Saturn circles our system in dark splendor with its mysterious rings, forcing us to be awakened to whatever we have neglected in the past. It will present real puzzles and problems to be solved, causing delays, obstacles, and hindrances. By doing so, Saturn stirs our own sensitivity to those areas where we are laziest.

Here we must patiently develop *method*, and only through painstaking effort can our ends be achieved. It brings order to a horoscope and imposes reason just where we are feeling least reasonable. By creating limitations and boundary, Saturn shows the consequences of being human and demands that we accept the changing cycles inevitable in human life. Saturn rules time, old age, and sobriety. It can bring depression, gloom, jealousy, and greed, or serious acceptance of responsibilities out of which success will develop. With Saturn there is nothing to do but face facts. It rules laborers, stones, granite, rocks, and crystals of all kinds.

THE OUTER PLANETS:
URANUS, NEPTUNE, PLUTO

Uranus, Neptune, Pluto are the outer planets. They liberate human beings from cultural conditioning, and in that sense are the lawbreakers. In early times it was thought that Saturn was the last planet of the system—the outer limit beyond which we could never go. The discovery of the next three planets ushered in new phases of human history, revolution, and technology.

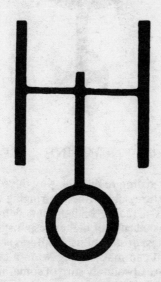

URANUS

Uranus rules unexpected change, upheaval, revolution. It is the symbol of total independence and asserts the freedom of an individual from all restriction and restraint. It is a breakthrough planet and indicates talent, originality, and genius in a horoscope. It usually causes last-minute reversals and changes of plan, unwanted separations, accidents, catastrophes, and eccentric behavior. It can add irrational rebelliousness and perverse bohemianism to a personality or a streak of unaffected brilliance in science and art. It rules technology, aviation, and all forms of electrical and electronic advancement. It governs great leaps forward and topsy-turvy situations, and *always* turns things around at the last minute. Its effects are difficult to predict, since it rules sudden last-minute decisions and events that come like lightning out of the blue.

NEPTUNE

Neptune dissolves existing reality the way the sea erodes the cliffs beside it. Its effects are subtle like the ringing of a buoy's bell in the fog. It suggests a reality higher than definition can usually describe. It awakens a sense of higher responsibility often causing guilt, worry, anxieties, or delusions. Neptune is associated with all forms of escape and can make things seem a certain way so convincingly that you are absolutely sure of something that eventually turns out to be quite different.

It is the planet of illusion and therefore governs the invisible realms that lie beyond our ordinary minds, beyond our simple factual ability to prove what is "real." Treachery, deceit, disillusionment, and disappointment are linked to Neptune. It describes a vague reality that promises eternity and the divine, yet in a manner so complex that we cannot really fathom it at all. At its worst Neptune is a cheap intoxicant; at its best it is the poetry, music, and inspiration of the higher planes of spiritual love. It has dominion over movies, photographs, and much of the arts.

PLUTO

Pluto lies at the outpost of our system and therefore rules finality in a horoscope—the final closing of chapters in your life, the passing of major milestones and points of development from which there is no return. It is a final wipeout, a closeout, an evacuation. It is a distant, subtle but powerful catalyst in all transformations that occur. It creates, destroys, then recreates. Sometimes Pluto starts its influence with a minor event or insignificant incident that might even go unnoticed. Slowly but surely, little by little, everything changes, until at last there has been a total transformation in the area of your life where Pluto has been operating. It rules mass thinking and the trends that society first rejects, then adopts, and finally outgrows.

Pluto rules the dead and the underworld—all the powerful forces of creation and destruction that go on all the time beneath, around, and above us. It can bring a lust for power with strong obsessions.

It is the planet that rules the metamorphosis of the caterpillar into a butterfly, for it symbolizes the capacity to change totally and forever a person's lifestyle, way of thought, and behavior.

THE MOON IN EACH SIGN

The Moon is the nearest planet to the Earth. It exerts more observable influence on us from day to day than any other planet. The effect is very personal, very intimate, and if we are not aware of how it works it can make us quite unstable in our ideas. And the annoying thing is that at these times we often see our own instability but can do nothing about it. A knowledge of what can be expected may help considerably. We can then be prepared to stand strong against the Moon's negative influences and use its positive ones to help us to get ahead. Who has not heard of going with the tide?

The Moon reflects, has no light of its own. It reflects the Sun—the life giver—in the form of vital movement. The Moon controls the tides, the blood rhythm, the movement of sap in trees and plants. Its nature is inconstancy and change so it signifies our moods, our superficial behavior—walking, talking, and especially thinking. Being a true reflector of other forces, the Moon is cold, watery like the surface of a still lake, brilliant and scintillating at times, but easily ruffled and disturbed by the winds of change.

The Moon takes about 27⅓ days to make a complete transit of the Zodiac. It spends just over 2¼ days in each sign. During that time it reflects the qualities, energies, and characteristics of the sign and, to a degree, the planet which rules the sign. When the Moon in its transit occupies a sign incompatible with our own birth sign, we can expect to feel a vague uneasiness, perhaps a touch of irritableness. We should not be discouraged nor let the feeling get us down, or, worse still, allow ourselves to take the discomfort out on others. Try to remember that the Moon has to change signs within 55 hours and, provided you are not physically ill, your mood will probably change with it. It is amazing how frequently depression lifts with the shift in the Moon's position. And, of course, when the Moon is transiting a sign compatible or sympathetic to yours, you will probably feel some sort of stimulation or just be plain happy to be alive.

In the horoscope, the Moon is such a powerful indicator that competent astrologers often use the sign it occupied at birth as the birth sign of the person. This is done particularly when the Sun is on the cusp, or edge, of two signs. Most experienced astrologers, however, coordinate both Sun and Moon signs by reading and confirming from one to the other and secure a far more accurate and personalized analysis.

For these reasons, the Moon tables which follow this section (see pages 86–92) are of great importance to the individual. They show the days and the exact times the Moon will enter each sign of the Zodiac for the year. Remember, you have to adjust the indicated times to local time. The corrections, already calculated for most of the main cities, are at the beginning of the tables. What follows now is a guide to the influences that will be reflected to the Earth by the Moon while it transits each of the twelve signs. The influence is at its peak about 26 hours after the Moon enters a sign. As you read the daily forecast, check the Moon sign for any given day and glance back at this guide.

MOON IN ARIES
This is a time for action, for reaching out beyond the usual self-imposed limitations and faint-hearted cautions. If you have plans in your head or on your desk, put them into practice. New ventures, applications, new jobs, new starts of any kind—all have a good chance of success. This is the period when original and dynamic impulses are being reflected onto Earth. Such energies are extremely vital and favor the pursuit of pleasure and adventure in practically every form. Sick people should feel an improvement. Those who are well will probably find themselves exuding confidence and optimism. People fond of physical exercise should find their bodies growing with tone and well-being. Boldness, strength, determination should characterize most of your activities with a readiness to face up to old challenges. Yesterday's problems may seem petty and exaggerated—so deal with them. Strike out alone. Self-reliance will attract others to you. This is a good time for making friends. Business and marriage partners are more likely to be impressed with the man and woman of action. Opposition will be overcome or thrown aside with much less effort than usual. CAUTION: Be dominant but not domineering.

MOON IN TAURUS
The spontaneous, action-packed person of yesterday gives way to the cautious, diligent, hardworking "thinker." In this period ideas will probably be concentrated on ways of improving finances. A great deal of time may be spent figuring out and going over

schemes and plans. It is the right time to be careful with detail. People will find themselves working longer than usual at their desks. Or devoting more time to serious thought about the future. A strong desire to put order into business and financial arrangements may cause extra work. Loved ones may complain of being neglected and may fail to appreciate that your efforts are for their ultimate benefit. Your desire for system may extend to criticism of arrangements in the home and lead to minor upsets. Health may be affected through overwork. Try to secure a reasonable amount of rest and relaxation, although the tendency will be to "keep going" despite good advice. Work done conscientiously in this period should result in a solid contribution to your future security. CAUTION: Try not to be as serious with people as the work you are engaged in.

MOON IN GEMINI
The humdrum of routine and too much work should suddenly end. You are likely to find yourself in an expansive, quicksilver world of change and self-expression. Urges to write, to paint, to experience the freedom of some sort of artistic outpouring, may be very strong. Take full advantage of them. You may find yourself finishing something you began and put aside long ago. Or embarking on something new which could easily be prompted by a chance meeting, a new acquaintance, or even an advertisement. There may be a yearning for a change of scenery, the feeling to visit another country (not too far away), or at least to get away for a few days. This may result in short, quick journeys. Or, if you are planning a single visit, there may be some unexpected changes or detours on the way. Familiar activities will seem to give little satisfaction unless they contain a fresh element of excitement or expectation. The inclination will be toward untried pursuits, particularly those that allow you to express your inner nature. The accent is on new faces, new places. CAUTION: Do not be too quick to commit yourself emotionally.

MOON IN CANCER
Feelings of uncertainty and vague insecurity are likely to cause problems while the Moon is in Cancer. Thoughts may turn frequently to the warmth of the home and the comfort of loved ones. Nostalgic impulses could cause you to bring out old photographs and letters and reflect on the days when your life seemed to be much more rewarding and less demanding. The love and understanding of parents and family may be important, and, if it is not forthcoming, you may have to fight against bouts of self-pity. The cordiality of friends and the thought of good times with them that

are sure to be repeated will help to restore you to a happier frame of mind. The desire to be alone may follow minor setbacks or rebuffs at this time, but solitude is unlikely to help. Better to get on the telephone or visit someone. This period often causes peculiar dreams and upsurges of imaginative thinking which can be helpful to authors of occult and mystical works. Preoccupation with the personal world of simple human needs can overshadow any material strivings. CAUTION: Do not spend too much time thinking—seek the company of loved ones or close friends.

MOON IN LEO

New horizons of exciting and rather extravagant activity open up. This is the time for exhilarating entertainment, glamorous and lavish parties, and expensive shopping sprees. Any merrymaking that relies upon your generosity as a host has every chance of being a spectacular success. You should find yourself right in the center of the fun, either as the life of the party or simply as a person whom happy people like to be with. Romance thrives in this heady atmosphere and friendships are likely to explode unexpectedly into serious attachments. Children and younger people should be attracted to you and you may find yourself organizing a picnic or a visit to a fun-fair, the movies, or the beach. The sunny company and vitality of youthful companions should help you to find some unsuspected energy. In career, you could find an opening for promotion or advancement. This should be the time to make a direct approach. The period favors those engaged in original research. CAUTION: Bask in popularity, not in flattery.

MOON IN VIRGO

Off comes the party cap and out steps the busy, practical worker. He wants to get his personal affairs straight, to rearrange them, if necessary, for more efficiency, so he will have more time for more work. He clears up his correspondence, pays outstanding bills, makes numerous phone calls. He is likely to make inquiries, or sign up for some new insurance and put money into gilt-edged investment. Thoughts probably revolve around the need for future security—to tie up loose ends and clear the decks. There may be a tendency to be "finicky," to interfere in the routine of others, particularly friends and family members. The motive may be a genuine desire to help with suggestions for updating or streamlining their affairs, but these will probably not be welcomed. Sympathy may be felt for less fortunate sections of the community and a flurry of some sort of voluntary service is likely. This may be accompanied by strong feelings of responsibility on several fronts and health may suffer from extra efforts made. CAUTION: Everyone may not want your help or advice.

MOON IN LIBRA

These are days of harmony and agreement and you should find yourself at peace with most others. Relationships tend to be smooth and sweet-flowing. Friends may become closer and bonds deepen in mutual understanding. Hopes will be shared. Progress by cooperation could be the secret of success in every sphere. In business, established partnerships may flourish and new ones get off to a good start. Acquaintances could discover similar interests that lead to congenial discussions and rewarding exchanges of some sort. Love, as a unifying force, reaches its optimum. Marriage partners should find accord. Those who wed at this time face the prospect of a happy union. Cooperation and tolerance are felt to be stronger than dissension and impatience. The argumentative are not quite so loud in their bellowings, nor as inflexible in their attitudes. In the home, there should be a greater recognition of the other point of view and a readiness to put the wishes of the group before selfish insistence. This is a favorable time to join an art group. CAUTION: Do not be too independent—let others help you if they want to.

MOON IN SCORPIO

Driving impulses to make money and to economize are likely to cause upsets all around. No area of expenditure is likely to be spared the ax, including the household budget. This is a time when the desire to cut down on extravagance can become near fanatical. Care must be exercised to try to keep the aim in reasonable perspective. Others may not feel the same urgent need to save and may retaliate. There is a danger that possessions of sentimental value will be sold to realize cash for investment. Buying and selling of stock for quick profit is also likely. The attention turns to organizing, reorganizing, tidying up at home and at work. Neglected jobs could suddenly be done with great bursts of energy. The desire for solitude may intervene. Self-searching thoughts could disturb. The sense of invisible and mysterious energies in play could cause some excitability. The reassurance of loves ones may help. CAUTION: Be kind to the people you love.

MOON IN SAGITTARIUS

These are days when you are likely to be stirred and elevated by discussions and reflections of a religious and philosophical nature. Ideas of faraway places may cause unusual response and excitement. A decision may be made to visit someone overseas, perhaps a person whose influence was important to your earlier character development. There could be a strong resolution to get away from present intellectual patterns, to learn new subjects, and to meet more interesting people. The superficial may be rejected in all its forms. An impatience with old ideas and unimaginative contacts could lead to a change of companions and interests. There may be an upsurge of religious feeling and metaphysical inquiry. Even a new insight into the significance of astrology and other occult studies is likely under the curious stimulus of the Moon in Sagittarius. Physically, you may express this need for fundamental change by spending more time outdoors: sports, gardening, long walks appeal. CAUTION: Try to channel any restlessness into worthwhile study.

MOON IN CAPRICORN

Life in these hours may seem to pivot around the importance of gaining prestige and honor in the career, as well as maintaining a spotless reputation. Ambitious urges may be excessive and could be accompanied by quite acquisitive drives for money. Effort should be directed along strictly ethical lines where there is no possibility of reproach or scandal. All endeavors are likely to be characterized by great earnestness, and an air of authority and purpose which should impress those who are looking for leadership or reliability. The desire to conform to accepted standards may extend to sharp criticism of family members. Frivolity and unconventional actions are unlikely to amuse while the Moon is in Capricorn. Moderation and seriousness are the orders of the day. Achievement and recognition in this period could come through community work or organizing for the benefit of some amateur group. CAUTION: Dignity and esteem are not always self-awarded.

MOON IN AQUARIUS

Moon in Aquarius is in the second last sign of the Zodiac where ideas can become disturbingly fine and subtle. The result is often a mental "no-man's land" where imagination cannot be trusted with the same certitude as other times. The dangers for the individual are the extremes of optimism and pessimism. Unless the imagination is held in check, situations are likely to be misread, and rosy conclusions drawn where they do not exist. Consequences for the unwary can be costly in career and business. Best to think twice and not speak or act until you think again. Pessimism can be a cruel self-inflicted penalty for delusion at this time. Between the two extremes are strange areas of self-deception which, for example, can make the selfish person think he is actually being generous. Eerie dreams which resemble the reality and even seem to continue into the waking state are also possible. CAUTION: Look for the fact and not just for the image in your mind.

MOON IN PISCES

Everything seems to come to the surface now. Memory may be crystal clear, throwing up long-forgotten information which could be valuable in the career or business. Flashes of clairvoyance and intuition are possible along with sudden realizations of one's own nature, which may be used for self-improvement. A talent, never before suspected, may be discovered. Qualities not evident before in friends and marriage partners are likely to be noticed. As this is a period in which the truth seems to emerge, the discovery of false characteristics is likely to lead to disenchantment or a shift in attachments. However, when qualities are accepted, it should lead to happiness and deeper feeling. Surprise solutions could bob up for old problems. There may be a public announcement of the solving of a crime or mystery. People with secrets may find someone has "guessed" correctly. The secrets of the soul or the inner self also tend to reveal themselves. Religious and philosophical groups may make some interesting discoveries. CAUTION: Not a time for activities that depend on secrecy.

NOTE: When you read your daily forecasts, use the Moon Sign Dates that are provided in the following section of Moon Tables. Then you may want to glance back here for the Moon's influence in a given sign.

MOON TABLES

CORRECTION FOR NEW YORK TIME, FIVE HOURS WEST OF GREENWICH

Atlanta, Boston, Detroit, Miami, Washington, Montreal,
Ottawa, Quebec, Bogota,
Havana, Lima, Santiago...............................Same time
Chicago, New Orleans, Houston, Winnipeg, Churchill,
Mexico City.. Deduct 1 hour
Albuquerque, Denver, Phoenix, El Paso, Edmonton,
Helena .... Deduct 2 hours
Los Angeles, San Francisco, Reno, Portland,
Seattle, Vancouver .... Deduct 3 hours
Honolulu, Anchorage, Fairbanks, Kodiak .... Deduct 5 hours
Nome, Samoa, Tonga, Midway.................... Deduct 6 hours
Halifax, Bermuda, San Juan, Caracas, La Paz,
Barbados...Add 1 hour
St. John's, Brasilia, Rio de Janeiro, Sao Paulo,
Buenos Aires, Montevideo.........................Add 2 hours
Azores, Cape Verde Islands...........................Add 3 hours
Canary Islands, Madeira, Reykjavik ....Add 4 hours
London, Paris, Amsterdam, Madrid, Lisbon,
Gibraltar, Belfast, Rabat...........................Add 5 hours
Frankfurt, Rome, Oslo, Stockholm, Prague,
Belgrade...Add 6 hours
Bucharest, Beirut, Tel Aviv, Athens, Istanbul, Cairo,
Alexandria, Cape Town, Johannesburg ....Add 7 hours
Moscow, Leningrad, Baghdad, Dhahran,
Addis Ababa, Nairobi, Teheran, Zanzibar.........Add 8 hours
Bombay, Calcutta, Sri Lanka.................... Add 10 ½ hours
Hong Kong, Shanghai, Manila, Peking, Perth...... Add 13 hours
Tokyo, Okinawa, Darwin, Pusan.................... Add 14 hours
Sydney, Melbourne, Port Moresby, Guam.......... Add 15 hours
Auckland, Wellington, Suva, Wake................. Add 17 hours

2003 MOON SIGN DATES—
NEW YORK TIME

JANUARY		FEBRUARY		MARCH	
Day Moon Enters		**Day Moon Enters**		**Day Moon Enters**	
1. Capric.	6:44 pm	1. Aquar.		1. Pisces	10:27 pm
2. Capric.		2. Pisces	2:56 pm	2. Pisces	
3. Aquar.	10:58 pm	3. Pisces		3. Pisces	
4. Aquar.		4. Pisces		4. Aries	8:31 am
5. Aquar.		5. Aries	12:45 am	5. Aries	
6. Pisces	5:58 am	6. Aries		6. Taurus	8:37 pm
7. Pisces		7. Taurus	1:00 pm	7. Taurus	
8. Aries	4:16 pm	8. Taurus		8. Taurus	
9. Aries		9. Taurus		9. Gemini	9:39 am
10. Aries		10. Gemini	1:46 am	10. Gemini	
11. Taurus	4:49 am	11. Gemini		11. Cancer	9:13 pm
12. Taurus		12. Cancer	12:20 pm	12. Cancer	
13. Gemini	5:09 pm	13. Cancer		13. Cancer	
14. Gemini		14. Leo	7:05 pm	14. Leo	5:07 am
15. Gemini		15. Leo		15. Leo	
16. Cancer	2:57 am	16. Virgo	10:24 pm	16. Virgo	8:54 am
17. Cancer		17. Virgo		17. Virgo	
18. Leo	9:30 am	18. Libra	11:49 pm	18. Libra	9:44 am
19. Leo		19. Libra		19. Libra	
20. Virgo	1:33 pm	20. Libra		20. Scorp.	9:39 am
21. Virgo		21. Scorp.	1:10 am	21. Scorp.	
22. Libra	4:24 pm	22. Scorp.		22. Sagitt.	10:34 am
23. Libra		23. Sagitt.	3:47 am	23. Sagitt.	
24. Scorp.	7:10 pm	24. Sagitt.		24. Capric.	1:49 pm
25. Scorp.		25. Capric.	8:12 am	25. Capric.	
26. Sagitt.	10:27 pm	26. Capric.		26. Aquar.	7:52 pm
27. Sagitt.		27. Aquar.	2:26 pm	27. Aquar.	
28. Sagitt.		28. Aquar.		28. Aquar.	
29. Capric.	2:31 am			29. Pisces	4:27 am
30. Capric.				30. Pisces	
31. Aquar.	7:45 am			31. Aries	3:06 pm

Summer time to be considered where applicable.

2003 MOON SIGN DATES—
NEW YORK TIME

APRIL		MAY		JUNE	
Day Moon Enters		**Day Moon Enters**		**Day Moon Enters**	
1. Aries		1. Taurus		1. Cancer	4:28 pm
2. Aries		2. Gemini	10:28 pm	2. Cancer	
3. Taurus	3:21 am	3. Gemini		3. Cancer	
4. Taurus		4. Gemini		4. Leo	2:26 am
5. Gemini	4:25 pm	5. Cancer	10:43 am	5. Leo	
6. Gemini		6. Cancer		6. Virgo	9:52 am
7. Gemini		7. Leo	8:47 pm	7. Virgo	
8. Cancer	4:37 am	8. Leo		8. Libra	2:31 pm
9. Cancer		9. Leo		9. Libra	
10. Leo	1:55 pm	10. Virgo	3:32 am	10. Scorp.	4:40 pm
11. Leo		11. Virgo		11. Scorp.	
12. Virgo	7:08 pm	12. Libra	6:43 am	12. Sagitt.	5:13 pm
13. Virgo		13. Libra		13. Sagitt.	
14. Libra	8:43 pm	14. Scorp.	7:15 am	14. Capric.	5:39 pm
15. Libra		15. Scorp.		15. Capric.	
16. Scorp.	8:17 pm	16. Sagitt.	6:44 am	16. Aquar.	7:42 pm
17. Scorp.		17. Sagitt.		17. Aquar.	
18. Sagitt.	7:53 pm	18. Capric.	7:04 am	18. Aquar.	
19. Sagitt.		19. Capric.		19. Pisces	12:58 am
20. Capric.	9:21 pm	20. Aquar.	10:02 am	20. Pisces	
21. Capric.		21. Aquar.		21. Aries	10:07 am
22. Capric.		22. Pisces	4:42 pm	22. Aries	
23. Aquar.	1:59 am	23. Pisces		23. Taurus	10:16 pm
24. Aquar.		24. Pisces		24. Taurus	
25. Pisces	10:03 am	25. Aries	3:00 am	25. Taurus	
26. Pisces		26. Aries		26. Gemini	11:14 am
27. Aries	8:55 pm	27. Taurus	3:33 pm	27. Gemini	
28. Aries		28. Taurus		28. Cancer	10:53 pm
29. Aries		29. Taurus		29. Cancer	
30. Taurus	9:27 am	30. Gemini	4:33 am	30. Cancer	
		31. Gemini			

Summer time to be considered where applicable.

2003 MOON SIGN DATES—
NEW YORK TIME

JULY		AUGUST		SEPTEMBER	
Day Moon Enters		**Day Moon Enters**		**Day Moon Enters**	
1. Leo	8:14 am	1. Virgo		1. Scorp.	
2. Leo		2. Libra	1:49 am	2. Sagitt.	1:33 pm
3. Virgo	3:17 pm	3. Libra		3. Sagitt.	
4. Virgo		4. Scorp.	5:13 am	4. Capric.	4:52 pm
5. Libra	8:21 pm	5. Scorp.		5. Capric.	
6. Libra		6. Sagitt.	8:12 am	6. Aquar.	9:16 pm
7. Scorp.	11:45 pm	7. Sagitt.		7. Aquar.	
8. Scorp.		8. Capric.	11:03 am	8. Aquar.	
9. Scorp.		9. Capric.		9. Pisces	3:08 am
10. Sagitt.	1:49 am	10. Aquar.	2:25 pm	10. Pisces	
11. Sagitt.		11. Aquar.		11. Aries	11:10 am
12. Capric.	3:22 am	12. Pisces	7:20 pm	12. Aries	
13. Capric.		13. Pisces		13. Taurus	9:51 pm
14. Aquar.	5:39 am	14. Pisces		14. Taurus	
15. Aquar.		15. Aries	3:01 am	15. Taurus	
16. Pisces	10:15 am	16. Aries		16. Gemini	10:33 am
17. Pisces		17. Taurus	1:53 pm	17. Gemini	
18. Aries	6:21 pm	18. Taurus		18. Cancer	11:08 pm
19. Aries		19. Taurus		19. Cancer	
20. Aries		20. Gemini	2:42 am	20. Cancer	
21. Taurus	5:49 am	21. Gemini		21. Leo	9:04 am
22. Taurus		22. Cancer	2:45 pm	22. Leo	
23. Gemini	6:43 pm	23. Cancer		23. Virgo	3:06 pm
24. Gemini		24. Leo	11:49 pm	24. Virgo	
25. Gemini		25. Leo		25. Libra	5:50 pm
26. Cancer	6:24 am	26. Leo		26. Libra	
27. Cancer		27. Virgo	5:28 am	27. Scorp.	6:53 pm
28. Leo	3:18 pm	28. Virgo		28. Scorp.	
29. Leo		29. Libra	8:42 am	29. Sagitt.	7:58 pm
30. Virgo	9:28 pm	30. Libra		30. Sagitt.	
31. Virgo		31. Scorp.	11:01 am		

Summer time to be considered where applicable.

2003 MOON SIGN DATES—
NEW YORK TIME

OCTOBER		NOVEMBER		DECEMBER	
Day Moon Enters		**Day Moon Enters**		**Day Moon Enters**	
1. Capric.	10:22 pm	1. Aquar.		1. Pisces	
2. Capric.		2. Pisces	2:53 pm	2. Aries	5:57 am
3. Capric.		3. Pisces		3. Aries	
4. Aquar.	2:46 am	4. Pisces		4. Taurus	5:31 pm
5. Aquar.		5. Aries	12:04 am	5. Taurus	
6. Pisces	9:21 am	6. Aries		6. Taurus	
7. Pisces		7. Taurus	11:30 am	7. Gemini	6:27 am
8. Aries	6:09 pm	8. Taurus		8. Gemini	
9. Aries		9. Taurus		9. Cancer	7:12 pm
10. Aries		10. Gemini	12:15 am	10. Cancer	
11. Taurus	5:06 am	11. Gemini		11. Cancer	
12. Taurus		12. Cancer	1:11 pm	12. Leo	6:41 am
13. Gemini	5:46 pm	13. Cancer		13. Leo	
14. Gemini		14. Cancer		14. Virgo	4:08 pm
15. Gemini		15. Leo	12:49 am	15. Virgo	
16. Cancer	6:42 am	16. Leo		16. Libra	10:48 pm
17. Cancer		17. Virgo	9:37 am	17. Libra	
18. Leo	5:42 pm	18. Virgo		18. Libra	
19. Leo		19. Libra	2:43 pm	19. Scorp.	2:21 am
20. Leo		20. Libra		20. Scorp.	
21. Virgo	1:02 am	21. Scorp.	4:25 pm	21. Sagitt.	3:17 am
22. Virgo		22. Scorp.		22. Sagitt.	
23. Libra	4:28 am	23. Sagitt.	4:04 pm	23. Capric.	2:56 am
24. Libra		24. Sagitt.		24. Capric.	
25. Scorp.	5:10 am	25. Capric.	3:32 pm	25. Aquar.	3:14 am
26. Scorp.		26. Capric.		26. Aquar.	
27. Sagitt.	4:56 am	27. Aquar.	4:49 pm	27. Pisces	6:11 am
28. Sagitt.		28. Aquar.		28. Pisces	
29. Capric.	5:38 am	29. Pisces	9:26 pm	29. Aries	1:09 pm
30. Capric.		30. Pisces		30. Aries	
31. Aquar.	8:42 am			31. Aries	

Summer time to be considered where applicable.

2003 PHASES OF THE MOON— NEW YORK TIME

New Moon	First Quarter	Full Moon	Last Quarter
Jan. 2	Jan. 10	Jan. 18	Jan. 25
Feb. 1	Feb. 9	Feb. 16	Feb. 23
March 2	March 11	March 18	March 24
April 1	April 9	April 16	April 23
May 1	May 9	May 15	May 22
May 30	June 7	June 14	June 21
June 29	July 6	July 13	July 21
July 29	Aug. 5	Aug. 11	Aug. 19
Aug. 27	Sept. 3	Sept. 10	Sept. 18
Sept. 25	Oct. 2	Oct. 10	Oct. 18
Oct. 25	Oct. 31	Nov. 8	Nov. 16
Nov. 23	Nov. 30	Dec. 8	Dec. 16
Dec. 23	Dec. 30	Jan. 7 ('04)	Jan. 15 ('04)

Each phase of the Moon lasts approximately seven to eight days, during which the Moon's shape gradually changes as it comes out of one phase and goes into the next.

There will be a solar eclipse during the New Moon phase on May 30 and November 23.

There will be a lunar eclipse during the Full Moon phase on May 15 and November 8.

2003 FISHING GUIDE

	Good	Best
January	10-15-18-19-20-21	2-16-17-25
February	1-15-16-17-18-23	9-13-14-19
March	11-15-16-17-18	3-19-20-21-25
April	1-13-14-19-23	9-15-16-17-18
May	1-9-16-17-18-31	13-14-15-19-23
June	7-13-14-17-21	11-12-15-16-29
July	10-11-14-15-16-21-29	7-12-13
August	10-11-12-15-20-27	5-9-13-14
September	3-7-8-11-12-13-18	9-10-26
October	9-10-11	2-7-8-12-13-18-25
November	1-6-7-10-11-12-17-23	8-9-30
December	7-8-9-16-30	5-6-10-11-23

2003 PLANTING GUIDE

	Aboveground Crops	Root Crops
January	3-7-11-12-13-16-17	23-24-25-26-29-30
February	3-4-8-9-13-14	19-20-21-22-26
March	3-7-8-12-13	2-19-20-21-25-26-29-30
April	3-4-8-9-15	17-18-21-22-26-27
May	2-6-7-13-14-15	19-23-24-28-29
June	2-3-9-10-11-12-30	15-16-19-20-24-25
July	6-7-8-9-12	17-18-22-23-27
August	2-3-4-5-9-30-31	13-14-18-19-23-24
September	1-5-6-9-26-27-28-29	14-15-19-20
October	2-3-7-8-26-30	12-13-17-18-23-24
November	3-4-8-26-30	9-13-14-20-21-22
December	1-5-6-23-24-28	10-11-17-18-19-20

	Pruning	Weeds and Pests
January	25-26	1-19-20-21-27-28
February	21-22	17-18-23-24-28
March	2-21-29-30	1-23-27-28
April	17-18-26-27	19-20-23-24-28-29
May	23-24	17-21-25-26-30
June	19-20	17-18-22-23-27-28
July	17-18-27	15-19-20-24-25
August	13-14-23-24	12-15-16-20-21-25-26
September	19-20	12-13-17-18-22-23-24-25
October	17-18	10-14-15-19-20-21-22
November	13-14-22	10-11-15-16-17-18
December	10-11-19-20	9-13-14-15-16-21-22

MOON'S INFLUENCE OVER PLANTS

Centuries ago it was established that seeds planted when the Moon is in signs and phases called Fruitful will produce more growth than seeds planted when the Moon is in a Barren sign.

Fruitful Signs: Taurus, Cancer, Libra, Scorpio, Capricorn, Pisces
Barren Signs: Aries, Gemini, Leo, Virgo, Sagittarius, Aquarius
Dry Signs: Aries, Gemini, Sagittarius, Aquarius

Activity	Moon In
Mow lawn, trim plants	**Fruitful sign:** 1st & 2nd quarter
Plant flowers	**Fruitful sign:** 2nd quarter; best in Cancer and Libra
Prune	**Fruitful sign:** 3rd & 4th quarter
Destroy pests; spray	**Barren sign:** 4th quarter
Harvest potatoes, root crops	**Dry sign:** 3rd & 4th quarter; Taurus, Leo, and Aquarius

MOON'S INFLUENCE OVER YOUR HEALTH

ARIES	Head, brain, face, upper jaw
TAURUS	Throat, neck, lower jaw
GEMINI	Hands, arms, lungs, shoulders, nervous system
CANCER	Esophagus, stomach, breasts, womb, liver
LEO	Heart, spine
VIRGO	Intestines, liver
LIBRA	Kidneys, lower back
SCORPIO	Sex and eliminative organs
SAGITTARIUS	Hips, thighs, liver
CAPRICORN	Skin, bones, teeth, knees
AQUARIUS	Circulatory system, lower legs
PISCES	Feet, tone of being

Try to avoid work being done on that part of the body when the Moon is in the sign governing that part.

MOON'S INFLUENCE OVER DAILY AFFAIRS

The Moon makes a complete transit of the Zodiac every 27 days 7 hours and 43 minutes. In making this transit the Moon forms different aspects with the planets and consequently has favorable or unfavorable bearings on affairs and events for persons according to the sign of the Zodiac under which they were born.

When the Moon is in conjunction with the Sun it is called a New Moon; when the Moon and Sun are in opposition it is called a Full Moon. From New Moon to Full Moon, first and second quarter—which takes about two weeks—the Moon is increasing or waxing. From Full Moon to New Moon, third and fourth quarter, the Moon is decreasing or waning.

Activity	Moon In
Business: buying and selling new, requiring public support	Sagittarius, Aries, Gemini, Virgo 1st and 2nd quarter
meant to be kept quiet	3rd and 4th quarter
Investigation	3rd and 4th quarter
Signing documents	1st & 2nd quarter, Cancer, Scorpio, Pisces
Advertising	2nd quarter, Sagittarius
Journeys and trips	1st & 2nd quarter, Gemini, Virgo
Renting offices, etc.	Taurus, Leo, Scorpio, Aquarius
Painting of house/apartment	3rd & 4th quarter, Taurus, Scorpio, Aquarius
Decorating	Gemini, Libra, Aquarius
Buying clothes and accessories	Taurus, Virgo
Beauty salon or barber shop visit	1st & 2nd quarter, Taurus, Leo, Libra, Scorpio, Aquarius
Weddings	1st & 2nd quarter

Virgo

VIRGO

Character Analysis

People born under the sign of Virgo are generally practical. They believe in doing things thoroughly; there is nothing slipshod or haphazard about the way they do things. They are precise and methodical. The man or woman born under this sixth sign of the Zodiac respects common sense and tries to be rational in his or her approach to tasks or problems.

Virgo is the sign of work and service. It is the symbol of the farmer at harvest time, and so the man or woman born under this sign is sometimes called the Harvester. These people's tireless efforts to bring the fruits of the Earth to the table of humanity create great joy and beneficence. Celebration through work and harvest is the characteristic of the sign of Virgo.

Sincerity, zeal, and devotion mark the working methods of the Virgo man and woman. They have excellent critical abilities; they know how to analyze a problem and come up with a solution. Virgo is seldom fooled by superficialities, and can go straight to the heart of the matter.

Virgo knows how to break things down to the minutest detail; he or she prefers to work on things piece by piece. Inwardly, he is afraid of being overwhelmed by things that seem larger than life. For this reason, one often finds the Virgo occupied with details. His powers of concentration are greatest when he can concentrate on small, manageable things.

The Virgo person believes in doing things correctly; he's thorough and precise. He's seldom carried away by fantasy; he believes in keeping his feet firmly on the ground. People who seem a bit flighty or impractical sometimes irritate him.

Virgo knows how to criticize other people. It is very easy for him to point out another's weaknesses or faults; he is seldom wrong. However, Virgo is sometimes a bit sharp in making criticisms and often offends a good friend or acquaintance. The cultivated Virgo, however, knows how to apply criticism tactfully. He or she is considerate of another's feelings.

The Virgo person believes in applying himself in a positive manner to whatever task is set before him. He is a person full of purpose and goodwill. He is diligent and methodical. He is seldom given to impulse, but works along steadily and constructively.

Anything that is scientific, technological, and practical arouses Virgo's interest. The technical and craft aspects of the arts impress these people, and many Virgos become expert designers, graphic artists, and handicrafters. The precision so important to these disciplines is a quality Virgo possesses in abundance. Combined with imagination and flair, the attention to detail often makes Virgos first-rate artists.

Whether or not individual Virgos are talented in artistic areas, most of these people are usually very interested in anything of an artistic nature. Virgos also are great readers. They have a deep appreciation for the way the intricacies of life weave together, then unravel, and finally are rewoven into a new fabric or design. Virgos also possess an innate verbal ability that is especially suited to the study of a language, whether the language is a machine language such as in computers or a tongue spoken by other people. Virgo has no trouble applying his or her native intelligence and skill either in a learning or teaching capacity. Virgos enjoy school. They often study a wide range of subjects, but not in great depth, in order to have a well-rounded education. Virgos like friends and colleagues to be as well-informed as they are if not more so. Virgo has a deep respect for culture, education, and intellect.

Usually, Virgo takes in stride whatever comes into his or her life. Basically, he is an uncomplicated person, who views things clearly and sharply. He has a way of getting right down to the meat of the matter. Generally a serious-minded person, he believes in being reliable. He is not one who will take great risks in life as he has no interest in playing the hero or the idealist. Virgo believes in doing what he can, but without flourishes.

Quite often he is a quiet, modest person. He believes that appearance is important and thus does his best to look well-groomed. He feels that being neat is important and dislikes untidiness in anything.

The Virgo man or woman likes to deal with life on a practical level and they usually look for the uncomplicated answer or solution to any problem or dilemma. Even if Virgos are urged to look into the mystical side of existence, they may dismiss it as being either unfounded or irrelevant.

On the whole, the Virgo person is even-tempered. He or she does not allow himself to become angry easily. He knows how to take the bitter with the sweet. But if someone does him a wrong turn, he is not likely to forget it. His good nature is not to be abused.

Health

Many persons born under this sign are amazingly healthy. They frequently live to see a ripe old age. This longevity is generally due to the fact that people born under this sign take all things in moderation. Virgo is not the type of person who burns the candle at both ends. They acknowledge their limits and avoid excess.

Frequently Virgos are small and neat-featured. Virgo women are sometimes quite attractive in a sort of dry way. Both men and women of this sign have a youthful appearance throughout life. When young, Virgos are generally very active. However, as they reach middle age and beyond they have a tendency to put on a bit of weight.

The Virgo person usually enjoys good health, although some have a tendency to be overly concerned about it. They imagine ailments they do not really have. Still, they do manage to stay fit. Other Virgos see themselves as being rather strong and resourceful, even when they are ill. For that reason they seldom feel moved to feel sorry for another ailing Virgo. Actually, serious illnesses frighten Virgos. They will do all they can to remain in good health.

The medicine cabinet of someone born under this sign is often filled with all sorts of pills, tablets, and ointments. Most of them will never be used.

As a rule, Virgo watches his diet. He stays away from foods that won't agree with him. He keeps a balanced diet and is moderate in his drinking habits. Virgos need plenty of exercise to keep the body fit. Most Virgos do not have a particular liking for strenuous sport. But the wise Virgo always will get some kind of energetic exercise, preferably a brisk and long walk, or a daily workout. Another thing that Virgos need is rest. They should get at least eight hours sleep per day.

On the whole, Virgo is a sensitive person. His nerves may be easily affected if he finds himself in a disagreeable situation. The stomach is another area of concern. When a Virgo becomes sick, this area is usually affected. Digestion complaints are not rare among persons born under this sign. Regular meals are important for the Virgo. Quick snacks and fast food may play havoc with his digestive system. In spite of this particular weakness, Virgos manage to lead normal, healthy lives. They should try to avoid becoming too concerned with ups and downs. Many of their illnesses may turn out to be imaginary.

Occupation

Virgos delight in keeping busy. They are not afraid of hard work. By nature, they are ambitious people and are happiest when they are putting their talents and abilities to good use. They can best be described as goal-directed; they never lose sight of their objective once committed. They are very thorough in whatever they undertake. Even routine work is something that they can do without finding fault. In fact, work that is scheduled—or that follows a definite pattern—is well suited to their steady natures. Virgos will put aside other things, if necessary, in order to attain a goal. They prefer to work under peaceful conditions, and will seldom do anything to irritate their superiors.

They learn well and are not afraid to undertake any kind of work—even the most menial—if it is necessary. Sometimes, however, they neglect their own conditions because they are so involved in their work. For this reason, Virgos occasionally fall ill or become a bit nervous. Any kind of work that allows them to make use of their talent for criticism will please them.

Virgo men and women usually shine as bookkeepers, accountants, teachers, and pharmacists. The cultivated Virgo person often turns to the world of science where they are likely to do well. Some great writers and poets have been born under this sixth sign of the Zodiac.

It is very important that Virgo has the kind of work that is suited to his personality. It may take a while before he actually finds his niche in life, and he may have to struggle at times in order to make ends meet. But because he is not afraid of work, he manages to come out on top.

Virgo is a perfectionist. He or she is always looking for ways to improve the work scheme or technique. He is never satisfied until things are working smoothly. He will even do more than his share in order to secure regularity and precision in a job he is doing. It is not unusual for the average Virgo to have various ideas about how to better the job they are doing, how to streamline things. They are extremely resourceful people as far as energy is concerned. In most cases, they can work longer than others, without letting it show. Because Virgo is so concerned with detail, they may seem obsessive or compulsive to co-workers.

The enterprising Virgo can go far in business if a partner is somewhat adventurous and enthusiastic, qualities which tend to balance those of the Virgo person. At times, Virgo can be quite a worrier. Battling problems large and small may prevent him from making the headway he feels is necessary in his work. A partner who knows how to cut the work and worries in half by taking advantage of shortcuts is someone the average Virgo businessperson could learn to value. People enjoying working with Virgo men and women, because they are so reliable and honest. They usually set a good example for others on the job.

If not careful, the ambitious Virgo can become the type of person who thinks about nothing else but the job. They are not afraid of taking on more than the average worker. But they can make the mistake of expecting the same of others. This attitude can lead to conflict and unpleasantness. Generally, Virgo does achieve what he sets out for, because he knows how to apply himself. He is seldom the envy of others because he is not the type of person who is easily noticed or recognized.

Virgo is a quiet person. He or she enjoys working in peaceful and harmonious surroundings. Conflict at work is bound to upset him and affect his nerves. He works well under people. He is not against taking orders from those who prove themselves his superiors. On the whole, the man or woman born under this sign does not like to be delegated with the full responsibility of a task or project. He or she would rather have a supporting or a subordinate role.

Virgo men and women frequently excel in a trade. They often make good metalsmiths and carpenters, jewelers and wood carvers. They can work in miniature, creating a variety of pleasing items.

The Virgo person is one who is very concerned about security. Now and again he may have cause to worry about his financial position. On the whole, he is conscious of the value of money. He or she is a person who will never risk security by going out on a limb. He knows how to put money away for a rainy day. Many times he will scout about for new ways of increasing his savings. Bettering his financial situation is something that constantly concerns him. When he does invest, it usually turns out to his advantage. He generally makes sure that the investment he makes is a sure thing. He does not believe in gambling or taking big risks.

Sometimes the Virgo, because of his keen interest in money and profit, is the victim of a fraud. Dishonest people may try to take advantage of his interest in monetary gain. The well-off Virgo is extremely generous and enjoys looking after the needs of others. He sees to it that those he cares for live in comfort.

Not all Virgos are fortunate enough to become extremely wealthy, but all of them work hard for what they achieve.

Home and Family

People born under this sign are generally homebodies. They like to spend as much time as possible surrounded by the things and the people they enjoy. They make excellent hosts and enjoy entertaining guests and visitors. It is important to Virgos that the people around them be happy and content. Virgo is most at ease when companions behave correctly, that is, if they are respectful of individuals' needs and property. Virgos do not like people to take advantage of their hospitality or to abuse what they consider a privilege. But on the whole Virgos are easygoing. The demands they may make of guests and family are reasonable.

A harmonious atmosphere at home is important to the person

born under this sign. As long as this can be guaranteed, Virgo remains in good humor. They are likely to have a number of insurance policies on the home, family, and possessions. They believe that you can never be safe enough.

In spite of their love of home, Virgo is likely to have an avid interest in travel. If they cannot make many changes in their environment, they are bound to make them in their home. The Virgo homemaker never tires of rearranging things. Generally, Virgos have a good sense of beauty and harmony. They know how to make a room inviting and comfortable. Change is always of interest to the person born under this sign. They like to read of faraway places, even if they never get a chance to visit them. A new job or a new home address from time to time can brighten Virgo's spirits immeasurably.

The Virgo woman is as neat as a pin. Usually she is an excellent cook, and takes care that her kitchen never gets out of order or becomes untidy even while she is working in it. She believes that everything has its proper place and should be kept there. Because she is so careful with her possessions, they often appear brand new.

Others may feel that the Virgo man or woman, because of his or her cool, calm ways, is not especially cut out to be a good parent. But the opposite is true. Virgo people know how to bring up their youngsters correctly. They generally pass on their positive qualities to their children without any trouble. They teach them that honesty and diligence are important. They instill them with an appreciation for common sense in all matters.

Although the Virgo father or mother may deeply love their children, they have a tendency to be rather strict. They are always concerned that their children turn out well. Sometimes they expect too much of them. Some of them can be old-fashioned and believe that a child belongs in a child's place. They expect this not only of their own youngsters but also of other people's children.

Social Relationships

The Virgo man or woman is particular about the friends he makes. He is fond of people who have a particular direction in life. He is inclined to avoid drifters or irresolute people. Those who have made their mark win his admiration. Virgo likes intelligent people, those who are somewhat cultured in their interests.

As a good friend, Virgo is invaluable; there is nothing he or she would not do to help someone in need. Virgo stands by friends even in their most difficult moments. The only demand he makes is that his interest in another's affairs be valued. He does not like to feel that his help is not appreciated. It is important that Virgo be thanked for even the slightest favor.

Quite often people born under this sign are rather timid or at least retiring; they have to be drawn out by others. After Virgos get to know someone well, however, they bloom. In spite of their initial shyness, they do not enjoy being alone. They like company; they like to be reassured by people. They prefer intelligent, informed people as companions. Virgo can overlook negative qualities in someone if they feel that person is basically sincere toward others. The Virgo person needs friends. In solitude, the average Virgo is apt to feel stranded or deserted. They enjoy having someone around who will make a fuss over them, no matter how small.

Virgo is a perfectionist. Sometimes they criticize others too strongly for their faults, and as a result, they may not have as many friends as they would like.

Virgo can be cliquey, enjoying a fairly closed circle of friends and acquaintances. Gossip and intrigue might be a mainstay of such a clique. The smaller the circle, the more comfortable Virgo will feel and the more chances there will be for Virgo to orchestrate the social and recreational activities. In an intimate group setting Virgo's shyness disappears, giving way to the delicious wit and clever turn of phrase basic to this verbal, mental sign.

Gala parties with lots of hangers-on and freeloaders are not Virgo's style. A typical noisy blast can be a turn-off to one who is finicky and fastidious. The mere sight of overindulgence and overfamiliarity can make Virgo long for the glamour of posh surroundings accompanied only by a lover or close friend.

Frequent home entertaining also can be a problem. The fussy Virgo will fret about all the details that must be arranged to host a successful social. Then the neat, tidy Virgo will worry about the mess created in the house after a perfect get-together. On the whole, Virgo men and women prefer socializing in a few select places known for gracious service and fine food.

Of all the signs in the Zodiac, Virgo is most drawn to human welfare issues, a fact that leads these men and women into groups whose goal is to improve people's lot in life. The Virgo dedication to a cause is remarkable. Their example is an inspiration for everyone to follow. Doing someone a good turn comes naturally to Virgo. Their qualities of service and kindness are genuine, as friends who admire and respect them will testify.

Love and Marriage

In love and romance, the person born under the sign of Virgo is not inclined to be overly romantic. To a partner, they may seem reserved and inhibited. Their practical nature prevails even in affairs of the heart. They are least likely to be swept off their feet when in love. Chances are they may flirt a bit in the beginning of a relationship, but soon thereafter they settle down to the serious side of love. Virgo standards are very high, and it may be some time before they find someone who can measure up to them. As a consequence, Virgo frequently marries rather late in life.

It is important for the Virgo man or woman to find the right person because they are easily influenced by someone they love. On the other hand, Virgo has a protective side to their nature. When in love they will try to shield the object of their affection from the unpleasant things in life.

The person born under the sign of Virgo may be disappointed in love more than once. People whom they set great store in may prove to be unsuitable. Sometimes it is Virgo's own fault. They may be too critical of small weaknesses that a partner or lover has.

Some Virgos seem prim and proper when it comes to romance. They would prefer to think that it is not absolutely necessary and that intellect is everything. It may take some doing to get such a Virgo to change this attitude. At any rate, they are not fond of being demonstrative as far as affection goes. They do not like to make a show of love in front of others.

If their lover is too demanding or forceful in the relationship, they may feel inclined to break off the affair. Virgo appreciates gentleness and consideration in love life. On the whole, they are not easy to approach. The person who finds him or her interesting will have to be very tactful and patient when trying to convince Virgo of their love.

In married life, Virgo is apt to be very practical. They are interested in preserving the happiness they have found and will do everything in their power to keep the relationship alive. It is quite important that the Virgo man or woman marry someone with a similar outlook. Someone quite opposite may misinterpret Virgo's calm and cool manner as being unfeeling. Virgo makes a faithful mate. He or she can always be depended upon. They know how to keep things in the home running smoothly. They will do what they can to preserve harmony because they dislike discord and unpleasantness. A cooperative person, Virgo is willing to make concessions if they seem necessary. In short, the Virgo man or woman can make a success of marriage if they have had the good fortune to choose the right person.

Romance and the Virgo Woman

The Virgo woman is often a serious person. She knows what she wants out of life and what to expect from people. She is discrim-

inating in her choice of men. It may take considerable time before
she will admit to herself that she is in love. She is not afraid to
wait in matters of romance; it is important to her that she select
the right person. She may be more easily attracted to an intelligent
man than to a handsome one. She values intellect more than physical attributes.

It is important for the Virgo woman to trust someone before
she falls in love with him. She will allow a relationship to develop
into a love affair only after she has gotten to know the man well
on strictly a companionship basis at first.

The Virgo woman is reputed to be prim and proper about sex.
But this description does not tell the whole story, or even the right
story. In fact, Virgo can exhibit extremes in sexual attitudes and
behavior. It is an age-old dilemma, contrast, contradiction—call it
what you will—between the madonna and the hooker. There is
Virgo the Virgin, whose purity is renowned and whose frigidity is
assumed. Then there is Virgo the Harvester, whose promiscuity is
whispered and whose fruitfulness is celebrated.

Indeed, the difference between an old-fashioned Virgo and a
liberated Virgo are remarkable but very hard to discern in the
beginning of an affair. One thing is sure, though. Cheat on your
Virgo woman, and you can kiss the relationship good-bye. That
is, unless you have discussed the possibility of having an open
relationship—on both sides and managed in good taste. Remember, no matter what her sexual proclivities are, the Virgo woman
cannot stand vulgarity in any form.

The Virgo woman generally makes a good wife. She knows how
to keep the household shipshape. She likes looking after people
she loves. She is efficient and industrious. There is almost nothing
she will not do for the man she loves. She is capable of deep
affection and love, but must be allowed to express herself in her
own way.

As a mother, she is ideal. She teaches all her youngsters to be
polite and well-mannered, and constantly worries about their
health and welfare. Fearing all manner of mishaps, injuries, illnesses, and minor ailments, the Virgo mother may tend to restrict
the kids' freedom at play and in school. However, she always has
the children's best interests at heart.

Romance and the Virgo Man

The Virgo man, practical and analytical as he is in most matters,
is rather cautious when it comes to love and romance. He is not
what one would call romantic. He may be shy and hesitant. It may
be up to the female to begin the relationship. He may prefer not

to start an affair until he has dated for a while.

Virgo is particular. If his love partner makes one false move, he is likely to dissolve the relationship. An understanding and patient woman can help him to be a little more realistic and open in his approach to love. But first she must know what kind of man she is dealing with.

The witty, talkative Virgo man enjoys flirting. But he will never press his luck nor take advantage of a compromising situation. He won't accuse you of stringing him along. It may seem as if he is waiting for you to make the next move. And you probably have to be the aggressor if the dating relationship is to get beyond the holding-hands stage and into serious lovemaking. Make sure, though, you don't go overboard with physical demonstrations of affection—especially in public places. Virgo is easily embarrassed by touching and kissing in front of other people. Any degree of sexual intimacy is strictly reserved for the bedroom.

The strong, silent Virgo type usually appeals to women who like the challenge of overcoming his apparent resistance to her feminine charms. Little does she know that he might be scared silly of making a fool of himself or of being criticized. Virgo projects his own personality traits onto people who get close to him. So he naturally believes that a woman who approaches is just as critical and faultfinding as he is. Fortunately, though, he doesn't project the egotism and chauvinism that could turn many a woman off. So if you want to play the seduction game, you will thrill to the ultimate conquest of winning this hard-to-get, nearly perfect guy.

The Virgo man enjoys family life and does everything he can to keep his wife and children happy and secure. He may want to have a hand in running the household because he feels he is more efficient than his mate. He is a calm, steady, and faithful person.

As a father he could be a bit of a fussbudget. He may not know how to communicate with his children effectively in some matters. However, he is loving and responsible. He does what he can to see that they have a proper upbringing.

Woman—Man

VIRGO WOMAN
ARIES MAN

Although it's possible that you could find happiness with a man born under the sign of the Ram, it's uncertain as to how long that happiness would last.

An Aries who has made his mark in the world and is somewhat steadfast in his outlooks and attitudes could be quite a catch for you. On the other hand, men under this sign are often swift-footed and quick-minded. Their industrious mannerisms may fail to impress you, especially if you feel that much of their get-up-and-go often leads nowhere.

When it comes to a fine romance, you want someone with a nice, broad shoulder to lean on. You are likely to find a relationship with someone who doesn't stay put for too long somewhat upsetting.

Aries may have a little trouble in understanding you, too, at least in the beginning of the relationship. He may find you a bit too shy and moody. An Aries tends to speak his mind; he's likely to criticize you at the drop of a hat.

You may find a man born under this sign too demanding. He may give you the impression that he expects you to be at his constant beck and call. You have a lot of patience at your disposal, and he may try every last bit of it. He may not be as thorough as you in everything he does. In order to achieve success or a goal quickly, he may overlook small but important details, then regret the oversight when it is far too late.

Being married to an Aries does not mean that you'll have a secure and safe life as far as finances are concerned. Not all Aries are rash with cash, but they lack the sound head you perhaps have for putting away something for that inevitable rainy day. He'll do his best, however, to see that you're adequately provided for, even though his efforts may leave something to be desired as far as you're concerned.

With an Aries man for a mate, you'll find yourself constantly among people. An Aries generally has many friends—and you may not heartily approve of them all. People born under the sign of the Ram are often more interested in interesting people than they are in influential ones. Although there may be a family squabble from time to time, you are stable enough to take it in your stride.

Aries men love children. They make wonderful fathers. Kids take to them like ducks to water. The Ram's quick mind and behavior appeal to the young. Aries ability to jump from one activity to another will suit and delight a child's attention span.

VIRGO WOMAN
TAURUS MAN

Some Taurus men are strong and silent. They do all they can to protect and provide for the women they love. In general, the Taurus man will never let you down. He's steady, sturdy, and reliable. He's pretty honest and practical, too. He says what he means and means what he says. He never indulges in deceit and will always put his cards on the table.

The Taurus man is very affectionate. Being loved, appreciated, and understood is very important for his well-being. Like you, he is also looking for peace and security in his life. If you both work toward these goals together, you'll find that they are easily attained.

If you should marry a Taurus man, you can be sure that the wolf will never darken your door. He is a notoriously good provider and will do everything he can to make his family comfortable and happy.

He'll appreciate the way you have of making a home warm and inviting. A comfortable couch and the evening papers are essential ingredients in making your Taurus husband happy at the end of the workday. Although he may be a big lug of a guy, you'll find that he's fond of gentleness and soft things. If you puff up his pillow and tuck him in at night, he won't complain.

You probably will like his friends. Taurus tends to seek out individuals who are successful or prominent. You also admire people who work hard and achieve their goals.

The Taurus man doesn't care too much for change. He's a stay-at-home of the first order. Chances are that the house you move into after you're married will be the house you'll live in for the rest of your life.

You'll find that the man born under the sign of the Bull is easy to get along with. It's unlikely that you'll have many quarrels or arguments.

Although he'll be gentle and tender with you, your Taurus man is far from being a sensitive type. He's a man's man. More than likely, he loves such sports as fishing and football. He can be earthy as well as down to earth.

The Taurus father loves the children, but he will do everything he can not to spoil them. He believes that children should stay in their place and, in adult company, should be seen but not heard. The Taurus father is an excellent disciplinarian. Your youngsters will be polite and respectful.

VIRGO WOMAN
GEMINI MAN

The Gemini man is a good catch. Many a woman has set her cap for him and failed to bag him. Generally, Gemini men are intelligent, witty, and outgoing. Many of them tend to be versatile.

On the other hand, some of them seem to lack that sort of common sense that you set so much store in. Their tendency to start a half-dozen projects, then toss them up in the air out of boredom may do nothing more than exasperate you.

One thing that causes a Twin's mind and affection to wander is a bore. But it is unlikely that an active woman like you would ever allow herself to be accused of being one. The Gemini man who has caught your heart will admire you for your ideas and intellect, perhaps even more than for your homemaking talents and good looks.

A strong-willed woman could easily fill the role of rudder for her Gemini's ship-without-a-sail. The intelligent Gemini is often aware of his shortcomings and doesn't mind if someone with better bearings gives him a shove in the right direction—when it's needed. The average Gemini doesn't have serious ego hang-ups and will even gracefully accept a well-deserved chewing out from his mate or lover or girl friend.

A successful and serious-minded Gemini could make you a very happy woman, perhaps, if you gave him half a chance. Although he may create the impression that he has a hole in his head, the Gemini man generally has a good head on his shoulders. Some Geminis, who have learned the art of being steadfast, have risen to great heights in their professions.

Once you convince yourself that not all people born under the sign of the Twins are witless grasshoppers, you won't mind dating a few to test your newborn conviction. If you do wind up walking down the aisle with one, accept the fact that married life with him will mean your taking the bitter with the sweet.

Life with a Gemini man can be more fun than a barrel of clowns. You'll never be allowed to experience a dull moment. Don't leave money matters to him, or you'll both wind up behind the eight ball.

Gemini men are always attractive to the opposite sex. You'll perhaps have to allow him a chance to flirt harmlessly. The occasion will seldom amount to more than that if you're his ideal mate.

The Gemini father is a pushover for children. See that you keep the young ones in line, otherwise they'll be running the house. He loves them so much, he generally lets them do what they want. Gemini's sense of humor is infectious, so the children will naturally come to see the fun and funny sides of life.

VIRGO WOMAN
CANCER MAN

The man born under the sign of Cancer may very well be the man after your own heart. Generally, Cancers are steady people. They are interested in security and practicality. Despite their seemingly grouchy exterior at times, men born under the sign of the Crab are sensitive and kind individuals.

Cancers are almost always hard workers and are very interested in making successes of themselves economically as well as socially. You'll find that their conservative outlook on many things often agrees with yours. They will be men on whom you can depend come rain or come shine. They will never shirk their responsibilities as providers. They will always see that their family never wants.

Your patience will come in handy if you decide it's a Cancer you want for a mate. He isn't the type that rushes headlong into romance. He wants to be sure about love as you do. If, after the first couple of months of dating, he suggests that you take a walk with him down lovers' lane, don't jump to the conclusion that he's about to make his great play. Chances are he'll only hold your hand and seriously observe the stars.

Don't let his coolness fool you, though. Beneath his starched reserve lies a very warm heart. He's just not interested in showing off as far as affection is concerned. Don't think his interest is wandering if he doesn't kiss you goodnight at the front door; that just isn't his style. For him, affection should only be displayed for two sets of eyes—yours and his. He's passionate only in private, which is something Virgo can understand and appreciate.

He will never step out of line. He's too much of a gentleman for that. When you're alone with him and there's no chance of being disturbed or spied upon, he'll pull out an engagement ring (the one that belonged to his grandmother) and slip it on your trembling finger.

Speaking of relatives, you'll have to get used to the fact that Cancer is overly fond of his mother. When he says his mother's the most wonderful woman in the world, you'd better agree with him, that is, if you want to become his wife.

He'll always be a faithful husband. A Cancer never pussyfoots around after he has taken that marriage vow. He doesn't take marriage responsibilities lightly. He'll see that everything in the house runs smoothly and that bills are paid promptly. He'll take out all kinds of insurance policies on his family and property. He'll arrange it so that when retirement time rolls around, you'll both be very well off.

Cancers make proud, patient, and protective fathers. But they can be a little too protective. Their sheltering instincts can interfere with a youngster's natural inclination toward independence. Still, the Cancer father doesn't want to see his kids learning about life the hard way from the streets.

VIRGO WOMAN
LEO MAN

To know a man born under the sign of the Lion is not necessarily to love him, even though the temptation may be great. When he fixes most girls with his leonine double-whammy, it causes their hearts to pitter-patter and their minds to cloud over.

You are a little too sensible to allow yourself to be bowled over by a regal strut and a roar. Still, there's no denying that Leo has a way with women, even sensible women like yourself. Once he's swept a girl off her feet, it may be hard for her to scramble upright again. Still, you are no pushover for romantic charm, especially if you feel it's all show.

He'll wine you and dine you in the fanciest places. He'll croon to you under the moon and shower you with diamonds if he can get ahold of them. Still, it would be wise to find out just how long that shower is going to last before consenting to be his wife.

Lions in love are hard to ignore, let alone brush off. Your resistance will have a way of nudging him on until he feels he has you completely under his spell. Once mesmerized by this romantic powerhouse, you will probably find yourself doing things of which you never dreamed. Leos can be vain pussycats when involved romantically. They like to be babied and pampered. This may not be your cup of tea exactly. Still when you're romantically dealing with a man born under the sign of Leo, you'll think up ways to make him purr.

Although he may be magnificent and magnanimous while trying to win you, he'll yowl or mew if he thinks he's not quite getting the tender love and care he feels is his due. If you keep him well supplied with affection, you can be sure his eyes will never gaze on someone else and his heart will never wander.

A Leo man often tends to be authoritarian. He can be depended upon to lord it over others in one way or another. If he is the top honcho at his firm, he'll most likely do everything he can to stay on top. If he's not number one, he's probably working on it and will be sitting on the throne before long.

You'll have more security than you can use if he is in a position to support you in the manner to which he feels you should be accustomed. He is inclined to be too lavish, though, at least by your standards.

You'll always have plenty of friends when you have a Leo for a mate. He's a natural-born wheeler-dealer and entertainer. He loves to let his hair down at parties.

As fathers, Leos tend to spoil their children. But they can also be strict when they think that the rules of the royal kingdom are being broken. You'll have to do your best to smooth over the children's roughed-up feelings.

VIRGO WOMAN
VIRGO MAN

The Virgo man is all business or so he may seem to you. He is usually very cool, calm, and collected. He's perhaps too much of a fussbudget to arouse deep romantic interests in a woman like you. Torrid romancing to him is just so much sentimental mush. He can do without it and can make that quite evident in short order. He's keen on chastity and, if necessary, he can lead a sedentary, sexless life without caring very much about the fun others think he's missing. In short, you may find him a first-class dud.

The Virgo man doesn't have much of an imagination; flights of fancy don't interest him. He is always correct and likes to be handled properly. Almost everything about him is orderly. There's a place for everything and everything in its place is an adage he'll fall upon quite regularly.

He does have an honest-to-goodness heart, believe it or not. The woman who finds herself strangely attracted to his cool, feet-flat-on-the-ground ways will discover that his is a constant heart, not one that goes in for flings or sordid affairs. A practical man, even in matters of the heart, he wants to know just what kind of person you are before he takes a chance on you.

The impulsive woman had better not make the mistake of kissing her Virgo friend on the street, even if it's only a peck on the cheek. He's not at all demonstrative and hates public displays of affection. Love, according to him, should be kept within the confines of one's home with the curtains drawn. Once he believes that you are on the level with him as far as your love is concerned, you'll see how fast he can lose his cool. Virgos are considerate, gentle lovers. He'll spend a long time, though, getting to know you. He'll like you before he loves you.

A romance with a Virgo man can be a sometime or, rather, a one-time thing. If the bottom ever falls out, don't bother reaching for the adhesive tape. Nine times out of ten he won't care about patching up. He's a once-burnt-twice-shy guy. When he crosses your telephone number out of his address book, he's crossing you out of his life for good.

Neat as a pin, he's thumbs-down on what he considers sloppy housekeeping. An ashtray with just one stubbed out cigarette in it can annoy him even if it's only two seconds old. Glassware should always sparkle and shine if you want to keep him happy. If you marry him, keep your sunny side up.

If you marry a Virgo man, instill a sense of order in the kids, or at least have them behaving by the time he gets home. The Virgo father wants his children to be kind and courteous and always helpful to the neighbors. The children should be kept as spotless as your house. Kids with dirty faces and hands displease him.

VIRGO WOMAN
LIBRA MAN

Men born under the sign of Libra are frequently too wrapped up in their own private dreams to be really interesting as far as love and romance are concerned. Many times, the Libra man is a difficult person to bring back down to earth. It is hard for him to face reality. Although he may be very cautious about weighing both sides of an argument, he may never really come to a reasonable decision about anything. Decision making is something that often makes the Libra man uncomfortable. He'd rather leave that job to someone else. Don't ask him why, he probably doesn't know himself.

Qualities such as permanence and constancy are important to you in a love relationship. The Libra man may be an enigma to you. One moment he comes on hard and strong with declarations of his love; the next moment you find he's left you like yesterday's mashed potatoes. It does no good to wonder what went wrong. Chances are it was nothing on which you can put your finger. It's just one of Libra's strange ways.

He is not exactly what you would term an ambitious person. You are perhaps looking for a mate or friend with more drive and fidelity. You are the type of person who is interested in making some headway in the areas that interest you. Libra is often content just to drift along. He does have drive, however, but it's not the long-range kind.

It's not that Libra is shiftless or lazy. He's interested in material things and he appreciates luxuries, but he may not be willing to work hard enough to obtain them. Beauty and harmony interest him. He'll dedicate a lot of time to arranging things so that they are aesthetically pleasing. It would be difficult to call the Libra man practical; nine times out of ten, he isn't.

If you do begin a relationship with a man born under this sign, you will have to coax him now and again to face various situations in a realistic manner. You'll have your hands full, that's for sure. But if you love him, you'll undoubtedly do your best to understand him, no matter how difficult this may be.

If you become involved with a Libra man, either temporarily or permanently, you'd better take over the task of managing his money. Often he has little understanding of financial matters. He tends to spend without thinking, following his whims.

The Libra father is gentle and patient. He can be firm without exercising undue strictness or discipline. Although he can be a harsh judge at times, with the kids he will radiate sweetness and light in the hope that will grow up imitating his gracious manner.

VIRGO WOMAN
SCORPIO MAN

Some people have a hard time understanding the man born under the sign of Scorpio. Few, however, are able to resist his fiery charm. When angered, he can act like the scorpion he is, ready to strike out and defend himself. His sting can leave an almost permanent mark. If you find yourself interested in the Scorpio man, you'd better learn how to keep on his good side.

The Scorpio man can be rather blunt when he chooses. At times, he may seem hard-hearted. He can be touchy every now and then, and this sensitiveness may get on your nerves after a while. When you feel as though you can't take it anymore, you'd better tiptoe away from the scene rather than chance an explosive confrontation. He's capable of giving you a sounding-out that will make you pack your bags and go back to Mother—for good.

If he finds fault with you, he'll let you know. He might misinterpret your patience and think it a sign of indifference. But you are the type of woman who can adapt to almost any sort of relationship or circumstance if you put your heart and mind to it.

Scorpio men are very perceptive and intelligent. In some respects, they know how to use their brains more effectively than most. They believe in winning, in whatever they do. Second place holds no interest for them. In business, they usually achieve the position they want through a combination of drive and intellect.

Your interest in home life probably won't be shared by him. No matter how comfortable you've managed to make the house, it will have very little influence on him with regard to making him aware of his family responsibilities. He does not like to be tied down, generally, and would rather be out on the battlefield of life, belting away at what he feels to be a just and worthy cause. Don't try to keep the home fires burning too brightly while you wait for him to come home from work; you might run out of firewood.

The Scorpio man is passionate in all things, including love. Most women are easily attracted to him and you are perhaps no exception. Those who allow themselves to be swept off their feet by a Scorpio man soon find that they're dealing with a carton of romantic fireworks. The Scorpio man is passionate with a capital P, make no mistake about that.

Scorpio men are straight to the point. They can be as sharp as a razor blade and just as cutting to anyone who crosses them.

Scorpio fathers like large families, generally. In spite of the extremes in his personality, the Scorpio man is able to transform conflicting characteristics when he becomes a father. He is adept with difficult youngsters because he knows how to tap the best in a child. He believes in preparing his children for the hard knocks life sometimes delivers.

VIRGO WOMAN
SAGITTARIUS MAN

The woman who has set her cap for a man born under the sign of Sagittarius may have to use a great deal of strategy before she can get him to drop down on bended knee. Although some Sagittarius may be marriage-shy, they're not ones to skitter away from romance. A high-spirited woman may find a relationship with a Sagittarius, whether a fling or the real thing, a very enjoyable experience.

As a rule, Sagittarius people are bright, happy, and healthy people. They have a strong sense of fair play. Often they're a source of inspiration to others. They're full of ideas and drive.

You'll be taken by the Archer's infectious grin and his light-hearted friendly nature. If you do wind up being the woman in his life, you'll find that he will treat you more like a buddy than the love of his life. It's his way.

You'll admire his broad-mindedness in most matters, including that of the heart. If, while dating you, he claims that he still wants to play the field, he'll expect you to enjoy the same liberty. Once he's promised to love, honor, and obey, however, he does just that.

A woman who has a keen imagination and a great love of freedom will not be disappointed if she does marry an Archer. The Sagittarius man likes to share his many interests, and he has a genuine belief in equality.

If he does insist on a night out with the boys once a week, he won't scowl if you decide to let him shift for himself in the kitchen while you pursue some of your own interests. He believes in fairness, and he is no male chauvinist.

The Sagittarius is not much of a homebody. Many times he's occupied with faraway places either in his dreams or in reality. He enjoys—just as you do—being on the go. A humdrum existence, especially at home, bores him. At the drop of a hat, he may ask you to take off with him into the wild blue yonder—his idea of a break from routine.

Sagittarius likes surprising people. He'll take great pride in showing you off to his friends. He'll always be a considerate mate; he will never embarrass or disappoint you intentionally. He's very tolerant when it comes to friends; you'll probably spend a lot of time entertaining people.

The Sagittarius father will dote on any son or daughter, but he may be bewildered by the newborn. The Archer usually becomes comfortable with youngsters once they have passed through the baby stage. As soon as the children are old enough to walk and talk, the Sagittarius dad encourages each and every visible sign of talent and skill.

VIRGO WOMAN
CAPRICORN MAN

The Capricorn man is frequently not the romantic lover that attracts most women. Still, with his reserve and calm, he is capable of giving his heart completely once he has found the right woman. The Capricorn man is thorough and deliberate in all that he does. His slow, steady approach is sure to win the one he loves.

He doesn't believe in flirting and would never lead a heart on a merry chase just for the game of it. If you win his trust, he'll give you his heart on a platter. Many times, it is the woman who has to take the lead when romance is in the air. As long as he knows you're making the advances in earnest, he won't mind—in fact, he'll probably be grateful.

But don't start thinking he's a cold fish; he isn't. Although some Capricorns are indeed very capable of expressing passion, others often have difficulty in trying to display affection. He should have no trouble in this area, however, once he has found a patient and understanding lover.

The Capricorn man is very interested in getting ahead. He's quite ambitious and usually knows how to apply himself well to whatever task he undertakes. He certainly isn't a spendthrift. Like you, he knows how to handle money with extreme care. You, with your knack for putting away pennies for that rainy day, should have no difficulty understanding his way with money.

The Capricorn man thinks in terms of future security. He wants to make sure that he and his wife have something to fall back on when they reach retirement age. There's nothing wrong with that; in fact, it's a plus quality.

The Capricorn man will want you to handle household matters efficiently. The fastidious Virgo woman will have no trouble doing so. If he should check up on you from time to time, don't let it irritate you. Once you assure him that you can handle everything to his liking, he'll leave you alone.

Although he's a hard man to catch when it comes to marriage, once he's made that serious step, he's inclined to become possessive. The Capricorn man needs to know that he has the support of his wife in whatever he does, every step of the way.

The Capricorn man wants to be liked. He may seem dull to some, but underneath his reserve there is sometimes an adventurous streak that has never had a chance to express itself. He may be a real daredevil in his heart of hearts. The right woman, the affectionate, adoring woman can bring out that hidden zest in his nature.

Capricorn makes a loving, dutiful father, even though he may not understand his children completely. The Goat believes that there are goals to be achieved, and that there is the right way to achieve them. The Capricorn father can be quite a scold when it comes to disciplining the youngsters. You'll have to step in and bend the rules sometimes.

VIRGO WOMAN
AQUARIUS MAN

You might find the Aquarius man the most broad-minded man you have ever met. On the other hand, you might find him the most impractical. Many times, he's more of a dreamer than a doer. If you don't mind putting up with a man whose heart and mind are as wide as the sky and whose head is almost always in the clouds, then start dating that Aquarius who has somehow captured your fancy. Maybe you, with your good sense, can bring him back down to earth when he gets too starry-eyed.

He's no dumbbell, make no mistake about that. He can be busy making some very complicated and idealistic plans when he's got that out-to-lunch look in his eyes. But more than likely, he'll never execute them. After he's shared one or two of his progressive ideas with you, you may think he's a nut. But don't go jumping to conclusions. There's a saying that Aquarius is a half-century ahead of everybody else in the thinking department.

If you decide to marry him, you'll find out how right his zany whims are on or about your 50th anniversary. Maybe the waiting will be worth it. Could be that you have an Einstein on your hands and heart.

Life with an Aquarius won't be one of total despair if you can learn to temper his airiness with your down-to-earth Virgo practicality. He won't gripe if you do. Aquarius always maintains an open mind. He'll entertain the ideas and opinions of everybody. But he may not agree with all of them.

Don't go tearing your hair out when you find that it's almost impossible to hold a normal conversation with your Aquarius friend at times. Usually chasing the big idea, he can overlook the vital details. Always try to keep in mind that he means well.

His broad-mindedness doesn't stop when it comes to you and your personal freedom. You won't have to give up any of your hobbies or projects after you're married. He will encourage you to continue them and to be as independent as he is.

He'll be a kind and generous husband. He'll never quibble over petty things. Keep track of the money you both spend. He can't. Money burns a hole in his pocket.

At times, you may feel like calling it quits. Chances are, though, that you'll always give him another chance.

The Aquarius is a good family man. He can be a shining example for the children because he sees them as individuals in their
own right, not as extensions of himself. Kids love him and vice
versa. He'll be tolerant with them as he is with adults.

VIRGO WOMAN
PISCES MAN

The man born under Pisces is quite a dreamer. Sometimes he's so
wrapped up in his dreams that he's difficult to reach. To the average, active woman, he may seem a little passive.

He's easygoing most of the time. He seems to take things in his
stride. He'll entertain all kinds of views and opinions from just
about everyone, nodding or smiling vaguely, giving the impression
that he's with them one hundred percent while that may not be the
case at all. His attitude may be why bother when he's confronted
with someone who is wrong but thinks he's right. The Pisces man
will seldom speak his mind if he thinks he'll be rigidly opposed.

The Pisces man is oversensitive at times. He's afraid of getting
his feelings hurt. He'll sometimes imagine a personal affront when
none's been made. More than likely, you'll find this complex of
his maddening. At times you may feel like giving him a swift kick
where it hurts the most. It won't do any good, though.

One thing you'll admire about this man is his concern for people
who are sickly or troubled. He'll make his shoulder available to
anyone in the mood for a good cry. He can listen to one hard-
luck story after another without seeming to tire. When his advice
is asked, he can be depended upon to offer some wise counsel.
He often knows what is upsetting someone before that person is
aware of it himself.

Still, at the end of the day, the Pisces man will want some peace
and quiet. If you've got a problem when he comes home, don't
unload it in his lap. If you do, you might find him short-tempered.
He's a good listener, but he can only take so much turmoil.

Pisces are not aimless although they may seem so at times. The
positive sort of Pisces man is often successful in his profession and
is likely to become rich and influential. Material gain, however, is
never a direct goal for a man born under the sign of the Fishes.

The weaker Pisces is usually content to stay on the level where
he finds himself.

Because of their seemingly laissez-faire manner, people under
the sign of Pisces are immensely popular with children. For tots,
the Pisces father plays the double role of confidant and playmate.
It will never enter his mind to discipline a child, no matter how
spoiled or incorrigible that child becomes.

Man—Woman

VIRGO MAN
ARIES WOMAN

The Aries woman may be a little too bossy and busy for you. Generally, Aries is an ambitious creature. She can become a little impatient with a Virgo who by nature is more thorough and deliberate than she is, especially if she feels you're taking too much time.

The Aries woman is a fast worker. Sometimes she's so fast she forgets to look where she's going. When she stumbles or falls, it would be nice if you were there to catch her. But Aries is a proud woman. She doesn't like to be criticized when she errs. The Virgo tongue lashings can turn her into a block of ice.

Don't begin to think that the Aries woman frequently gets tripped up in her plans. Many times she is capable of taking aim and hitting the bull's-eye. You'll be flabbergasted by her accuracy as well as by her ambition. On the other hand, you're apt to spot a flaw in her plans before she does.

You are perhaps somewhat slower than Aries in attaining your goals. Still, you are not inclined to make mistakes along the way. You're almost always well prepared.

The Aries woman can be sensitive at times. She likes to be handled with gentleness and respect. Let her know that you love her for her brains as well as for her good looks. Never give her cause to become jealous. When your Aries date sees green, you'd better forget about sharing a rosy future together. Handle her with tender love and care and she's yours.

The Aries woman can be giving if she feels her partner is deserving. She is no iceberg; she responds to the proper masculine flame. She needs a man she can admire and of whom she can feel proud. She can cause you plenty of heartache if you've made up your mind about her but she hasn't made up hers about you. The Aries woman is very demanding at times. Some tend to be highstrung. They can be difficult if they feel their independence is being hampered.

The cultivated Aries woman makes a wonderful homemaker and hostess. You'll find she's very clever in decorating and using color. Your house will be tastefully furnished; she'll make sure that it radiates harmony. The Aries wife knows how to make guests feel at home.

Although the Aries woman may not be keen on burdensome responsibilities, she is fond of children and the joy they bring. She is skilled at juggling both career and motherhood, so her kids will never feel that she is an absentee parent. In fact, as the youngsters grow older, they might want a little more of the liberation that is so important to her.

VIRGO MAN
TAURUS WOMAN
A Taurus woman could perhaps understand you better than most women. She is very considerate and loving. She is thorough and methodical in whatever she does. She is anxious to avoid mistakes.

Home is very important to the Taurus woman. She is an excellent homemaker. Although your home may not be a palace, it will become, under her care, a comfortable and happy abode. She'll love it when friends drop by for the evening. She is a good cook and enjoys feeding people well.

The Taurus woman is serious about love and affection. When she has taken a tumble for someone, she'll stay by him forever, if possible. She will try to be practical in romance, to some extent. When she decides she wants a certain man, she keeps after him until he's won her. Generally, the Taurus woman is a passionate lover, even though she may appear staid at first glance. She is on the lookout for someone who can return her affection fully. Taurus women are sometimes given to fits of jealousy and possessiveness. They expect fair play in the area of marriage. When it doesn't come about, they can be bitingly sarcastic and mean.

The Taurus woman is usually an easygoing person intent on keeping the peace. She won't argue unless she must. She'll do her best to keep your love relationship on an even keel.

Marriage is generally a one-time thing for Taurus. Once they've taken the serious step, they seldom try to back out of it. Taurus women need love and warmth. With the right man, they become ideal wives.

The Taurus woman will respect you for your steady ways. She'll have confidence in your common sense. She'll share with you all the joys and burdens of parenthood.

Taurus women seldom put up with nonsense from their children. It is not that they are strict, but rather that they are concerned. They like their children to be well behaved and dutiful. Nothing pleases a Taurus mother more than a compliment from a neighbor or teacher about her child's behavior.

Although some children may inwardly resent the iron hand of a Taurus mother, in later life they are often thankful that they were brought up in such an orderly and conscientious way.

VIRGO MAN
GEMINI WOMAN
You may find a romance with a woman born under the sign of the Twins a many-splendored thing. She will provide the intellectual companionship you often look for in a friend or mate. A Gemini partner can appreciate your aims and desires because she

travels pretty much the same road as you do intellectually, that is, at least part of the way. She may share your interests but she will lack your tenacity.

She suffers from itchy feet. She can be here, there, all over the place. Her eagerness to be on the move may make you dizzy. Still, you'll enjoy and appreciate her liveliness and mental agility.

The Gemini woman often has a sparkling personality. You'll be attracted to her warmth and grace. While she's on your arm you'll probably notice that many male eyes are drawn to her. She may even return a gaze or two, but don't let that worry you. All women born under this sign have nothing against a harmless flirtation once in a while. But if she feels she is already spoken for, she will never let it get out of hand.

Although she may not be as handy as you'd like in the kitchen, you'll never go without a tasty meal. The Gemini woman is always in a rush. She won't feel she's cheating by breaking out the instant mashed potatoes or the frozen peas. She may not be a good cook but she is clever. With a dash of this and a suggestion of that, she can make an uninteresting TV dinner taste like a gourmet meal. Then, again, maybe you've struck it rich and have a Gemini lover who finds complicated recipes a challenge to her intellect. If so, you'll find every meal a tantalizing and mouth-watering surprise.

When you're beating your brains out over the Sunday crossword puzzle and find yourself stuck, just ask your Gemini woman. She'll give you all the right answers without batting an eyelash.

Just like you, she loves all kinds of people. You may even find that you're a bit more discriminating than she. Often all that a Gemini requires is that her friends be interesting and stay interesting. But one thing she's not able to abide is a dullard.

Leave the party organizing to your Gemini sweetheart or mate, and you'll never have a chance to know what a dull moment is. She'll bring out the swinger in you if you give her half the chance.

A Gemini mother enjoys her children, which can be the truest form of love. Like them, she's often restless, adventurous, and easily bored. She will never complain about their fleeting interests because she understands the changes they will go through as they mature.

VIRGO MAN
CANCER WOMAN

The Cancer woman needs to be protected from the cold, cruel world. She'll love you for your masculine yet gentle manner; you make her feel safe and secure. You don't have to pull any he-man or heroic stunts to win her heart; that's not what interests her.

She's more likely to be impressed by your sure, steady ways—

that way you have of putting your arm around her and making her feel she's the only girl in the world. When she's feeling glum and tears begin to well up in her eyes, you have that knack of saying just the right thing. You know how to calm her fears, no matter how silly some of them may seem.

The woman born under the sign ruled by the Moon is inclined to have her ups and downs. You have that talent for smoothing out the ruffles in her sea of life. She'll probably worship the ground you walk on or put you on a very high pedestal. Don't disappoint her if you can help it. She'll never disappoint you.

The Cancer woman will take great pleasure in devoting the rest of her natural life to you. She'll darn your socks, mend your overalls, scrub floors, wash windows, shop, cook, and do just about anything in order to please you and let you know that she loves you. Sounds like that legendary good old-fashioned girl, doesn't it? Contrary to popular belief, there are still some around, and many of them are Cancers.

Of all the signs of the Zodiac, the Cancer-born are the most maternal. In caring for and bringing up children, Cancer women know just how to combine the right amount of tenderness with the proper dash of discipline. A child couldn't ask for a better mother. Cancer women are sympathetic, affectionate, and patient with their children.

While we're on the subject of motherhood, there's one thing you should be warned about: never be unkind to your mother-in-law. It will be the only golden rule your Cancer wife will probably expect you to follow. No mother-in-law jokes in the presence of your mate, please. They'll go over like a lead balloon. Mother is something pretty special for her. She may be the crankiest, nosiest old bat. But she's your wife's mother. You'd better treat her like she's one of the landed gentry. Sometimes this may be difficult to swallow. But if you want to keep your home together and your wife happy, learn to grin and bear it.

Treat your Cancer wife like a queen, and she'll treat you royally.

VIRGO MAN
LEO WOMAN

The Leo woman can make most men roar like lions. If any woman in the Zodiac has that indefinable something that can make men lose their heads and find their hearts, it's the Leo woman.

She's got more than a fair share of charm and glamour. She knows how to make the most of her assets, especially when she's in the company of the opposite sex. Jealous men are apt to lose their cool or their sanity when trying to woo a woman born under the sign of the Lion. The Lioness likes to kick up her heels quite often and doesn't care who knows it. She frequently makes heads turn and tongues wag. You don't necessarily have to believe any of what you hear—it's probably jealous gossip or wishful thinking. Still, other women in her vicinity turn green with envy and will try anything to put her out of the running.

Although this vamp makes the blood rush to your head and makes you momentarily forget all the things you thought were important and necessary in your life, you may feel differently when you come back down to earth and the stars are out of your eyes. You may feel that she isn't the type of girl you planned to bring home to Mother. Not that your mother might disapprove of your choice, but you might after the shoes and rice are a thing of the past. Although the Leo woman may do her best to be a good wife for you, chances are she'll fall short of your idea of what a good wife should be like.

If you're planning on not going as far as the altar with the Leo woman, you'd better be financially equipped for some very expensive dating. Be prepared to shower her with expensive gifts and to take her dining and dancing to the smartest spots in town. Promise her the moon if you're in a position to go that far. Luxury and glamour are two things that are bound to lower a Leo's resistance. She's got expensive tastes, and you'll have to cater to them if you expect to get to first base with her.

If you've got an important business deal to clinch and you have doubts as to whether you can swing it or not, bring your Leo woman along to the business luncheon. More than likely, with her on your arm, you'll be able to win any business battle with both hands tied. She won't have to say or do anything, just be there at your side. The grouchiest oil magnate can be transformed into a gushing, obedient schoolboy if there's a charming Leo woman in the room.

Leo mothers are sometimes blind to the faults of their children. On the other hand, the Leo mother can be strict when she wants them to learn something. She expects her youngsters to follow the rules, and she is a patient teacher. Being easygoing and friendly, she loves to pal around with the kids while proudly showing them off on every occasion.

VIRGO MAN
VIRGO WOMAN

The Virgo woman may be even too difficult for the Virgo man to understand at first. Her waters run deep. Even when you think you know her, don't take any bets on it. She's capable of keeping things hidden in the deep recesses of her womanly soul—things she'll only release when she's sure that you're the man she wants. But it may take her some time to come around to this decision. Virgos are finicky about almost everything. Many of them have the idea that the only people who can do things correctly are Virgos.

Nothing offends a Virgo woman more than slovenly dress, sloppy character, or a careless display of affection. Make sure your tie is not crooked and your shoes sport a bright shine before you go calling on this lady. Keep your off-color jokes for the locker room; she'll have none of that.

Take her arm when crossing the street, but don't rush the romance. Trying to corner her in the back of a cab may be one way of striking out. Never criticize the way she looks. In fact, the best policy is to agree with her as much as possible.

Still, there's just so much a man can take. All those dos and don'ts you have to observe if you want to get to first base with a Virgo may be just a little too much to ask of you. After a few dates, you may decide that she just isn't worth all that trouble. However, the Virgo woman is usually mysterious enough to keep her men running back for more. Chances are you'll be intrigued by her airs and graces.

If lovemaking means a great deal to you, you'll be disappointed at first in the cool ways of your Virgo woman. However, under her glacial facade there lies a hot cauldron of seething excitement. If you're patient and artful in your romantic approach, you'll find that all the caution was well worth the trouble. When Virgos love, it's all or nothing as far as they're concerned.

One thing a Virgo woman can't stand in love is hypocrisy. She doesn't care what the neighbors say. If her heart tells her to go ahead, she does. She is very concerned with human truths. If her heart stumbles upon another fancy, she will be true to that new heartthrob and leave you standing in the rain.

She's honest to her heart and will be as true to you as you are with her. Do her wrong once, however, and it's farewell.

The Virgo mother has high expectations for her children, and she will strive to bring out the very best in them. She is more tender than strict, though, and will nag rather than discipline. But youngsters sense her unconditional love for them, and usually turn out just as she hoped they would.

VIRGO MAN
LIBRA WOMAN
Libra invented the notion that it's a woman's prerogative to change her mind. Her changeability, in spite of its undeniable charm, could actually drive even a man of your patience up the wall. She's capable of smothering you with love and kisses one day, and on the next avoid you like the plague.

If you think you're a man of steel nerves then perhaps you can tolerate these sudden changes without suffering too much. However, if you admit that you're only a mere mortal who can take so much, then you'd better fasten your attention on a partner who's somewhat more constant.

But don't get the wrong idea. A love affair with a Libra can have a lot of pluses to it. The Libra woman is soft, very feminine, and warm. She doesn't have to vamp all over the place in order to gain a man's attention. Her delicate presence is enough to warm the cockles of any man's heart. One smile, and you're a piece of putty in the palm of her hand.

She can be fluffy and affectionate, which you will like. On the other hand, her indecision about which dress to wear, what to cook for dinner, or whether to redecorate could make you tear your hair out. What will perhaps be more exasperating is her flat denial of the accusation that she cannot make even the simplest decision. The trouble is that she wants to be fair or just in all matters. She'll spend hours weighing pros and cons. Don't make her rush into a decision; that will only irritate her.

The Libra woman likes to be surrounded by beautiful things. Money is no object when beauty is concerned. There will always be plenty of flowers in the house. She'll know how to arrange them tastefully, too. Women under this sign are fond of beautiful clothes and furnishings. They will run up bills without batting an eyelash, if given the chance.

Once she's involved with you, the Libra woman will do everything in her power to make you happy. She'll wait on you hand and foot when you're sick and bring you breakfast in bed Sundays. She'll be very thoughtful and devoted. If anyone dares suggest you're not the grandest man in the world, your Libra wife will give that person a good sounding-out.

The Libra mother works wonders with children. Gentle persuasion and affection are all she uses in bringing them up. It works. She is sensitive and sensible, with an intuitive understanding of what a child needs. Her youngsters will never lack for anything that could make their lives easier and richer. Still, you will always come before the children.

VIRGO MAN
SCORPIO WOMAN
When the Scorpio woman chooses to be sweet, she's apt to give the impression that butter wouldn't melt in her mouth but, of course, it would. When her temper flies, so will everything else that isn't bolted down. She can be as hot as a tamale or as cool as a cucumber when she wants. Whatever mood she's in, you can

be sure it's for real. She doesn't believe in poses or hypocrisy.

The Scorpio woman is often seductive and sultry. Her femme fatale charm can pierce through the hardest of hearts. The Scorpio woman can be a whirlwind of passion. But life with her will not be all smiles and smooth sailing. If you think you can handle a woman who is quick to retaliate and hold a grudge, then try your luck. Your stable and steady nature will probably have a calming effect on her. You're the kind of man she can trust and rely on. But never cross her, even on the smallest thing, or she'll make you pay for it.

Generally, the Scorpio woman will keep family battles within the walls of your home. When company visits, she can be depended upon to give the impression that married life with you is one big joyride. It's just her way of expressing her loyalty to you, at least in front of others. The Scorpio woman will certainly see that others have a high opinion of you both. She'll support you in whatever it is you want to do.

Although she's an individualist, after she has married, she'll put her own interests aside for those of the man she loves. With a woman like this behind you, you can't help but go far. She'll never try to take over your role as boss of the family and she'll give you all the support you need in order to fulfill that role. She won't complain if the going gets rough, for she is a courageous woman. She's as anxious as you to find that place in the sun for you both. She is as determined a person as you are.

Although the Scorpio mother loves her children, she will not put them on a pedestal. She is devoted to developing her youngsters' talents. The Scorpio mother is protective yet encouraging. The opposites within her nature mirror the contradictions within life itself. Under her skillful guidance, the children will learn how to cope with extremes and will grow up to become well-rounded individuals. She will teach her young ones to be courageous and steadfast.

VIRGO MAN
SAGITTARIUS WOMAN
You'll most likely never meet a more good-natured woman than the one under the sign of Sagittarius. Generally, she is full of bounce and good cheer. Her sunny disposition seems almost permanent and can be relied upon even on the rainiest of days.

The woman born under the sign of the Archer is rarely malicious. But she is often a little short on tact and says literally anything that comes into her head, regardless of the occasion. Sometimes the words that tumble out of her mouth are downright cutting and cruel. But no matter what she says, she means well.

Unfortunately, the Sagittarius woman is capable of losing some of her friends—and perhaps even some of yours—through such carelessness.

On the other hand, you will appreciate her honesty and good intentions. To you, these qualities play an important part in life. With a little patience and practice, you can probably help cure your Sagittarius of her loose tongue. In most cases, she'll give in to your better judgment and try to follow your advice.

Chances are, she'll be the outdoors type and sportswoman. Long hikes, fishing trips, and white-water canoeing will probably appeal to her. She's a busy person, one who sets great store in mobility. She won't sit still for one minute if it's not necessary.

She is very friendly and likes lots of company. When your buddies drop by for poker and beer, she won't have any trouble fitting in.

On the whole, she is a very kind and sympathetic woman. If she feels she's made a mistake, she'll be the first to call your attention to it. She's not afraid to own up to her own faults and shortcomings.

You might lose your patience with her once or twice. After she's seen how upset her shortsightedness and careless comments have made you, she'll do her best to please you.

The Sagittarius woman is not the kind who will pry into your business affairs. But she'll always be there, ready to offer advice if you need it.

The Sagittarius woman is seldom suspicious. Your word will almost always be good enough for her.

The Sagittarius mother is a wonderful and loving friend to her children. She is not afraid if a youngster learns some street smarts along the way. To bolster such knowledge, or to counteract it, she may preach a bit too much for the kids. Then you can switch the focus to the practical. But you will appreciate how she encourages the children to study in order for them to get a well-rounded and broad education.

VIRGO MAN
CAPRICORN WOMAN

The Capricorn may not be the most romantic woman of the Zodiac, but she's certainly not frigid when she meets the right man. She believes in true love. She doesn't appreciate flings. To her, they're just a waste of time. She's looking for a man who means business—in life as well as in love. Although she can be very affectionate with her lover or mate, she tends to let her head govern her heart. That is not to say she is a cool, calculating cucumber. On the contrary, she just feels she can be more honest about love if she consults her brains first.

The Capricorn woman is faithful, dependable, and systematic in just about everything she undertakes. She is very concerned with security and makes sure that every penny she spends is spent wisely. She is very economical about using her time, too. She does not believe in whittling away her energy on a scheme that is bound not to pay off.

Ambitious herself, she is often attracted to the ambitious man—one who is interested in getting somewhere in life. If a man with this temperament wins her heart, she'll stick by him and do all she can to help him get to the top.

The Capricorn woman is almost always diplomatic. She makes an excellent hostess. She can be very influential when your business acquaintances come to dinner.

The Capricorn woman is likely to be very concerned, if not extremely proud, of her family tree. Relatives are very important to her, particularly if they're socially prominent. Never say a cross word about her family members. She is likely to punish you by not talking to you for days.

As a rule, she's thorough in whatever she does. The Capricorn woman is well-mannered, well-groomed, and gracious, no matter what her background.

If you should marry a woman born under this sign, you need never worry about her going on a wild shopping spree. She understands the value of money better than most women. If you turn over your paycheck to her at the end of the week, you can be sure that a good hunk of it will wind up in the bank.

The Capricorn mother is very ambitious for her children. She wants them to have every advantage and to benefit from things she perhaps lacked as a child. She will train the youngsters to be polite and kind, and to honor traditional codes of conduct. She can be correct to a fault. But the meticulous Virgo mate will not find fault with the Capricorn mother's careful ways.

VIRGO MAN
AQUARIUS WOMAN

If you find that you've fallen head over heels for a woman born under the sign of the Water Bearer, you'd better fasten your safety belt. It may take you quite a while to actually discover what she is like. Even then, you may have nothing to go on but a series of vague hunches. The Aquarius woman is like a rainbow, full of bright and shining hues. She's like no one you've ever known. There is something elusive about her.

The Aquarius woman can be pretty odd and eccentric at times. Some say this is the source of her mysterious charm. You might think she's just a screwball, and you may be 50 percent right. The

Aquarius woman often has her head full of dreams. By nature, she is often unconventional; she has her own thoughts about how the world should be run. Sometimes her ideas may seem weird, but chances are they're just a little too progressive. Keep in mind the saying: The way the Aquarius thinks, so will the world in 50 years.

She'll probably be the most tolerant and open-minded woman you've ever encountered.

If you find that she's too much mystery and charm for you to handle, tell her so and say that you think it would be best to call it quits. She'll probably agree without making a scene yet still want to remain friends. The Aquarius woman is like that. Perhaps you'll both find it easier to get along in a friendship than in a romance.

The Aquarius woman is not a jealous person and, while you're romancing her, she won't expect you to be, either. You'll find her a free spirit most of the time. Just when you think you know her inside out, you'll discover that you don't really know her at all.

She's a very sympathetic and warm person. She is always helpful to those in need of assistance and advice.

She'll seldom be suspicious even when she has every right to be. If the man she loves makes a little slip, she's inclined to forgive and forget it.

The Aquarius mother is bighearted and seldom refuses her children anything. Her open-minded attitude is easily transmitted to her youngsters. They have every change of growing up as respectful and tolerant individuals who feel at ease anywhere.

VIRGO MAN
PISCES WOMAN

Many a man dreams of an alluring Pisces woman. You're perhaps no exception. She's soft and cuddly and very domestic. She'll let you be the brains of the family; she's contented to play a behind-the-scenes role in order to help you achieve your goals. The illusion that you are the master of the household is the kind of magic that the Pisces woman is adept at creating.

She can be very ladylike and proper. Your business associates and friends will be dazzled by her warmth and femininity. Although she's a charmer, there is a lot more to her than just a pretty exterior. There is a brain ticking away behind that soft, womanly facade. You may never become aware of it—that is, until you're married to her. It's no cause for alarm, however; she'll most likely never use it against you, only to help you and possibly set you on a more successful path.

If she feels you're botching up your married life through careless behavior or if she feels you could be earning more money than you do, she'll tell you about it. But any wife would, really.

She will never try to usurp your position as head and breadwinner of the family.

No one had better dare say one uncomplimentary word about you in her presence. It's likely to cause her to break into tears. Pisces women are usually very sensitive beings. Their reaction to adversity, frustration, or anger is just a plain, good, old-fashioned cry. They can weep buckets when inclined.

She can do wonders with a house. She is very fond of dramatic and beautiful things. There will always be plenty of fresh-cut flowers around the house. She will choose charming artwork and antiques, if they are affordable. She'll see to it that the house is decorated in a dazzling yet welcoming style.

She'll have an extra special dinner prepared for you when you come home from an important business meeting. Don't dwell on the boring details of the meeting, though. But if you need that grand vision, the big idea, to seal a contract or make a conquest, your Pisces woman is sure to confide a secret that will guarantee your success. She is canny and shrewd with money, and once you are on her wavelength you can manage the intricacies on your own.

Treat her with tenderness and generosity and your relationship will be an enjoyable one. She's most likely fond of chocolates. A bunch of beautiful flowers will never fail to make her eyes light up. See to it that you never forget her birthday or your anniversary. These things are very important to her. If you let them slip your mind, you'll send her into a crying fit that could last a considerable length of time.

If you are patient and kind, you can keep a Pisces woman happy for a lifetime. She, however, is not without her faults. Her sensitivity may get on your nerves after a while. You may find her lacking in practicality and good old-fashioned stoicism. You may even feel that she uses her tears as a method of getting her own way.

The Pisces mother totally believes in her children, and that faith never wavers. Her unconditional love for them makes her a strong, self-sacrificing mother. That means she can deny herself in order to fulfill their needs. She will teach her youngsters the value of service to the community while not letting them lose their individuality.

VIRGO
LUCKY NUMBERS 2003

Lucky numbers and astrology can be linked through the movements of the Moon. Each phase of the thirteen Moon cycles vibrates with a sequence of numbers for your Sign of the Zodiac over the course of the year. Using your lucky numbers is a fun system that connects you with tradition.

New Moon	First Quarter	Full Moon	Last Quarter
Jan. 2	Jan. 10	Jan. 18	Jan. 25
5 3 0 8	2 6 1 3	3 7 0 4	4 2 5 9
Feb. 1	Feb. 9	Feb. 16	Feb. 23
4 0 7 2	2 6 8 3	3 1 7 5	8 3 2 0
March 2	March 11	March 18	March 24
0 1 5 9	9 2 6 4	4 7 7 1	1 5 4 0
April 1	April 9	April 16	April 23
3 3 7 2	4 8 6 9	9 7 1 2	1 0 6 9
May 1	May 9	May 15	May 22
7 8 0 5	5 3 6 4	4 7 2 9	9 0 8 3
May 30	June 7	June 14	June 21
7 2 9 4	2 5 3 6	6 0 9 5	8 5 9 4
June 29	July 6	July 13	July 21
4 1 8 2	2 9 3 7	7 6 2 5	5 9 3 5
July 29	August 5	August 11	August 19
8 7 1 0	0 8 2 6	5 0 1 4	8 3 9 4
August 27	Sept. 3	Sept. 10	Sept. 18
6 2 5 3	6 0 9 5	0 8 3 7	9 4 2 3
Sept. 25	Oct. 2	Oct. 10	Oct. 18
3 9 4 7	2 1 0 6	9 4 8 1	0 5 3 9
Oct. 25	Oct. 31	Nov. 8	Nov. 16
9 7 1 5	4 0 5 3	7 2 4 8	8 6 9 0
Nov. 23	Nov. 30	Dec. 8	Dec. 16
1 8 7 0	3 6 1 5	5 7 2 9	9 3 1 9
Dec. 23	Dec. 30	Jan. 7 ('04)	Jan. 15 ('04)
9 5 3 8	2 6 1 0	2 5 3 8	1 0 3 7

VIRGO
YEARLY FORECAST 2003

Forecast for 2003 Concerning Business
and Financial Affairs, Job Prospects,
Travel, Health, Romance and Marriage
for Persons Born with the Sun
in the Zodiacal Sign of Virgo.
August 22–September 22

For those born under the influence of the Sun in the zodiacal sign of Virgo, ruled by Mercury, the planet of wit and intelligence, 2003 promises to be a comfortable and positive year. You should gain increasing confidence in your own abilities and appearance as the year progresses, inspiring luck and good fortune to come your way. While home life can be full of thrills and spills, relationships are sure to become deeper and more satisfying. Virgo business people will be worked hard, but the benefits should be long-lasting. Working practices might have to be revamped considerably as fresh perspectives and new techniques are adopted. Your personal finances will be better if you accept whatever overtime work is available. Spending on your home may be necessary, although this should be thought of as an investment in the future. The outlook for jobs suggests that you utilize your ability to shake things up a little. Routine work will not tend to appeal as much as more challenging prospects. Travel will mainly revolve around business trips, which can be illuminating but also a drain on your personal resources. Finding time for a relaxing vacation should also be a priority. Health matters will demand some of your attention. Changes in your daily routine are going to affect you throughout the year. A different diet may be wise, especially when your energy runs low. Where love and romance are concerned, a pragmatic approach is advisable. Love can strike out of the blue, but it may not be possible for you to respond to it. Deepening your understanding of the person closest to your heart can bring profound happiness.

The business world is full of exciting changes and opportunities, but only if you are open to taking advantage of them. It is important to find the balance between well-tested ways of working and new techniques for success. This is a year when your own role in the company will be consolidated. As you begin to exert more and more effort and authority, you will also get more in return. Hard work will keep your nose to the grindstone, but the rewards should be proportionate. Group decisions can be difficult to come by, and meetings may need to be steered in subtle ways if you are to get the results you want. Play the role of peacemaker to keep co-workers from forming factions, which would only weaken your enterprise. Financial constraints could suggest work being farmed out to workers who are not paid very high wages. Think carefully about the practical and moral implications before going with such a plan. This is a period when technological advances cannot be ignored, no matter how traditional the business may be. At the very least, consider new methods of making your presence known such as through an Internet website. Working practices are likely to change profoundly as fluctuating profits make the option of temporary staff seem more attractive. Relationships on the job may go through some ups and downs. It is vital to treat staff members with respect and dignity at all times. A period of stiff competition from a rival company is expected between March and September. It may not be possible to prepare beforehand with strategies that will ensure your enterprise keeps its share of the market. Try not to wear yourself out by identifying so strongly with the company that you take work and worry home with you every night. Keeping a clear head will be easier if you are able to switch off from thinking about business all the time. You will then be able to serve your enterprise more effectively.

This year should be reasonably stable where your personal finances are concerned. The trick is not so much spending less but earning more, which ought to be possible by taking on extra work. Even if this overtime pay is only for a short period, it can make a world of difference. You may have to spend a considerable sum on home maintenance that cannot and must not be avoided. If well done, this can be counted as an investment. Be sure to get comparative quotes for all work to ensure that you get the best deal available. Virgos with elderly parents may have to take on more responsibility for them, which could require money as well as time. This is one area of life where you want to give nothing but the best. Try to keep a firm hand on personal expenditure, even if it means occasionally missing out on expensive entertainment. As a Virgo you usually manage money effectively, and you ought to be able to keep on the straight and narrow quite easily this year.

The prospects for jobs and employment are fairly flexible, depending upon what you want. Even the most routine job offers chances to diversify. Break out of dull patterns of work, putting to use talents and skills that your employer never guessed you possessed. If you are doing more, do not forget that you are worth more. Virgos looking forward to a job change should try to be realistic. It is fine to have lofty aims, but far more satisfying in the long run to make sure your goals can actually be reached. If you have been out of regular employment for a while, consider working from home. There are many opportunities for people to work by computer without the hassle of regular commuting. There may be a period during which you feel you are working hard but receiving little reward. By the second half of the year you should certainly begin to reap the benefits of being responsible and reliable. Your sterling qualities will not go unnoticed, especially when they are so valuable in today's employment market.

Although Virgos are not always enthusiastic travelers, this year you can gain much pleasure from time spent away from home. Think of it as a prescription for good health; a relaxing trip can refresh and re-energize you as nothing else. Business trips are highlighted, with the possibility of more than one during the course of the year. Even though these may strain your nerves, you will gain insights into customers and suppliers that stay with you for many years to come. Some of your most profound travel-related experiences could arise from people you meet when far from your home base. Exchanging news and views ought to be highly stimulating. You may look forward to a vacation with friends, but arrangements are apt to be altered. Although this may cause a brief feeling of irritation, it will probably work out for the best. Whatever you do, relax and enjoy the people you encounter while traveling.

Your health this year will be a focus of attention at least for part of the time. You are inclined to take good care of yourself. Natural remedies could help with common digestive problems. A change of diet could be in order, especially if you are becoming concerned about the quality of the food you habitually eat. Organically grown products can be an expensive but worthwhile alternative. Hard work could take its toll on your nerves and energy, so make sure you get plenty of downtime on weekends. A herbal tonic or supplement may be useful during cold months when your natural resources are at full stretch. Guard against a cold or flu-like illness between the end of April and mid-May. Even if the weather is warm, take extra precautions, but without going over the top and becoming a health-freak. Lighten up a little if you feel you are getting obsessive in any way. A relaxed attitude to life will help keep you in the best of physical as well as mental health.

The year ahead is one in which love and romance figure quite prominently in your life. While it is wonderful to be in love, it is also necessary to recognize that sharing life with someone demands more than starry-eyed adoration. This is a time when you can throw aside the hearts-and-flowers vision of romance, and discover for yourself deep and lasting love. Virgos who recently ended a relationship will need a little while to get over the emotional upset. It would be unwise to rush right into someone else's arms just for the sake of companionship. Even the most settled and stable partnership is bound to go through a few rough periods. However, if handled right, these can actually strengthen the relationship. You may feel an uncharacteristic urge to become involved with someone totally different from you in every way, or even to start an affair. Rather than blindly acting on desire, try to take a step back and question your own motives. This will probably be enough to stop you before any damage is done. Keep in mind that whatever relationship you are in requires that you be emotionally honest with yourself, as well as with the other person. Staying true to your heart without sugarcoating your feelings or denying them altogether creates a far richer and more rewarding partnership, which will tend to last longer and give both partners great happiness.

VIRGO
DAILY FORECAST

January–December 2003

JANUARY

1. WEDNESDAY. Promising. You are apt to be concerned with your career or life goals all year, and this day is no exception. Although you are probably staying home today, you are likely to be running around. Your determined mood may lead you to do some housecleaning, whether literally or mentally. This is a great day to revise your goals and make some New Year's resolutions. Just do not be too unreasonable or you could end up feeling guilty because you are unable to follow through. Another very popular theme this year will be a search for deeper meaning in your life. You may get involved in metaphysical, spiritual, or religious pursuits, also learning that being of service to other people imparts joy to your life.

2. THURSDAY. Satisfactory. You should be very good at whatever you attempt to do. Dealing with family members or housemates can be productive, although you might have a tendency to go overboard offering your good advice. You are likely to see the world through parental eyes, which can be good providing you are not being too stern or acting like a know-it-all. For Virgos who are normally quite reserved and easygoing, this is a great day to stand up for yourself and your rights. Find the perfect balance and you will be very pleased. If you get the opportunity to be alone with your mate or to go on a date, this should be quite a romantic time. Candlelight, flowers, and dancing might set the stage for the rest of the evening.

3. FRIDAY. Surprising. Do not hesitate to go after what you want, particularly a secret desire involving your career or a pet project. Be enthusiastic and believe strongly in yourself. Picture what you want in your mind's eye. Visualize yourself having what you desire, no matter how far-fetched it may seem. Virgo singles who are looking for someone special to begin a relationship should try a different approach to meeting that perfect person. Computer or Internet dating, or a local singles' group, would be good options. If you feel uncomfortable meeting new people, perhaps you are taking it too seriously. Make your goal to have fun, and without too many expectations. Just enjoy yourself and see what develops.

4. SATURDAY. Diverse. Your creative mood this morning could lead you to make a change. Rearranging furniture or organizing a collection would be a great way to utilize this energy. Go out and buy some stylish new storage bins or baskets. If improving your health has been on your mind, this is a good time to get started. A different approach than those you have tried in the past might be more effective. Whatever your goal, take into account your whole lifestyle, not just your physical body. You can enhance your mind with education or self-hypnosis tapes and can soothe your spirit with prayer, meditation, or a walk in nature. A pet may need some extra attention and cuddling.

5. SUNDAY. Choppy. Housemates or family members could be getting on your nerves. All people, including you, may be a bit more critical than usual today. This mood could create some tough times if you let it. You might notice that small things bother you, like a dusty shelf or socks left on the floor. If this is the case, decide whether it is easier to clean it yourself or to make a comment. It may be best to stand up for your rights in a thoughtful manner, without placing any specific blame. If involved in a charitable event or organization, give freely of your time or money, and do not let group politics get to you. Think of the greater good, knowing that you are doing the right thing. A phone call may seem unusually thought-provoking.

6. MONDAY. Expansive. You could walk around as if in a fog. You may be prone to losing things. Try to keep your head on your shoulders and your wits about you. Turn that foggy feeling into an artistic or romantic one, and enjoy it. Virgos facing some detail work may want to put it off for a day or two and instead focus on something more creative. Do not be bashful when it comes to meeting new people. Someone you think is snobbish may simply be shy. Likewise, certain people could mistake you for having an attitude if you are not friendly enough. If thinking of formalizing a potential partnership, this is the time to get the ball rolling. Arrange a special private rendezvous.

7. TUESDAY. Variable. Virgos who are married or otherwise involved in a significant relationship should take a few minutes out to reflect on all that is most important in life. Consider whether things are going well, whether you are happy with your spouse and vice-versa. If anything does need to be discussed, this is a good day to get it out into the open. The general mood is one of compassion, helping to promote a mutually agreeable solution. The same goes for business partnerships. Keep a close eye on your important papers. This is one of those days when you may set something down and then not be able to find it again for a while. Check and recheck documents for spelling and mathematical errors.

8. WEDNESDAY. Spirited. Although Virgos are often a bit reserved, this is one day to attempt to more assertive. Think of it as a game. For practice, if you do not like the service you get in a restaurant, talk to the manager or do not leave a tip. If someone who is behind you in a line gets served ahead of you, make a comment. Do not let people get away with bullying or being pushy. Do not worry about being rude. Since it is only practice, enjoy it. Hone your negotiating skills, too. Make a lowball offer on an object, and allow yourself to be turned down so that you get used to rejection. In that way you will not take it personally every time. Enjoy a little romance tonight, being somewhat more aggressive in that department as well.

9. THURSDAY. Fair. Any or all of your close relationships can get out of balance. You may find yourself teetering between your desires and those of your loved one. The answer could be as simple as choosing to compromise. Being selfish could land you in hot water. Obtain the advice of a trusted relative or friend when it comes to complicated matters of the heart. Counseling may be useful despite your doubts or your mate's. If you feel overwhelmed by all of your duties, try to prioritize. Write down all that needs to be done right away, then number the items in order of importance. If you cannot get everything done today, start again tomorrow with a new list of priorities.

10. FRIDAY. Stimulating. Get out and work up a sweat. Do so outdoors if the weather permits. Skiing, running, or playing hockey can be a great way to work off any tension or aggression you are feeling. You may prefer to swim at an indoor pool, or drop by a gym. If you take a friend along, you will have a better time. Wake up early and do some household chores so you return to a clean home. If not feeling too well, rent a comedy video and enjoy a good belly laugh. You can really enjoy getting into a child's world. You may need to discuss jointly held investments, such as property or a checking account. Try to keep your mate or partner's needs and point of view in mind.

11. SATURDAY. Helpful. You may be expecting to go about your day without any surprises, but that is not likely. People may be a little touchy and quick to anger. If you are going on a trip, even just across town, take extra care with your timing. Leave early to allow for an unexpected detour or accident that slows you down. Be extra considerate when driving since other people could be impatient. Try to be as polite as possible to strangers. As soon as you can, get some rest and relaxation by taking an afternoon nap. Enjoy luxuries such as delicious food, a comfortable easy-chair, a nice back rub. If you stand firm when it comes to negotiating a deal, you could wind up with a great discount.

12. SUNDAY. Constructive. The groundwork you lay today can have a great effect on your future cash flow. Start making plans to improve your education and upgrade your skills. You might decide to go out of town or even to another country to get some advanced training. You may even decide to start teaching, probably at the community level. If you try to be the best in your chosen field of expertise or service, you are practically ensured success. You may become involved in publishing in some way, whether by placing a classified ad or submitting an article you wrote. Do so with confidence. Keep your social calendar open; you have a surprise visit or invitation coming your way.

13. MONDAY. Lively. You can expect people at the office to be friendly. You may engage in some interesting conversation with your boss or another higher-up. Meeting new people and networking should work well for you. If unsure what to talk about, start a conversation by asking about the person's early education. People always like talking about themselves, and that is especially true on this day. Curiosity could get the better of you if you are not careful, however. Do not overstep your bounds by putting your nose where it does not belong. Virgo students should find it easy to get started or continue writing an important paper. Research can pay off. Playing word games tonight can be fun as well as educational.

14. TUESDAY. Successful. If you apply yourself you can make good headway in achieving your career and life goals. A self-help book that a friend recently recommended may have some excellent ideas and motivational techniques for you to use. Follow the exercises in the book instead of skipping ahead. As a Virgo you have a tendency to flit around like a butterfly, trying this, that, and the other thing. Applying yourself in a systematic manner is vital for success. If you get the opportunity to attend a meeting or have lunch with some co-workers or other associates, by all means go along. Together you could come up with an amazing idea, so keep a pen and paper handy to jot down any interesting ones.

15. WEDNESDAY. Changeable. Control your activities closely. Procrastinating can get you in a lot of trouble. If you recently put off doing a certain job, you may now have to rush around trying to finish it. As a result you may make a mistake or otherwise have to cover for yourself. You do not need that anxiety, so decide early in the day what needs to be taken care of immediately, then do it. You might be asked to supervise a project or otherwise take on some extra responsibility. Your boss is apt to look over your shoulder, so make sure you can handle the work before you agree. One of your relatives could be trying to get in touch with you. Call to say a quick hello or send an e-mail message.

16. THURSDAY. Fulfilling. You are in the mood to be a romantic, gentle partner. Arrange to share some creative time with your loved one. Working together on an art project or to improve your home environment will be fulfilling. You may be attracted to someone at work, but give it lots of thought. You must not get caught up in office gossip. You can come up with some great ideas if you get together with like-minded people. Just be careful who you spend time with, since you are very sensitive to people who give off negative vibes. If you know someone recently lied to you or talked about you behind your back, this may be the time to start distancing yourself from the relationship. Make room for new people to come into your life.

17. FRIDAY. Rewarding. You could get farther than you think with a tough project. A club or other association may be able to help you. Friends can be a significant source of inspiration. If you have been working long and hard lately, take a break to restore your physical and mental health. Going outdoors to enjoy the fresh air can make you feel more energetic and enthusiastic. Play sports if possible, relishing the energy you get from a good workout. A new romance has more potential than you might think, although there is a slight danger that it is too good to be true for very long. Only time or maybe a good friend will tell you. Enjoy the relationship fully while it is in high gear.

18. SATURDAY. Volatile. Do not trust your own judgment exclusively. An overly idealistic or enthusiastic viewpoint can lead you to make errors as well as promises you cannot keep. You might feel like going ahead with a plan or project now, but hold out until tomorrow if you can. A premature move could send you two steps back. Overconfidence can lead to exposing your hand when you are not quite ready. Although it is nice to be enthusi-

astic, being overly so can actually work against you. You are better off to be silent in your power. The time is coming very soon
when you can make your big move. Being alone with your
thoughts is the best approach this evening.

19. SUNDAY. Reassuring. Like it or not, you may have to do an
unpleasant chore or job. Your attitude toward the work can make
all the difference. Try to complete the task and be proud of yourself. Creative or artistic projects can be especially rewarding and
inspiring. Physically, you could experience heightened tension.
You may find that you are working too much and for too few
rewards. If you have been penned up indoors, try to get out and
take a long walk or go to the gym. Relaxation exercises such as
yoga, controlled breathing, or gentle stretching can help you get
centered and focused. You might be asked to go out with a friend
tonight. Do not let a recent disappointment stop you from having
a good time.

20. MONDAY. Fruitful. You are strong and self-assured; take
advantage of this. Once you know what you really want out of
life, you can take the steps necessary to get it. Do not give up.
With effort and persistence you should be able to succeed at anything you choose to tackle. You may get an opportunity to catch
up on paperwork and household chores. Do not put off scheduling
a routine doctor or dentist appointment or a vision check. Offer
a kind word to those you rarely think of, such as clerks and ticket
takers. If a co-worker is having a bad day, offer your compassion.
You may not be able to solve the problem, but your understanding is bound to be appreciated.

21. TUESDAY. Cautious. You need to be aware of a heightened
tendency to procrastinate. Set aside a few minutes today to take
care of the things you would rather put off. You might even decide
to give up your lunch break in order to do it. Handle an emotional
co-worker with kid gloves. This is a great day to get some exercise.
A long walk could be ideal, or racket sports with a friend who is
a good competitor. Watch the time if speaking on the phone long-
distance; you are likely to run up quite a bill if you are not paying
attention. You could receive good news from a business contact.
Visit the local library and you may find a book that opens up a
new world of possibilities for you.

22. WEDNESDAY. Disquieting. Turn your thoughts to money
matters. If you are in a financial pinch because you overspent
recently, you might have to pay less than the full amount due on
your credit card, which will force up your interest payments. It
could be time to admit that you need some help dealing with

budgeting. Do not be hard on yourself. A credit counseling service can teach you how to manage your finances, and they will probably do it for free. If you are managing well, think about extra savings for a rainy day, a child's education, or your own retirement. When investing your money, be careful to diversify.

23. THURSDAY. Favorable. You might decide to do something a little out of character. A friend might be a little apprehensive at first but probably will not really mind. You can work well as part of a team, together making great progress with an ongoing project. You may enter into an unusual contract that is a bit out of the ordinary, but that is okay. A younger person may be able to handle more than you think. Focus on improving your physical condition. Go for a long walk on your lunch hour or play sports after work. Being on a team provides camaraderie as well as good physical conditioning. Enjoy an exciting action movie or television show tonight.

24. FRIDAY. Fortunate. Enjoy celebrating a recent business success. Luck is with you. Use caution, however, when taking a big risk. Friends can be supportive, and you will enjoy their smiling faces. Make plans for an evening out to party. Make sure you mark the date of an upcoming birthday on your calendar so you do not forget. You may as well also create or purchase a gift, to save you the trouble of worrying about it. You could make a crucial arrangement with a loved one later in the day. Be prepared to compromise a little by deciding in advance which issues are truly important and which ones you can easily let go. Romance should be memorable after dark.

25. SATURDAY. Troublesome. A neighborhood problem is coming to a head, but try not to deal with it right now if you can avoid it. Be honest with a friend or neighbor concerning behavior that you can no longer put up with. Find a way to take care of the matter without placing blame or being overly aggressive. Start writing in a journal about your hopes and your concerns. If you intend to be totally honest in what you write, find a hiding place for it. Or you may want to develop a personal shorthand to foil prying eyes. This can be an excellent time for letting romantic feelings out in the open; be ready for a wonderful response. Do not make an unnecessary trip if you are not pressed to do so.

26. SUNDAY. Mixed. Your good Virgo sense of humor can work to your advantage if you happen to make an embarrassing move. You may be ready to start a personal improvement project. If you have thought about some major home renovations, work on the planning a bit more before you jump in if big expense is involved.

Try not to get exasperated with a relative. Although you are likely to be rather short-tempered or even grumpy, you will regret saying something unpleasant that you cannot take back. Try to let go of angry feelings for a day or two. If you really feel you have been the victim of injustice, bring it up only when you have had a chance to cool off.

27. MONDAY. Helpful. You may be getting all worked up about a situation over which you have little or no power. You will probably be quite pleasantly surprised to see that everything is going to be okay. You can thrive under adverse conditions. Trouble can actually be stimulating for you, making you step out of your safety zone. Put matters into perspective by thinking about how boring life gets when everything stays the same for days or weeks. Challenges are really opportunities. You can make a difference to a neighbor if willing to do a little bit of work together. Think fast on your feet and you might be shocked how quickly the answers you have been seeking are provided to you.

28. TUESDAY. Worrisome. Your mind is not likely to be on your work but rather on domestic matters. Force yourself to pay close attention to details. Not doing so could lead to sloppiness which causes you to make errors that harm your well-earned reputation. There is no get-rich-quick method that will work for you at this time. Slow, steady progress is the only way. Overtime hours you put in can cause some strife when you are not able to fulfill your responsibilities at home. Think of what you can do to make up for it. Repay money or favors. Keep your accounts up to date as well. A clean slate should be your goal. Get to bed earlier than usual tonight.

29. WEDNESDAY. Frustrating. This day could be somewhat difficult. Your mate may not agree on certain household rules or even on major issues like child or pet discipline. If this is the case, make sure you do not argue too long or loud. You may need to both talk to a third party, such as a good friend whose opinion you both trust. Your child may incur a large expense that you will ultimately be responsible for paying. Asking your own parents or another relative for money may not be a good idea. You need to make a decision whether to incur any more personal debt. A romance may not be turning out exactly the way you hoped. Your attempts might be met with rejection that is hard to accept.

30. THURSDAY. Deceptive. You might be tempted to do something that makes you uncomfortable. If you know the activity is illegal or immoral, simply do not do it. People could be preoccupied, so do not be surprised if a mistake gets compounded. You can change a negative situation with your own kind words or deeds. Do not let another person put you under pressure when it comes to making an important decision about your job. You could be susceptible to environmental particles such as pet dander or solvents. Alcohol and drugs can take a real toll on your system, so avoid them. A workmate may entice you to have a longer than usual lunch, which could lead to a reprimand from the boss.

31. FRIDAY. Calm. Even if you stayed up late last night, make sure you get out of bed as soon as you turn off your alarm. Otherwise you might fall back asleep and end up late for work. Your boss will not be very tolerant. You could encounter a challenge at work and need someone else to help you out. It is vital to recognize your own responsibilities. You may have to labor through your lunch hour in order to catch up with your work, but at least you will have the satisfaction of a job well done. Bring a brown bag lunch just in case you cannot get to the cafeteria or restaurant. Try not to schedule important meetings for today as people may cancel out at the last minute.

FEBRUARY

1. SATURDAY. Beneficial. You are likely to be more courageous than usual, making this an exceptionally good time for starting a major project. Health matters should be relatively easy to get under control. There could be a certain herb, vitamin, or nutritional supplement that will benefit you at this time. Make an appointment to see your doctor if concerned about a chronic condition or a new symptom you have recently noticed. Consider taking a class to further your marketable skills. Sign up today in order to avoid being disappointed when the class is full. Traveling could be a bit tricky if you misplace your ticket or get caught in a traffic jam. Allow at least an extra hour.

2. SUNDAY. Enjoyable. If you are planning to host or to attend a party or other get-together today, you could be in for a real treat. Loosen up. Tell all your favorite jokes, no matter how corny or old they are. Friends and family members will enjoy a sing-along or a game of charades. Ask people to bring any musical instrument they play, then have a jam session. If a close friend needs support, offer it but do not try to solve the problem or give any definite advice. This is a great day to get some exercise; a long walk in the woods would be ideal. Spend the evening with that special person in your life, cozying up by the fire or otherwise lounging around, reminiscing and making plans for the future you envision.

3. MONDAY. Tiring. Do not let one person's rejection stop you from asking others for help. You might have to make a few such requests before getting what you need. Do not give up. Physically, you could be stressed and experience signs of tension such as a headache. This could be caused by a power issue or anger with a family member. It is very important that you get some time alone to sort out your thoughts. Find positive ways to blow off steam. You may be motivated to take care of a long-standing issue with your business partner, but tone down your words. Although tempting to move forward at your own pace, you have to consider the position that other people are taking and their reasons for doing so.

4. TUESDAY. Demanding. A project that you are working on with other people may require a few changes. Partners may not agree, however, regarding what to do. You might have to put your foot down in order to make any progress; do not hesitate to do so. You may need a day or two away from work, a mini-vacation. You may have a friend who lives in another area of the country who you could visit, for the pleasure of the company and to get a change of scenery. You may get a chance to clear up miscommunication. Do not be too proud to risk revealing what is in your heart and on your mind. If you are upset with a friend, work through it right away so neither of you will harbor resentment toward the other.

5. WEDNESDAY. Promising. You might have to deal with some uncomfortable feelings involving money and personal relationships. You may have recently been given a valuable gift or received an inheritance. Someone in your family or circle may not be pleased with their share. People can be quite greedy when it comes to cash, property, or other material goods, but do not let anyone make you feel guilty for your good luck. You have probably earned it in one way or another. If life starts to seem overwhelming, try to get away from it all. Relax and take good care of your own needs. Whether you want time alone or want to be with other people, do what feels right and good to you.

6. THURSDAY. Calm. Meditation and reflection are useful methods of gaining insight into your relationships. Think about your current circumstances. The way you present yourself could have a lot to do with how other people have been treating you lately. There are many things you can do to try to improve your self-confidence, to make yourself more successful and popular. If you have been wearing the same hairstyle for years, you might get a real boost from a new color or cut. If you regret not earning a certain degree or certificate, you do not have to wait for the school term to learn. You could educate yourself with audiotapes on different subjects or take a course via the Internet.

7. FRIDAY. Comforting. Try to spend the day with people you care about. Communications should improve as long as you do not insist you are right all the time. Answer mail and return phone calls. A visit to a museum or library with a good friend will be comforting and satisfying. A potentially difficult situation at work can easily be diffused with a little honesty and extra consideration. Romance is in the air. Plan a date with that special person in your life. Pretend you have just met. The perfect date could be a light meal followed by a romantic movie or perhaps dancing at a club. This could even be the right night to have an important talk about the future. Your loved one should be open-minded and eager to please you.

8. SATURDAY. Stimulating. Just about anything can be a learning experience. If you are traveling, notice the differences between your culture and the one you are visiting. Try to eat authentic local food. Pay attention to the way people dress, and how their daily routine varies from your own. Taking a class or studying a favorite subject are other starred ways of spending this stimulating day. As a Virgo you have a tendency to be on the stubborn side. Once you make up your mind it can be quite difficult to get you to change it. You are probably very opinionated as well, although you might think other people are so. The strange behavior of someone else may be a mirror of your own attitudes and actions.

9. SUNDAY. Changeable. You could be too philosophical for your own good. If loved ones roll their eyes at your statements, or if you find you are constantly arguing with other people, listen to what you are saying. You may be preaching rather than talking. You may have a disagreement with a loved one over vacation plans. Leave the details to the other person once you find some common ground. You are gifted with intuition, but you still need to check facts if you intend to accuse someone of wrongdoing. You are likely to find real inspiration at a spiritual meeting providing you agree with what the speaker is saying. Enjoy an adventure film this evening.

10. MONDAY. Pressured. Although you are eager to succeed, it may not be that simple. Try to find a need that is not being met at work, or a problem to solve. Your boss may not recognize your contribution right now but will on another day, so do not get upset over lack of appreciation. Follow your intuition when dealing with a parent or other elder who has been on your mind. If you have not visited lately, now is the time to do so. You may not even realize what it means for this person to hear your voice. Making a romantic move tonight could lead to disappointment, but it never hurts to try. If you do not make some kind of effort you will never know what might have been.

11. TUESDAY. Auspicious. Your reputation precedes, so hopefully you have been good lately. Unseen forces are helping you succeed in your chosen line of work or study. Focus on your own abilities rather than believing that other people always know how to do things better than you. Draw on your natural leadership skills if asked to teach or lead more than a few people. Tap into your authority and your experience. You may feel your personal life has been put on hold. This is a good time to reexamine what you really want out of relationships. However, do not make too much effort to change current friendships. Just think about what you want to be doing a year or a decade from now. Be confident; you can do whatever you wish.

12. WEDNESDAY. Good. Your good mood should continue today. Being around a group of people becomes more fulfilling and enjoyable. Your friends should be calling, and you will enjoy sharing stories of happenings at home or at work. A long telephone call could cost a fortune if you do not watch the time. A friend you have not seen in a while would be very happy to hear from you. Consider ways of making this evening more fun than usual. Entertaining friends at home could lead to a great evening of conversation. A co-worker's interesting story may captivate you. You are likely to be admired for a recent accomplishment, but give credit where it is due.

13. THURSDAY. Sensitive. A group meeting that you attend may not be in your best interests. If spending or investing money is involved, beware. A loan that you made in good faith a while ago may be causing some frustration because it might not be possible to collect the cash. Think long and hard if someone asks for money now; you do not want to be burned twice. Hearing of someone from your past, perhaps an old schoolmate, who has had some misfortune should cause you to count your blessings. Channel your energy into a physical project such as washing the car, vacuum cleaning, or sweeping the front walk. Pent-up emotions are not something you want to carry around.

14. FRIDAY. Quiet. A good friend may need some comfort. Put off activities that are not necessary in order to help. Take an honest look at all that is going on in the world around you. When you examine the realities some people have to live with, your sensitivity will increase. Find charity in your heart, either to give some of your time or your money to help make a difference. If you are in a position to use the media to reach a large group of people, take advantage by urging other people to join you in good works. When writing your personal goals, identify an unselfish or altruistic ideal to which you can contribute. Keep in mind that charity begins at home.

15. SATURDAY. Fair. Your impulsive mood could lead to spending frivolously. You might be tempted to indulge in shopping as a form of therapy. If you must do so, buy only a few items. Going to a thrift or secondhand store would be much better than going to a mall. You might hear of a friend or family member's new romance or engagement. Congratulate the happy couple right away, before they get too preoccupied. Miscommunication between you and a special friend may be nothing more than a misunderstanding. Find a way to set the record straight without coming on too strong. Although you might be tempted to take a shortcut today, it could lead to a dead end.

16. SUNDAY. Tricky. You might be on edge as you worry about some details that have not fallen into place. Do not force the issue now. A cooperative spirit will be effective, so be prepared to give more than you take. Refrain from mixing business with pleasure or you might make the wrong impression on someone important. If you want to encourage a person who you believe needs help, you may feel like disclosing something personal. Doing so could be a mistake, however. It is vital to know when to have compassion and when you are being suckered; the difference at this time can be a very fine line. Spend a quiet evening alone in creative reflection. Focus on goals for the week ahead.

17. MONDAY. Erratic. People can get uptight and upset while discussing even minor matters, such as the best way to unroll toilet paper or which sports team is likely to win the championship. Just bite your tongue instead of engaging in an argument. Enjoy getting away for a few minutes of solitude. A walk holding hands with your mate or partner would also be ideal. You are likely to find out whether your relationship is based on wishful thinking or if you both really feel the same way. Keep in mind that no relationship is perfect. You may have to be a little more patient. Work from behind the scenes rather than seeking to be in the spotlight.

18. TUESDAY. Frustrating. If someone at work is causing difficulties that are expensive for the company, it could be up to you to resolve the matter. Now is the time to take care of it before it is blown out of all proportion. If you need to have an important discussion with someone regarding job performance, do so privately and gently. If you are the one creating the problem, you are the one who should solve it. This is not a good day to procrastinate or try to pass the buck. The more productive you can be, the better. Any health concerns could be due to unwise lifestyle choices such as poor nutrition or not getting enough exercise. Make an appointment to see your family doctor if worried.

19. WEDNESDAY. Profitable. This is an excellent day for starting to earn more money. An idea you came up with earlier in the year could be quite profitable if you go about it in the right way. This is a starred time for selling excess items you have accumulated. Place an ad in your local paper or tack your offer on a bulletin board. In order to make sure you get a fair price, ask for slightly more than what you might be willing to take. You may find all kinds of opportunities if out looking for a new job. Contact companies that you would like to work for to see what they have available. One of their current employees may be retiring or resigning from a position that is perfect for you.

20. THURSDAY. Difficult. After yesterday, when things were quite positive, this day could seem like a letdown. It is time to take a hard look at your spending habits. If you have literally been blowing money into the wind, you must find a way to cut expenses. Carpooling is one good option; buying groceries in bulk is another. If planning something special for a loved one, you might get discouraged when you are criticized or turned down. Consider the source. Some people need a hug rather than a snarl. If your self-esteem is weak, try to get to the source of the problem. Accomplish something worthwhile and you are bound to feel better.

21. FRIDAY. Deceptive. Any activities that involve word processing or pen and paper are favored. Catch up on all of your communications. You may be in such high demand that you have to take the phone off the hook in order to complete tasks by the deadline. You can no longer afford to procrastinate. The focus this evening is on home. Enjoy all your wonderful toys and gadgets. Be very gentle if you have to criticize a family member, a neighbor, or a community leader. Things are not always as they seem, and looks can be deceiving. Do not sign any new financial

document if you can avoid doing so. If you cannot avoid it, make
sure you read and understand all of the clauses and fine print.

22. SATURDAY. Complicated. Doubt can cloud an otherwise
good day. A real problem in your neighborhood may not be easy
to solve, but that does not mean you should not try. Be persistent
and in the end you will succeed. Do not attempt to force matters
by outwitting someone, or you may start verbal warfare. Avoid
being too spontaneous when it comes to starting a new relationship. First find out if anyone you know has information about the
person you are interested in getting to know. Someone who lives
close to you might come into your yard without permission. Say
something about it rather than remaining mute and angry.

23. SUNDAY. Variable. You might not be able to trust a certain
older person. Although it is unlikely that this person would intentionally mislead you, that chance does exist. Your long-term career plans may have to be placed on hold due to a relationship
or personal problem that needs immediate undivided attention. It
probably will not damage your reputation as long as you are truthful at the onset. Do not be too controlling with family members
in regard to domestic matters or you may alienate just the person
you really need on your side right now. Start thinking about making plans for the future, but do not make any moves today. Parents or other relatives can seem critical or overly demanding.

24. MONDAY. Diverse. This is a good time to choose a new
color scheme for your home or office. Try to create a feeling of
warmth and comfort. Consider adding a water feature, mirrors,
plants. You do not have to spend a lot of money hiring a con-
sultant; just read a book. Also avoid spending a lot on new household projects, at least right now. If planning a major renovation,
get some professional help from a contractor or from a friend who
is experienced. If you have a performance coming up or a paper
that is due, try it out on family members. You can count on them
to be honest and gently truthful.

25. TUESDAY. Mixed. Keep your sense of humor intact when
you get challenged by someone who only is trying to be funny.
Sometimes jokes made at the expense of others are not humorous
at all, and this can be one of those occasions. Work on a creative
project that brings you pleasure. All work and no play can make
you grouchy as well as dull. Stress may stem from a promise that
you have yet to keep. Vow to uphold your end of a bargain. Love
is likely to be on your mind, but you do not really know what you
want. One minute you think settling down sounds great, the next

you feel like being footloose and fancy-free. Since you cannot have both, you must decide.

26. WEDNESDAY. Fruitful. Go ahead and take a risk when it comes to sharing your unique creativity. The response you receive is apt to be even better than you imagined or hoped. A child who has been exhibiting some disturbing behavior lately needs to be gently guided. Setting a good example will probably work better than being a strict disciplinarian. Most of all, remember that love is the best teacher. Romantic feelings toward someone may come out today, even though you try to hold them in. If you have a crush on someone it can be tough to hide your feelings. When you are ready to start dating, go for it by being upfront rather than shy.

27. THURSDAY. Interesting. You may witness an event that makes the news, or learn about an activity that becomes a new hobby or sport for you. Check out some fun activities such as dancing, fencing, or playing a musical instrument. Phone your friends to share your good news. If participating in a new sport, make sure you receive proper instruction so that you do not accidentally sprain or bruise your ankle or wrist. New people who you meet today could be quite eccentric as well as creative. You will enjoy the conversation, so do not be timid. Aim to have a little fun. Matters of the heart are featured after the lights go out.

28. FRIDAY. Slow. A quiet start to the day may not be what you were hoping for. Although you have big plans for getting a lot done and being productive, you may be disappointed. If you absolutely must complete an important project, take frequent breaks, or cut your day in two with a rest period in between. Repetitive tasks that require little conscious thought can be almost like meditating. You may get valuable insight that seems to come out of nowhere. If you are consciously or unconsciously doing something that might harm your health, try to come to terms with it today. Avoid anything that might poison your system such as alcohol, nonprescription drugs, or contaminated water.

MARCH

1. SATURDAY. Auspicious. You might be struck by a story or a phrase in a newspaper or on television that goes straight to your heart. What you learn about yourself as a result could eliminate certain worries for good. Breathe a big sigh of relief. This is a good time to ask for help to give a project just the momentum it needs in order to keep going. People are likely to give you a hand in whatever way they can. Get out for some exercise this evening. Work up a sweat, then maintain the pace for a while if you can. If you bring along your mate or partner, you may be motivated to begin a regular fitness program together. You can be a very positive influence on each other.

2. SUNDAY. Erratic. Try to be realistic about what is actually going on between you and your closest friend or ally. You may be upset about a recent discussion that unexpectedly ended on a bad note. This is your chance to figure out what went wrong and try to make it right again. Ideally you should arrange to have some time alone today, but your mate or partner may want to spend quality time with you. Try to find a balance by doing both. Discussing important life-impacting issues is not the best idea right now. Instead, do something light like shopping or going to see a movie together. Aim to pay more attention to the positive qualities of other people rather than always noticing the negative.

3. MONDAY. Changeable. If thinking of going into business with a partner, spend a little time together hashing out the details. If you begin to get down on yourself or critical of other people, take a break and relax. You may simply be overworked. Get together with your best friend or a close relative who will encourage you to push forward through your fears and worries about a decision you need to make soon. A minor cycle beginning now puts the focus on all of your closest relationships. Consider what you can do to make them run smoothly and fairly for everyone involved. Do not forget to stop and pick up a few groceries or dry cleaning on the way home this evening.

4. TUESDAY. Surprising. Try not to leave a lot undone this morning. Someone who works with or for you will resent cleaning up after you. This is an excellent day to discuss important matters, with the goal of making your life smoother and easier. A new acquaintance might turn out to be a great business contact or even a partner in some way. Make sure you are your most charming Virgo self when meeting new people. Look extra good if going out tonight. Buy a bright and bold article of clothing to be sure you are noticed. There could be someone very attractive who gives you the eye. Practice your flirting techniques but do not let your expectations rise too high too fast.

5. WEDNESDAY. Successful. Go ahead and make the major change in your life that you have been contemplating. The time is prime for all types of beginnings, especially for future plans that concern a partner. Discussing money and what to do with it can produce good results. At the same time you should probably check your insurance coverage to be sure it is sufficient based on replacement value. You might need additional for an expensive new item you recently bought. Go over your budget to be sure you are not spending money for extra things that you do not need. Dealing with inheritance matters in proper fashion is crucial. Your relatives are counting on you to do the right thing.

6. THURSDAY. Helpful. Do not postpone dealing with a nagging question or problem that you just have not been able to solve until now. There are tricks you can use to figure out the answer. Start by writing down the question this morning, telling yourself that you want an answer by the end of the day at the latest. Keep your question at the back of your mind, notice any possible solutions that come into your head, and write them down. If you do not have an answer by bedtime, you will probably dream it tonight. If you feel a strong desire to travel, it may be time to plan a vacation. A cruise or a train trip may be in your future. Shy away from normal tourist routine.

7. FRIDAY. Upbeat. A renewed sense of optimism is just what you need in order to cope with a situation that involves someone overseas. Making contact by phone or e-mail could set your mind at ease. Luck can come from following a hunch, but do not become overly confident or take a big risk. Spontaneity and impulsiveness are fine as long as you do not go overboard. Try to develop patience when it comes to dealing with people who disparage some of your beliefs. At least these are modern times when people are not persecuted for being different. Having dinner at a foreign restaurant or with someone from a different culture could be a lot of fun. For a real change, try cooking an exotic meal.

8. SATURDAY. Variable. If you've indulged in wishful thinking in regards to a vacation, this is the day to get down to the realities of the situation. You may still have big plans, but you will probably have to find a discount ticket and affordable accommodations. You might be able to rent out your home for a month and recoup some of your expenses in that way. You might feel like getting a total head-to-toe makeover, but you would be better off not to even try. Settle for less than major changes, like a new hair color or style. Virgo students may have to study extra hard to get a passing grade on a test. Keep evening plans simple. Avoid going out as part of a large group.

9. SUNDAY. Uncertain. You need to handle a delicate situation with kid gloves. Resolving it completely is probably not going to happen today, but at least you can appease some hurt feelings and reduce the emotional damage. Instinctively you know what should be done at any given time, but your judgment may be questioned by people who do not agree with you. It is too soon to tell if a certain project is a pass or fail. You will probably enjoy a quiet evening at home more than going out. Rent a movie, make some popcorn, and curl up on the couch with a cozy quilt. Turn off the ringer on the phone and enjoy some peace and quiet. Show your mate or partner the depth of your feelings and devotion.

10. MONDAY. Challenging. Certain factors outside of your control are affecting your job performance. Pay attention to subtle clues from your boss, who may not want to talk about problems directly. You might ask if your work is satisfactory and, if not, what you can do to remedy the situation. Someone influential should be willing to mentor you, but do not expect this person to volunteer. You are going to have to ask for the favor and be willing to accept positive criticism. Try to remain optimistic no matter how you actually feel. No one can really tell what you are thinking, but some sensitive people will probably intuit how you are feeling.

11. TUESDAY. Tricky. You may get involved in the life of one of your friends more than you would prefer. A triangle formed with you and two other people could seem a little treacherous if one person has turned against another. Do not let anyone coerce you into saying negative words about someone you respect and care about. If you do so, it could be used against you later on. If going for a job interview, do not hesitate to drop names. In fact, who you know could be more important than your real qualifications when it comes to a certain job opening. It might seem as if you are being drawn into a complicated social circle. Do not participate in gossip that is malicious or spread a rumor you have not personally verified.

12. WEDNESDAY. Manageable. Your alliance with a group or association could lead to a new opportunity when you are introduced to someone quite by chance. Use caution, however, as you are apt to be emotionally vulnerable. Put up your guard and do not be overly open in expressing what is on your mind. If it seems that someone is trying to take unreasonable advantage of your kindness, take a step back. A how-to book can give you the information and skills you need in order to move forward while standing on your own two feet. A problem that is coming between friends could actually resolve itself without your effort, so try not to get involved unless specifically asked to do so. Do not let anyone intimidate you, even if it means you must leave the room.

13. THURSDAY. Demanding. Friends may be the most important people in your life. If you have been caught up in career, relationship, or personal issues recently, you may not have had much time to be in contact with them. Even if you are too busy to go out together for lunch or plan a day together, you can at least call and say hello. Concerns about the direction of your life may be unfounded, but review it anyway. Even if you made a bad choice in the recent past, do not view life as hopeless. Do whatever is necessary in order to redeem yourself. Never hold back an apology because of pride. Making amends will be easier than you think if you start right away.

14. FRIDAY. Eventful. Go forward with plans that involve a group of people, especially if they are your friends. Get interested in participating in networking, which would definitely be profitable. Getting together with like-minded people can advance your self-growth and development. Taking up a hobby such as public speaking or acting would be excellent if you are on the timid side. Recognition and honor could be coming your way for recent work you completed or a good deed done within the past six months. A party invitation that you receive is a definite go. You may not be able to see how today's actions can affect you in the future, but you will be pleasantly surprised.

15. SATURDAY. Calm. Spend some time alone, reading or catching up on a hobby or collection. If you must complete some routine tasks, play some inspiring music while doing so. You can have a lot of pleasure even while doing things you usually avoid. If you have to go to work, keep cool and project a good attitude. Otherwise your co-workers might pick up on your negative feelings and turn the whole day into a downer. Forgetfulness is very possible. Write down crucial names and dates so you do not cause any problems. Ask a family member to help you remember birthdays, anniversaries, and other important dates.

16. SUNDAY. Mixed. Do not underestimate the difficulty of a personal project, nor let it stop you from going ahead with it. Hiring someone to help you might be a good idea, or getting a friend to volunteer temporary services. Working with numbers should be easier than usual. Complex computer programming or detailed handwork will not faze you. You may not get much routine housework done. Give yourself a break. Becoming anxious about things like dirty laundry or an unmowed lawn is a waste of your energy. You probably will be motivated for any activity that involves self-improvement. You could write an excellent article, report, or proposal.

17. MONDAY. Sensitive. People may be asking too much of you, taking advantage of your abilities. You need to learn when to say no and when it is okay to help. Setting up boundaries can save you a lot of headaches later on. Getting away from the rat race can be wonderful, especially if you get some pampering at a spa or salon. Beautiful clothing and jewelry are sure to appeal, but shopping is likely to feel more like a chore than a pleasure. Honestly appraise what you would most like to have happen over the next week or month, then set about to make your hopes come true. The first step is always the hardest.

18. TUESDAY. Lively. Follow up on business already started rather than beginning any new projects. A partner or friend may have some useful and interesting information for you. What you do with it is up to you. Follow your good Virgo intuition for the best results; your instincts should be right. Try to return all phone messages. Being a perfectionist or overly critical while at work will not benefit you or anyone else right now. Try not to complain too much about your job. Give your co-workers a break. Negative words might reach the wrong ears and could even affect your promotion possibilities.

19. WEDNESDAY. Happy. This day can be outstanding if you allow it to be. Try to schedule some time to be alone with that special person in your life. If you are longing for love but have no one special, check out a dating service or club. If you have an opportunity to go out with someone new but are only mildly interested, go anyway; you could have a very good time. Pamper yourself with as much luxury as you can afford. At the very least, wake up early so you can have a leisurely breakfast. Take some time for meditation. The busier you are, the more you need to relax. Reflecting on life and planning your day will help you feel and look more confident and in control.

20. THURSDAY. Excellent. Life could seem better than ever these days. The challenges that you are now facing seem minor compared to how you viewed them a month or even a week ago. Keep on your toes, however; being overly optimistic can blind you to some realities that need your attention. At least you will not avoid taking care of things. This is a very good time to make a financial proposal, such as asking for a raise at work or bidding on a new job or contract. Be sure you are armed with facts and figures to support why you deserve what you are asking for; you should not be denied if you are well informed. Be sure to clarify any terms you are unfamiliar with before signing a document or filing legal papers.

21. FRIDAY. Rewarding. Go ahead and speak your mind. People will listen to you more intently than they have recently. Those close to you need to know what you are planning. If you let it be a surprise, you might be refused, rejected, or repressed. New community goals are worth the challenge it is going to take to implement them. However, be realistic about how much energy and what type will be necessary to make things happen. Gathering signatures is one way to get the attention of government officials; media attention may work much faster. Create a well-worded letter stating your position, and fax it off to newspapers and to radio and television stations in town. Follow up with a phone call and a gathering of supporters.

22. SATURDAY. Fair. If you enjoy gardening, take advantage of this time to start seeds indoors and to plan your vegetable plot and flower beds. Opt for something really colorful. You may want to try growing a few unique plants. Consider joining a gardening club in order to exchange seeds and plants. If you have not bought any decorative item for your home recently, go to some garage sales or thrift stores and look around. You will feel better if you do something to make your living environment nicer. Relatives can be argumentative, so you might find yourself having to act as peacemaker. Diffuse any such situations as quickly as possible. Look at both sides before deciding who to support.

23. SUNDAY. Good. A distant relative is eager to hear from you. If you haven't talked to your favorite aunt or uncle in a while, make a call. Time goes by too quickly between visits. Local socializing could be taking too much of your time away from domestic life. Your friends will understand if you explain your situation rather than just disappear. They will feel cut off if you

simply quit calling. You may want to work from a home office. If
your company does not offer such an option, explore alternatives.
Check books and magazines with information on home-based
businesses. Do some research if that is what you want sometime
in the future. Right now you can be building up contacts.

24. MONDAY. Improving. Doing chores around the house may
not be your idea of early morning fun, but you will be pleased
when you return home to a nice clean environment. This day offers a wonderful opportunity to get closer to a child. Virgo parents
of a youngster who is feeling under the weather should try to
arrange to take the day off from work to stay home. Remember
how it felt when you were young and your mother or father took
care of you; try to recreate that special feeling. Your thoughts may
turn to love this evening. If you are considering going on a blind
date, take a chance and make the arrangements.

25. TUESDAY. Tricky. A little extra caution is needed in a few
areas because you are likely to be somewhat careless or sloppy.
Someone who does not have your best interests in mind could
mislead you. An attraction to the glamorous side of life can be
seductive, but pure pleasure seeking can bring more pain than it
is worth. Find a balance between having fun and being totally self-
centered. You might think you are invincible, which is great for
the ego but could trip you up if you fail to pay attention to such
things as safety rules and good manners. Judge your abilities by
your accomplishments, not by compliments you receive from
those who have their own agenda.

26. WEDNESDAY. Tranquil. If you want to win the heart of a
potential mate, try being shy. It may sound a little corny, but this
is a fun way of letting someone know you are interested. Making
eye contact and then looking down quickly once you are noticed
can be a subtle way of saying you are interested. Virgos who are
already involved in a romantic relationship can take this time to
add a little spice to love. Whatever your sweetheart enjoys most,
make it a point to offer it. Encourage kids to be more creative.
Arts and crafts, painting, singing, and dancing are just a few ex-
amples of activities that will open up and enrich their worlds, especially if you participate side by side.

27. THURSDAY. Manageable. Deal with a worrisome health issue rather than putting it off. If you have been trying to break a
nasty habit, this could be the day when doing so is easier for you.
Environmental contaminants and allergens can weaken your system. Consider an air cleaner as one of your therapies. News of a
job opening that is specifically suitable for your talents could be

music to your ears. Make sure you have a professional-looking resume and cover letter ready to ship off as soon as you hear of the position. It would be wise to leave the room or hang up the phone if one of your colleagues is being unreasonable.

28. FRIDAY. Confusing. Closely monitor what you say. A tendency toward impulsive speech means you can put your foot in your mouth in a flash. At the same time, your mental sharpness helps you excel at problem solving and working with figures. Jumping to conclusions is not the way to obtain truthful answers. Get some exercise, using it to burn off steam if you feel frustrated or angry. It will give you a natural high that lasts for hours. Trying an alternative health method can bring relief for a minor medical condition, but do not choose a practitioner by just looking in the phone book. Get a recommendation from a friend, relative, or coworker.

29. SATURDAY. Surprising. Your mate or partner may be arranging something special, so try to act like you are oblivious. Your super-generous mood could find you at the mall buying expensive gifts for loved ones. However, if you go overboard on the spending you will be in for a shock when you receive your credit card or bank statement. Doing chores around the house with your loved one can be a cozy way to spend the morning hours. Play the kind of music you used to listen to when you were first dating. The resulting rush of memories could lead to a wonderful romantic moment. You can shine this evening at a party or other social event. Wear your favorite outfit and fragrance.

30. SUNDAY. Easygoing. Play hooky from your domestic responsibilities. Focus instead on your primary relationship. A conversation regarding business with your teammate or partner is likely to yield just the satisfaction you are seeking. You can pin the other person down to an agreement that will work well for both of you. Your optimistic outlook makes it easy to get attention and respect from someone you admire. If a chance to share a friend's good fortune comes up, enjoy the celebration. If you have been trying to juggle many things recently, this could be the day when you finally see the light at the end of the tunnel. Delegating some responsibility is not a bad idea.

31. MONDAY. Volatile. Recent progress you made with a partner could hit a snag. You will have to do some quick thinking in order to get back on the right track. Luckily this should not be too difficult for you today. It can be hard to maintain a positive attitude when loved ones do not understand all that you have been going through. You need to be patient. You might think someone is out to get you, when actually the person is just going through some difficult times and needs a scapegoat. Stay in tonight rather than go to a scheduled meeting, especially if money matters are to be discussed. If you must attend, have all your facts and figures available in written form and be ready for a lot of questions.

APRIL

1. TUESDAY. Favorable. You should not have any trouble convincing your mate or partner to go along with your plans as long as you both will benefit from the potential outcome. In order to increase your chances of success, do not beat around the bush. State your case clearly and in easy to understand terms. Also make sure you include all the possible ways the day could turn out. You may be able to earn good dividends from investing in an insurance policy, but investigate it first to be sure it is a recommended one. Do not wait any longer to make the changes necessary in order to turn your life around. Break free from a codependent relationship, or at least take initial steps to make it better.

2. WEDNESDAY. Stimulating. You have what it takes to put the spark back into your life and your most important relationship. Do not settle for a boring existence. Live with passion. If you have an idea or a plan that you have wanted to try for a long time but were afraid to do by yourself, this is a starred time to find a partner to help you. Sharing expenses will be easier than going it alone. A one-sided infatuation is not fair for anyone. You can temper hurt feelings by showing compassion to someone who has a crush on you. Your interest in the occult or metaphysics could increase when you read a book that delves into the unseen workings of the universe.

3. THURSDAY. Exciting. Look around you and you will probably spot some exceptional opportunities. Take swift action in order to establish a place for yourself. If planning to further your education, you may be eligible for a grant or scholarship. Investigate what is available but not publicized. Attending school in a different country can be the thrill of a lifetime. Getting in touch with a loved one who is living overseas could provoke a conversation that answers some vital questions. Meeting new people who share philosophies similar to your own can be rewarding. Taking up a new sport will prove exhilarating but also quite physically demanding.

4. FRIDAY. Pressured. Your nerves might be on edge if you have to handle a lot of paperwork. Constant interruptions could cause you to make a crucial mistake unless you are extra careful. Hold all your calls, and tell co-workers to bother you only if necessary. Opposition from someone who does not share your basic beliefs could get you down, but do not take it to heart. Venture into uncharted waters and you could wind up over your head. Do not let your high energy level go to waste. Go out jogging, mow the lawn, or take the dog for a long walk. It makes good sense to get into the best possible shape before summer arrives. You will want to look good in a bathing suit or shorts.

5. SATURDAY. Productive. As a Virgo you probably have a list of things that need to be done today and every day. Do not concern yourself too much with activities that are not really necessary. Take care of only those that are causing you to worry. Then get outdoors and enjoy the day. Hiking or playing sports with a good friend can make you feel like a new person. Although April showers may come your way, you will not mind too much if enjoying yourself. Tonight take in a theater, concert, or opera performance. Dressing up can be a pleasure in itself. You might run into someone who will be quite impressed by your appearance.

6. SUNDAY. Happy. This day offers an excellent chance to spend some quality time with an older person who is of great importance in your life. If you do not have any senior relatives, you can get a lot out of volunteering at a nursing home or for some other service. While attending a seminar or workshop you could be introduced to a new concept that causes you to shift your career goals. If you do any networking while you are out and about, you should benefit in a big way from the folks you meet. Take full advantage at this time of any connections that will further your ambitions. Who you know can be as important as what you do.

7. MONDAY. Demanding. You may have to admit a mistake you recently made, but doing so can put you in good light with those who really count. A supervisor might get on you about a problem that you had nothing to do with. Rather than become angry or frustrated, offer to help in whatever way you can. A better paying job or promotion may require you to work more hours than what you consider ideal. Weigh your options carefully before making a decision and announcing it. The job might be worth it in the long run if it looks good on your resume. Although being in the public eye is something you may have always secretly desired, you could find that being even a minor celebrity has certain drawbacks.

8. TUESDAY. Active. Your public life is more important than ever. Express your ideas and plans to the right people and you will be very happy with the feedback you receive. If given the green light to go ahead on a pet project, make sure you keep control of the details. Group activities may be on the agenda. Although you may not be entirely comfortable with these at first, you will probably fit right in. Do not reveal your intentions if doing so might harm your chances of success. Be aware that certain people are jealous or will recognize a good idea and steal it for themselves. If your idea or product can be legally protected, follow up on that now.

9. WEDNESDAY. Mixed. Be careful what you wish for since you just may get it today. Your extra personal magnetism virtually guarantees romantic success. You will be unusually popular in your social circle and might receive an invitation for a very exclusive event happening this weekend. Children might not be pleased if you spend the evening with friends, but they will just have to understand. Do not let your hopes go down the drain. Take some time out to examine the reasons you are not making progress in achieving your dreams. Writing affirmations on a regular basis might help you get over negative thought patterns that can squash your initiative. Be as kind to yourself as you are to other people.

10. THURSDAY. Spirited. This can be a very important day if you play your cards right. You have exceptional opportunities to increase your circle of friends and acquaintances; act on these right away. Do not be overly enthusiastic or confident, however, or you could alienate someone you would like to have on your side. Emotional relationships are intense and compelling. You might profess love before you feel truly committed, or otherwise be too emotionally generous. If you can control your words you can make good headway in nearly anything you choose. Just do not promise more than you are sure you can deliver, or at least include an escape clause that will free you if necessary.

11. FRIDAY. Challenging. You may feel ready to proceed with some pretty ambitious plans, but it might actually be better to slow down and become better prepared. If outside forces seem to place obstacles in your way, look for a convenient detour or an escape route. It does absolutely no good to be resentful of anyone who does not think exactly like you. Guard against taking more work than you can handle. Try to be tolerant of people who seem to be demanding too much from you. You are apt to be especially sensitive, which might lead you to think you could do well on your own. If that is what you think, you should give it a try sometime, but not now. Get extra rest this evening.

12. SATURDAY. Inspiring. This can be a very inspiring day if you slow down and spend some time meditating or reflecting. Longing for a deep connection with a soulmate could make you feel lonely if you do not currently have a partner or special friend. Take some time to consider exactly what you want from a relationship and why you are not getting it. Be gentle with yourself. If you do not come up with any immediate answers, a visit to the library to find books on the subject would be very helpful. Be prepared for more give-and-take in all of your existing relationships. You may not be able to count on someone who has let you down in the past. Be wary of getting caught up in other people's problems.

13. SUNDAY. Disappointing. Someone who is very close to you could disappoint you, but do not cast any blame. The person may have some heavy-duty worries and therefore not able to meet your needs. Some people might be cold or distant due to their personal circumstances. Aim for patience and compassion. If you take the moods of other people personally, you are apt to only make matters worse. A social gathering could be a letdown, although you can make it better by being pleasant and cheering up others. Plans could have to be abandoned or rescheduled, but you probably will not mind. Easy activities such as reading or writing may be the best bet as you prepare for the workweek.

14. MONDAY. Buoyant. If you do not feel a surge of energy this morning, an extra cup of coffee or some inspirational music could get you on track. Investing your time, money, and talent in a personal project could end up being profitable, but do it for love, not money. Value your ideas and what you have to offer. If you feel you are not special, you probably just have not found your own calling. Although somewhat impatient to get things moving, slow down and consider the long-term consequences and probabilities. Get in touch with people who can either help you save money or are willing to donate their expertise. Enjoy the finer little things of life such as good food, soft fabrics, and sweet smells.

15. TUESDAY. Harmonious. Focus on your finances and future wealth. Make budgeting your priority. Although you may feel like spending a lot on a luxury item that you really do not need, you would be better off putting it into a savings account and forgetting about it. As a Virgo you are probably very good at putting money aside but do not know enough about investing. A high interest-bearing account could serve you well. You will probably be more comfortable investing on the conservative side rather than risking your hard-earned money. Going out to lunches and dinners with friends might claim more of your budget than you realize, so keep track for a few weeks.

16. WEDNESDAY. Variable. Continue to work on bottom-line money issues. You could probably benefit from taking a class for investment strategy. Community classes offer such subjects as money managing, retirement accounts, and buying on credit. While checking out what courses are being offered, see if anything piques your interest but is more for recreation. Quilting, wood-working, or landscape painting might appeal. A long-standing squabble with a sibling will not be close to resolving until you forgive past injustices. Determine what you really feel. If you are still angry, seek a way to let it go once and for all. Maintaining a grudge can hurt you more than the other person.

17. THURSDAY. Tricky. Your physical energy is at a peak but you need to use extra caution if involved in any activities that have safety concerns. Dangerous sports should be put off until another day. If driving a vehicle or operating any type of heavy machinery, be aware of your surroundings at all times. Do not even use a car if the brakes are run-down or the tires are thread-bare. Use your energy in a constructive manner, cleaning up ac-cumulations that really bother you or making a change you do not want to put off any longer. Do not make impulsive decisions, especially in a fit of anger. You are likely to be frustrated by a neighbor or a local issue that makes you feel helpless.

18. FRIDAY. Erratic. Although you could run into some com-munication difficulties, do not let them frustrate you too much. There is probably very little you can do to keep every message from going haywire, but you can take some basic precautions. If you want to give directions or complicated instructions, tell them yourself rather than trusting a subordinate. Do not rely on out-dated equipment if it has been causing problems; upgrade instead. Make a real effort to be especially pleasant to anyone you really do not like; they all of a sudden might become nicer people. A cousin or friend who recently moved is thinking of you. Arrange to get together soon.

19. SATURDAY. Rewarding. Old family stories can be compel-ling. Contact some of your elderly relatives and collect several tales for posterity's sake. Discovering what some of them lived through will probably amaze you. Think about making some changes to your home. Whatever you choose to do, you need to prepare properly. For both major and minor renovations, try to find a handyman or a contractor through a referral from a friend, rather than selecting at random from the telephone book or newspaper. If planning on handling the work yourself, enlist a friend or two to help. You can always foot the bill for a dinner on the town to show your gratitude for their assistance.

20. SUNDAY. Bumpy. A change of residence at this time could be untimely. If you must move, keep the preparations as smooth as possible. Hire professional movers if you can afford them; make sure they are insured and bonded. An outsider may seem like a threat to your family security but is probably weaker than you think. Do not risk a confrontation. Let the person know who is boss, without alienating a loved one. A thorough check of environmental dangers in the home may be needed if you live in an older area where they are common. If you have not changed the batteries in your smoke alarm or checked your fire extinguisher in a while, this is a good day to do so.

21. MONDAY. Exciting. Today the general mood changes from introverted to extroverted. You are likely to feel more creative, assertive, and energetic. Co-workers and even the boss can be quite entertaining. Do not be timid about sharing some of your favorite jokes and stories with them. Try a new approach to doing a boring job and you may stumble onto something very useful. For Virgo singles, dating can be wonderful. However, if you have more than one love interest you had better watch out; both of them may decide to visit you today. Get outside for some vigorous physical exercise. If you are into running, cycling, or other athletic endeavors, you might now be ready to get more serious about the sport on a competitive level.

22. TUESDAY. Interesting. You are apt to be somewhat sensitive and emotional, but not in a negative way. If you can get past your own instant desires and move onto a more productive and creative level, you are likely to enjoy yourself the most. If you become moody or temperamental, focus on simple jobs that require little thinking. Play some pleasant music and enjoy some incense or aromatherapy oils. Children can be rather aggressive. Rather than flying off the handle because of their behavior, consider this a challenge on how to be a better caregiver. Taking care of family needs can be fulfilling. You should be in the mood for love this evening but may be too tired to express yourself.

23. WEDNESDAY. Volatile. Camaraderie with workmates is vital at this time. Just use your discretion, since one of them may not be trustworthy or could have some serious personal problems. Getting suckered into doing someone else's dirty work is a possibility. If you sense that is happening, set up boundaries immediately before it is too late. Guard your health by taking a good look at what makes you weak, then decide how best to avoid it. If you have been working too hard or pushing yourself emotionally, you may be susceptible to a cold or virus. Get extra rest. A romance with a co-worker may be enjoyable but not in your best interests.

24. THURSDAY. Fair. Get to work earlier than usual. This is a starred time to take care of the little things you have been putting off, like cleaning out drawers and filing away important papers. If your boss asks you to do tedious work that you feel is beneath you, bite your tongue and do it anyway. Let other people take the spotlight. Learn more about preventive medicine and various types of natural therapies. Take control of your own health. Not only will you feel better, but you could also save yourself a lot of money. Dealing with a sick pet could be part of your day; a trip to the veterinarian should not be too much of a hassle. You may meet someone interesting while out walking the dog or searching for a strayed cat.

25. FRIDAY. Eventful. Your mate or steady date might make an announcement that will impact your family in a big way. Even if your patience is low at this time, try to be supportive of what a relative has in mind. Routine business is likely to be disrupted at some point and may seem out of your control. Do what you can to obtain some assistance from those who are closest to you. If you allow yourself to be drawn into a confrontation that is none of your concern, you may be opening yourself up to criticism or retaliation. A special invitation may come quite suddenly. You might have to call a babysitter or cancel a planned outing. If you have no particular plans, invite a few friends to drop by to play cards.

26. SATURDAY. Good. The normal ups and downs of any relationship may leave you feeling jaded or bored. However, you will realize exactly why certain people pair even if they do not seem compatible to an outsider. Working out some concerns with your mate or partner will give you more peace of mind. Consciously pinpoint the good qualities of the special people in your life and keep them in mind. This will make you more appreciative of the wonderful relationships you have. If there are chores to do around the house or you are working on a project that is too big for you to handle on your own, you can rely on a friend to help you. Remember to show your gratitude and return the favor when asked.

27. SUNDAY. Sensitive. You may tend to brood and sulk, especially if you are worried or if you feel that someone close to you is not pulling their own weight. Try not to get angry and brood. Instead, be honest with yourself and others. Do what you can to restore the balance in your relationship, then let it go. Focus instead on what makes you feel good. Follow your special passion, whether it is a hobby, reading a book, or competing in a sport. Enjoy doing what you do best. A little romance this evening will make the day even better. Just be aware of the potential of envying someone who seems more successful than you but probably is no happier. Do not reject any offer of friendship.

28. MONDAY. Lucky. You are likely to be lucky in love as well as money. Do not stay shut up in the house when you could be out taking advantage of this rare day. Consider sprucing up your appearance by getting your hair cut or colored. Buying clothes is a featured activity; get something classic that you will want to wear for years. Do not bother buying anything made with cheap materials or questionable workmanship. Spending a little extra is worth it. Married Virgo couples may decide to renew their vows, and some lovers will announce an engagement. If you have been thinking of asking an all-important question, this is the time to do so. If the answer is yes, you can immediately start making plans.

29. TUESDAY. Successful. Exciting financial news that affects both you and your loved one provides reason to celebrate. Your mate or partner could finally agree on some plans you have had in mind for a long time. If you recently broke up with your steady date or are going through a divorce, you may see the good in it for the first time. Once you can take responsibility in all matters involving your relationships, you will discover a personal power you never knew you had. Take the time to ask yourself what you are getting out of a certain friendship; you may find you would rather spend the time alone. A legal matter that is being debated this time will probably be decided in your favor, much to your relief.

30. WEDNESDAY. Favorable. Arrange to have a meeting with someone important to discuss a matter that has been on your mind for a long time. Get your priorities straight first. Prepare for all potential responses in order to increase your chances for success. Virgo salespeople should find it easy to get new accounts, but do not be too intent or you will push customers away. Try to schedule some time for exercise and fresh air. An old friend may call to talk about the good old days. A get-together with a colleague after work can be pleasant and informative. If you drive a car or ride a motorcycle, be extra cautious. Allow extra time when traveling in heavy traffic or through a construction zone.

MAY

1. THURSDAY. Lively. A chance to travel overseas for work or a vacation could come from out of the blue. Try not to miss out on such an opportunity or you might regret it later. You may have been feeling a little grouchy lately without understanding why. It could be that you are nervous about paying the bills this month and then not having enough left over to get that something special you desire. Worrying about something over which you have little control is not likely to help. Look into obtaining a debt consolidation loan at a lower interest rate than what you are currently paying on your credit cards. This could clear up your problems and help you reach the goal of being debt-free.

2. FRIDAY. Challenging. Your supervisor may offer you everything if only you agree to take on a monumental task. When it really comes down to it you may end up with nothing. Although you generally avoid being evasive, in this situation it will be in your best interest not to do so. Keep a low profile if you want a promotion or a new job. Higher-ups will sense your eagerness and are not likely to respond in the way you hope. Stand aside and let those who are racing past you run against the brick wall. It is better not to run with the bunch. Keep to yourself and no one can blame you. Daydreaming can be productive if you come up with a great idea and present it to your superiors.

3. SATURDAY. Fulfilling. A very active day awaits you. Older relatives expect you to be at their beck and call. Go out of your way to enjoy their company while you can. If one elder in particular tends to get on your nerves and you find it hard to be around, do not avoid them, just see that their needs are met. You will feel good about yourself for having spent the time together. A boss or supervisor from your past could offer you a job. If it involves a pay hike, give the job offer some real consideration. You may be coming up to the wire on a deadline, so finish the necessary preparations before even considering going out this evening.

4. SUNDAY. Problematic. Do not believe everything that everyone says. As a Virgo you have a tendency to be gullible. You could even be ripped off by a con artist, illegal investment scheme, or a shoddy product unless you are careful. You might be disappointed to discover that one of your goals is unrealistic. Laugh it off, then try to figure out what went wrong. A disappointment can become a major life lesson if you are willing to look at it that way. If not, you could wallow in your own misery unnecessarily. Making a major decision is not likely to be easy. Too many options lead to confusion. If you do not have to choose today, put off deciding until later in the week.

5. MONDAY. Variable. A group discussion involving politics could be fascinating. However, one particular person could get out of control with excitement. Do not let it be you, or you are likely to offend someone who you would rather have on your side. Sometimes it is better just to listen quietly and try to learn something rather than speak out with every little thought that comes into your mind. Efforts to advance your career goals may be profitable, although you are probably going to have to work harder than you would like. Your social life may be more like work than play, but your friendships are well worth it. Do not start an argument about religious beliefs or practices.

6. TUESDAY. Helpful. Spending the day being lazy just will not do. You may have to be a little tough on yourself in order to get going this morning. If you feel really ill, take the day off work in order to get some substantial rest. Dreams can come true if you believe in them and go after them with a passion. Be realistic about your goals and you have a much better chance of attaining them. Allow a close friend to assist you in resolving a difficult matter. Do not let your pride or prejudice stand in the way. Treating one child as special can upset another. It may be necessary to bribe a child in certain instances, but try other options first. Keep in mind who is the adult.

7. WEDNESDAY. Dynamic. You can be a major help to someone who is having trouble at home. If two married friends are breaking up, it is important that you support each person individually. However, you do not have to discuss what is said with the other person. Work on developing new, more interesting friends, whether you are conscious of doing this or not. As you meet people, notice those with whom you would like to strike up a friendship and then pursue the relationship. Take some time before bed to review your hopes and fears for the future. When you list the potential outcome of things that you are worried about, you will probably find you are going to be okay no matter what happens.

8. THURSDAY. Disruptive. Emotional peace depends on your ability to keep cool in stressful situations. A co-worker could taunt you by bringing up a mistake you made in the distant past. Your patience is needed to avoid a confrontation with someone who is being belligerent or abusive. Although you will not feel like it at the time, turning the other cheek can save you a lot of anxiety in the future. Your pride may be hurt but your reputation will stay intact. Do not hesitate to tackle a big clean-up job. Go through boxes of stuff you never use. Having a garage sale will give you some extra income as well as extra room. Donate all the sale leftovers to a worthwhile local charity or thrift store.

9. FRIDAY. Inspiring. This is a good day to talk to folks who share your spiritual beliefs. You will be inspired to move forward with plans you previously shelved. Be creative and you can find a solution to a complex personal dilemma. Wait before jumping into a major new investment. Hidden annoyance may cause you to lash out at a colleague. There is nothing much you can do about your work situation today, so do not make a big deal of negative aspects. You will be better off doing a simple job alone rather than involving someone who may do it differently than you. You will resent being told what to do. Artistic activities can give you a sense of beauty and wonder.

10. SATURDAY. Easygoing. Relax and enjoy hanging around the house without any particular agenda. Talking over financial plans with someone in the know can be very beneficial. Shop for a special gift for yourself or for a loved one, but do not overspend. If plans to buy a big-ticket item have been postponed, consider alternatives such as renting or substituting. You can win points with a family member or your steady date if you cook a gourmet meal. Do not hesitate to include a special dessert. If you give subtle hints that you want a favor, you might be able to avoid asking for it outright. This is a wonderful time to get your hands into the garden soil and plant some seeds or seedlings.

11. SUNDAY. Fair. This day can be confusing if you have many things going on all at once. You are unusually popular within a certain social circle. A phone call requesting your company at an unscheduled event might catch you by surprise. By all means attend; it could be profitable. You might have to button your lip when someone gives you information that borders on gossip. It is human nature to want to share sensational news with other people, but keep in mind that someone's feelings or reputation may be at stake. Be careful with electronic equipment if working around water. Do not do any dangerous job that really requires someone who is well trained and licensed.

12. MONDAY. Erratic. Discount a third of what you hear or are told today. Communications could be frustrating, particularly any that involve money. Be very careful not to exaggerate what you are willing to spend. Virgo people who are in sales might be tempted to stretch the truth a little in order to close a deal. Doing so could backfire, however, if the person returns the merchandise or files a complaint. You might feel somewhat bored and be tempted to spend your cash on something glamorous, only to feel ridiculous afterward. Getting lost in an unfamiliar neighborhood is a possibility, so make sure you have an up-to-date map before you head out to unknown places.

13. TUESDAY. Steady. A conservative approach is better than taking a gamble when it comes to finances. Balance your checkbook and pay bills if you get the chance. You will be pleased to find that you have more money in your account than you thought, but make sure you have subtracted your automatic withdrawals. Hanging around with someone who talks too much can drive you almost out of your mind. Be courteous, however, so as not to start a squabble. Young people in general might be so energetic that they annoy you. Put them to work doing things around the house or completing homework before giving them privileges such as watching TV or playing computer games.

14. WEDNESDAY. Important. You are likely to feel a vague sense of confusion or anxiety because your imagination is in overdrive and can be hard to control. If you are able to discipline yourself past the point of worrying about things you cannot change, you can tap into your well of creativity and inspiration. A problem at work may be more dramatic than it really is. Do not let yourself get drawn into a complicated scheme involving many people. You may be asked to speak for others, but you will be better off refusing to do so since you might not be able to relate what they truly want to say. Put your energy into helping those who are less fortunate than you but are trying equally hard to succeed.

15. THURSDAY. Sensitive. If you think you can avoid a colleague's badgering, you are probably wrong. Try to have patience and compassion for people who frustrate you on a daily basis.

Judging others does not help matters. Educational pursuits are favored; if you are considering taking a class, look into your options. Sign up before the roster is filled. Exercise caution if tempted to use drugs or drink to excess in a social situation, especially if you then have to drive. You are much more sensitive than usual and not likely to get away with such behavior. Sudden insight could lead you to phone the newspaper editor or the mayor regarding a problem happening in your town. Remain anonymous if possible.

16. FRIDAY. Demanding. You are likely to be asked to fulfill a promise you made within the last month but may be forced to renege due to family responsibilities. Although you have a valid excuse, that will not make it any easier when you have to let down a friend. An evening get-together is likely to be fun. However, if alcohol is involved, make sure it is not you who people are laughing at. You are susceptible to mood changes. You could get quite emotional if you let yourself lose control in the first place. Slow, gentle physical activities such as yoga, stretching, or walking can be very beneficial to your general health and well-being. Your imagination is strong now.

17. SATURDAY. Beneficial. You should feel good about a decision recently made affecting your family in a substantial manner. You are apt to be in the right place at the right time and wind up being interviewed on television or radio. Working with the public can lead to new friendships. You need a few minutes to yourself at some point in the day. Intense relationships with relatives could mean you either strengthen a good bond or weaken a bad one. A certain female is likely to be a powerful influence on you; take her advice with the certainty of good results. You may have a tendency to try to hide your true feelings, but to no avail. People will read between the lines of what you write.

18. SUNDAY. Exciting. Have friends over for an impromptu gathering, and ask each of them to bring a friend or two. You are likely to meet some new people who are quite dynamic and unique, and you might forge a long-lasting friendship with one of them. Financial benefits could be yours when you meet someone who has a good business connection for you. People are inclined to be generous at this time. If a project of yours needs help, do not be shy about asking for it. You may receive a gift from someone you love. You do not have to buy or make one in return right away; allow yourself just to be on the receiving end. You probably deserve more than you give yourself credit for.

19. MONDAY. Tricky. Expanded optimism will not do you much good if you gamble more than you can afford to risk. If you become too confident you might blow a job interview or turn off a potential date. Someone you are interested in romantically does not want to see you bragging, so tone it down when trying to impress a potential mate. This is an excellent time to challenge your mind through teaching, learning, traveling, or reading. Just do not make any final decisions for a few more days; you are likely to get more information that could cause you to change your mind. Signing a contract or other legally binding document is not recommended at this time.

20. TUESDAY. Pleasant. Get up early, ready for a pleasant day. Your creative abilities are at their height. Your sense of humor should not be kept to yourself; share it with colleagues and friends. You can brighten up the day of someone who has just received some bad news. A romance is likely to put you on cloud nine, but you might not be a good match intellectually; only time will tell. Any activity involving kids is favored. Playing competitive word games will stimulate you mentally as well as being fun. For an entertaining night, go to a theatrical production in town or catch a concert or funny movie. Try to get to bed at a normal hour.

21. WEDNESDAY. Deceptive. This morning starts with enthusiasm regarding business and work matters, but soon turns confusing rather quickly. A certain colleague you are counting on may lack the ability to do what you want, delaying your project by a day or two. It might be difficult to communicate with people who do not speak your language. However, be creative and you can find ways to break that barrier. A business trip could lift your spirit but probably will require more effort or expense than is justified by the potential results. A sales pitch you receive for a product designed to make your life easier is apt to be overrated as well as overpriced.

22. THURSDAY. Reassuring. Get right down to work in the morning hours in order to finish as quickly as possible. Working alone will probably produce the best results. Try figuring out a way to do two jobs at once. By afternoon you will be in a more sociable mood, ready to discuss partnership matters. Know what you want to say beforehand or you may be caught off guard. When your mate or partner comes to you for a discussion, do not say you are too busy. An opportunity that comes from a friend, probably a woman, should not be ignored; it may contain the key that unlocks the door to your fortune. Enjoy sharing stories with someone who has an unusual or eccentric outlook. Look for signs today; everything around you is filled with meaning.

23. FRIDAY. Changeable. A tendency to blame another person for a current problem in your life could have you running around in circles. If you feel obsessed with something that someone else did, reexamine the situation more closely. Figure out how you contributed to the situation, or at least why this came into your life at this time. After doing so, you can forgive and be free. Your mate or partner may be quite busy and under a lot of pressure. If you feel left out, try not to make a big deal of it. Relish the few moments you do get to spend together. Taking time to consider the needs of other people will endear you to those who really matter. Be sure to show affection to a pet also.

24. SATURDAY. Difficult. Do not attempt to run away from a difficult situation or you will be adding the element of resentment when you finally face it. You may at last make contact with someone who admires your accomplishments. You can afford to be generous in order to show your gratitude toward those you care about, but do not do so in place of stating how appreciative you are. Take time to reinforce the love you feel toward your mate or partner. Virgo relationships could be in a holding pattern. If you want to move forward, you will have to be the one to take control. You have some hidden emotions that could cause you to lash out, so watch what you say when angry.

25. SUNDAY. Intense. As a Virgo you will be very sensitive today, but you will not be the only one. Everyone is vulnerable to dramatic outbursts and confusing feelings. Relationships are the prime area of life where you are particularly susceptible to these emotions. Your tendency when faced with something you do not understand will be to speak out in anger or to run and hide. Try to find the middle ground, and remember that you are not alone. Turn to a friend or older family member for comfort. People can be hard to figure out, so do not even try. There is a real danger that you will be deceived or taken for a ride. Do not hand over money or authority to anyone. Draw from your inner strength.

26. MONDAY. Eventful. Partners may have some major issues to work out in regard to shared assets. Some matters are probably not what they seem, which you are about to discover. Draw on the love in your heart. Be compassionate to those who you see as weak, ineffective, or downright dumb. You never know what someone else is going through in life, and in some cases you are probably better off not knowing. Matters of the heart can be very intriguing. Virgo singles who are getting involved should be aware of a tendency for love to be unreal, taking on a fairy-tale quality. When the rose-colored glasses come off, you may be left with a lot of explaining to do.

27. TUESDAY. Encouraging. There is definitely an emotional undercurrent to deal with today. Do not expect to feel comfortable; just persevere. Put one foot in front of the other and keep going. You are motivated to get ahead in your career. Be quite active in all of your efforts. Teaching a class is a possibility, as is public speaking. You may be making a presentation to company bigwigs or to an entire class of students. You may feel like a rookie, but everyone has to start somewhere so give yourself a break. A colleague or associate may be jealous of your recent promotion or accomplishments but do not let it get you down.

28. WEDNESDAY. Pressured. A sudden change of plans or some other disappointment could shatter your day, but only if you let it. A feeling of betrayal or rejection may wash over you, but it does not have to. If you can manage to think philosophically, you should be able to see how one door closes and another opens. You may not know where the other door will lead, but be confident. Being alone to pursue your desires, to study your next moves, and to daydream will be a wonderfully useful thing. If stuck with someone who chatters away about anything and everything, find a reason to change your venue. Watch what comes out of your own mouth, too, for it may be misunderstood or misconstrued.

29. THURSDAY. Choppy. Virgos with too much to do could turn into a walking bundle of nerves. Performing vigorous activities can relieve moody restlessness or anxiety. Unless you use your energy constructively rather than internalizing it, you could wind up with a headache, sore neck and shoulders, or heartburn. If you tend to have a short temper it could blow unless you keep it under tight control. Quarrels over a domestic situation are likely to be over as quickly as they begin. Children may be more active than usual, and you may have to calm one who has been angered or is suffering hurt feelings. This is a good time to get your education or travel plans finalized for the summer period.

30. FRIDAY. Uncertain. Try to find the balance between your professional responsibilities and the needs of your family. A perfect answer to a matter involving your long-term career is possible, but you are not likely to get it today. There are many ways in which you can start moving forward, although they may not be clear at this time. Do not let feelings of hopelessness linger for long. By tomorrow things will seem clearer and you will be more optimistic. An international situation that has been in the news could make you anxious, especially if you have a loved one in the area. To put your mind at ease, make an effort to get in contact through personal or official channels.

31. SATURDAY. Fortunate. Today begins a month-long cycle when your goals and aspirations become more attainable. Take some time this morning to list what you would like to get rid of and what you would like to include in your life. Meditate on small steps you could take now to start working toward fulfilling your desires. Taking a course or joining a professional networking group can get you started. A social event that you attend this evening could put you face-to-face with someone who could offer you new opportunities. Dress up, but not too much. You will have fun while meeting new people.

JUNE

1. SUNDAY. Variable. Your hopes for the future should seem charmed when you realize how much progress you have made lately. If this is not the case, it is never too late to start in earnest. While talking with a friend, you could confess a sensational secret about something that happened a long time ago. If you are thinking of doing so, think again. You will not feel good if your personal life gets spread all over town. Do not participate in gossipy conversations involving an acquaintance. These have a way of hurting not only the person involved but those doing the talking as well. A televised documentary is apt to be so inspiring that you want to make a donation to the cause.

2. MONDAY. Exciting. This is a better day than most for making a presentation or starting a publicity campaign. Get in touch with the media if you think the public would be interested in hearing about your effort. You probably cannot count on a co-worker who promises to lend you a hand, but you can bank on a friend coming through for you. An invitation in the mail may request your company at a friendly, fun event. If you met someone recently who you would like in your social circle, do not be timid about pursuing the friendship. Be open, honest, and flattering and you will soon be the best of friends. You will be clearly in charge at a meeting, so proceed the way you want despite initial opposition.

3. TUESDAY. Tricky. The focus is now on your public life. Your reputation could be at stake due to someone with whom you have been associating lately. Distance yourself from a person who is acting immorally, illegally, or unethically and you can redeem your respect and self-image. A competitor or someone you work with may attempt to blackmail you, so cover your tracks as best you can. Friends may try to talk you into spending your hard-earned cash on a risky venture; beware and do not get involved. You are apt to have great expectations regarding a matter that may not be realistic at this time. Be wary of making promises you may not be able or willing to keep. Strive to maintain your excellent reputation for reliability.

4. WEDNESDAY. Buoyant. An event that you were looking forward to may be cancelled, but something better could come up. A few minutes alone with your thoughts can help you set new priorities. You may have less interest in the day-to-day matters of life like work and routine chores. Instead, a burst of creativity seeps in to provide imaginative answers to tough questions. Arrange to go to bed early. You have a tendency to want to sleep more. Your physical body is especially sensitive to what you eat and drink. A health issue may be a matter of lifestyle or nutrition more than anything else, but it might take a real scare to get you to make meaningful changes.

5. THURSDAY. Stormy. If you are closely involved with a volunteer organization you may have to face some of the politics and intrigue of the group. Keep in mind that even humans with the best of intentions have egos that demand expression. No one is perfect, even you. If you can be sympathetic toward someone who is being a bully, you may be able to turn the situation around. Attending a spiritual meeting will be both inspirational and comforting, although there may be one or two people there you would rather not see. Do not let their presence keep you away, however. Typical Virgo guilt could get the best of you if you insist on being a perfectionist. Learn to go with the flow in selected situations, especially when you are not in control.

6. FRIDAY. Challenging. Aggressive, irritating people can rain on your parade. It can be very challenging to maintain a sense of peace and serenity when there is lots of excitement around you. If you can arrange to be alone you will probably have a better day than if you have to work cooperatively. Members of the opposite sex can get on your nerves because you will be especially aware of the differences between you. Your social life can be disappointing. A date could be cancelled at the last minute. If romantic attention comes from the wrong person, make it clear right away that you are not interested. Otherwise the scenario will just get worse with time.

7. SATURDAY. Frustrating. As a Virgo you tend to want what you want when you want it. If you have been denied lately, you could be quite frustrated. It might be good to just start a fight with your mate or partner so that you can kiss and make up. Engaging in sports, whether on a team or one-on-one, is also a good way to work out frustrations. Play for the physical challenge, not just to prove that you can excel. If you play an instrument or are engaged in any crafts or art, this is a day to let your creative energies flow. If angry and brooding, you can do real damage to a relationship. Be honest and direct. Your goal should be to solve the problem. Someone you recently met is hoping you will keep the promise you made.

8. SUNDAY. Mixed. Try to be as flexible as possible today because events may not turn out as you had planned. Inspiration in the morning can lead you to pursue a new course of action. It is good to be excited, but be sure to look clearly ahead to see if there is something blocking your way. Ask a trusted friend to explain why some things seem to be harder for you than they are for others. You might not be interested in day-to-day activities, but you will enjoy renting some videos or reading an epic novel. You could be worried about your physical condition. You might be pushing yourself too hard with excessive dieting and exercising. Ease up a little and take that much needed break.

9. MONDAY. Problematic. You could be asked to work beyond your maximum potential in order to finish an important task. Doing so might negatively affect your health, so make sure you take frequent breaks, eat sensibly, and drink lots of water. Taking proper care of yourself is the most important job right now. An inability to express yourself and present your ideas might make you frustrated. Do not get involved in a battle of wills with an authority figure at this time or you may get caught in the middle of the problem. Examine your personal goals to see if you are on the right path. If you are on the wrong road, make the necessary adjustments before you have gone too far.

10. TUESDAY. Auspicious. Powerful forces now in place allow you to transform your financial style. One of your primary concerns should be having enough money in the bank or invested for retirement and your family's future. You may have to face some personal dilemmas or change some of your values. If you are still operating on the same old budget, or without one, now is the time to reevaluate. Write down how much money regularly comes in, how much goes out, and where it goes. If your expenses are more than your income, you may need to get a part-time job or eliminate some frills from your life. Do not hesitate to ask for help if you need to consolidate your debts.

11. WEDNESDAY. Choppy. Keep close control of your feelings. In all that you do, a deep emotional sensitivity is likely to color your words and actions. You will not be weak or ineffective. In fact, your power may surprise you, perhaps to the extreme. Personal passion can make you headstrong, especially when it comes to matters that hit close to home. You could be very effective as a public speaker, particularly when fighting for a special cause. A certain family member could be testing you. Being flexible rather than limiting your options will be a major challenge. Use your Virgo energy to stand up for what you believe in. Writing to politicians or a newspaper is the perfect way to make your views known.

12. THURSDAY. Manageable. Keep a close eye on your female friends and relatives, a sister in particular. Women may use subtle tactics in order to get their way against your wishes. You can expect to lose out, but try hard anyway. Insights into your own behavior could become clear if you examine your childhood environment. Your place in the birth order might explain some of your feelings and attitudes. Surprisingly, it can make a real difference if you were the oldest, middle, or youngest child. An interest in motivations can lead you to books that help you understand yourself and your place in the world at large.

13. FRIDAY. Good. It is all too easy to be lazy today, thereby missing out on some beautifully sentimental moments. Use this time to benefit from idealistic daydreams. There should be brief opportunities to improve your domestic life. Bring in some new appliances, or make the necessary changes to provide greater comfort, ease, and even luxury in your home. Things such as artwork and sculpture, music, plants, and scented candles can be inexpensive but make a world of difference. Family relationships will be more harmonious thanks to your personal efforts. Be extra considerate of someone who has suffered a recent letdown. Provide a shoulder to cry on and words of consolation.

14. SATURDAY. Sensitive. You are likely to sense your limitations quite keenly as people and events put a damper on the day. Pessimism is a negative emotion that does not serve you well. Getting caught up in it will only make matters worse. Parents or other older relatives can seem to thwart your every move, but do not blame them for your bad mood. Avoid putting off household chores. Get them over with as soon as possible so you can continue with your day. If you are able to take full responsibility for yourself and your own actions you will be a step ahead of the game. This is actually a great day to work toward fulfilling educational and professional goals. Immerse yourself in studying or writing. A late-night invitation may be irresistible.

15. SUNDAY. Changeable. If you drowned your sorrows last night you will pay for it today. However, if you wake up feeling ill for no apparent reason, you may be developing allergies or a virus. Get some extra rest in preparation for the busy week ahead. Also make time for recreation. You may want to rent a romantic comedy or read a romance novel. Virgo students need to study harder. You could be surprised with a pop quiz soon, so avoid goofing off. If you have a paper to write but have not yet even started, now is the time. Apply yourself and energy will seem to come from out of nowhere to get the job done. Aim to do a little more than absolutely necessary.

16. MONDAY. Diverse. You have what it takes to work hard, putting in long hours to complete a big job. Of course, if you are feeling ill you should probably stay home in bed. Detail work will come easier than usual. Around the house you may even enjoy cleaning. As children become more independent, you might get a little nostalgic when you see how fast they are growing up. Spend some time with them doing crafts. Making things with your hands can be very satisfying as well as a lot of fun. Include your kids, even if it means just being in the same room together. You can now reach the next skill level in an activity that is becoming more than a hobby for you.

17. TUESDAY. Fair. There is a tendency to be somewhat inactive or confused. You may have to force yourself to get out of bed and begin working on a certain project. Procrastination is your worst enemy; if it comes to call, do not let it in the door. A co-worker could be in some personal trouble, and your understanding can make all the difference. Someone who is weak or sad will be drawn to your sympathetic energy. Root for the underdog. Let other people stand up and take the accolades while you stay in the shadows supporting them. When the right time comes, they will do the same for you. Creativity in business matters could lead to promising new methods that put you far ahead of the competition.

18. WEDNESDAY. Varied. Events can happen rather quickly. If you feel a bit of anxiety, that is probably why. Stay on your toes when working on an intricate job. If you make a mistake, someone new to the company may question your competence. Trust your primary relationship. Your mate or partner is sure to be very supportive. If you are considering leaving your present job in order to move on to greener pastures, this is an auspicious time to begin taking the necessary first steps. Collect references, update your resume, talk to headhunters, and check the Internet for job listings. Do not make any sudden changes, however, or you could wind up in a lesser position than the one you have now.

19. THURSDAY. Exciting. You are ready to start on the next phase of the main project you have been working on. Work that has been shelved may begin again. Resolve to really accomplish something this time and you will. Unforeseen circumstances may cut into your day, but a little chaos can be quite creative if you are able to look past the surface. An opportunity to spend significant quality time with your mate or partner needs to be weighed against the value of completing a big job. Ideally, choose the morning and afternoon hours to work, then devote the entire evening to romance. Cultivate self-discipline for the best results in whatever you choose to undertake.

20. FRIDAY. Eventful. Sudden changes in your working life can leave you feeling perplexed. Do not be a worrywart. You can be sure that whatever happens today will be for the best. Being completely responsible and dedicated will insure success. Get your affairs in order so that you are not caught off guard. A certain license may be expiring soon; take care of it right away. Purchasing a new car or a major appliance may be on your mind. For once you and your mate or partner will probably agree on which model to buy. You could meet someone who adds a spark of excitement to your life. A new colleague who has just been hired is sure to be not only fun to work with but full of up-to-date ideas.

21. SATURDAY. Volatile. Relationships can become unstable if some basic values are not agreed upon. Partnership trouble that involves finances is brewing. The secret to avoiding this upset is to be forthcoming, completely honest, and honorable, dedicated to solving the problem rather than casting blame. If you are going through a difficult time in your love life, trust that you are doing the right thing. Let go of those things you have outgrown or that no longer create the life you desire. It is time to move on. Changes in your profession are in the works. These may include new company management taking over, a sudden change of position for you, or even a new mix of job responsibilities.

22. SUNDAY. Pleasant. You may have some negative experience of life, which is not likely to be too upsetting. In fact, you could find it quite intriguing. A close look at your own personality can be enlightening, but do not let it shock you. Everyone has strange tendencies of some kind, but that does not mean you have to act them out in a way that is harmful to you or to other people. Acknowledge your own faults, then move on. You may be involved in a rather exciting romance that is a little on the unconventional side. Or you may be experimenting with some rather unique or unusual way of living. Just be sure you are not going overboard.

23. MONDAY. Cautious. Some matters are out of your hands as circumstances beyond your control lead you to a new career destination. This is likely to be a jolt but nevertheless important. You may be examining the purpose of life as signs point you in a different direction. If you are where you are supposed to be, life will flow. If not, you will encounter a series of obstacles in your path that force you to make some major changes. Communication could be difficult. Taking a narrow viewpoint can make it hard to get your point across. A business partner may give you advice that would put you in an awkward position if you accept it. You may get or give an ultimatum. Nothing is quite as it seems. Be alert for a hint of what is to come.

24. TUESDAY. Pressured. This day is critical as far as your ambitions are concerned. You are likely to be very serious if not critical. Some negative truths about your present situation as far as career, professional goals, and the future go may appear, but do not let them get you down or frustrated. You need to consolidate and structure your goals and ambitions. This is not a day to waste. If you are disciplined, you can make excellent progress and impress influential people. Do not overwork, however, or you could wind up exhausted. Your energy level is not as high as it could be. Someone from outside the country may be a distraction at work or at home.

25. WEDNESDAY. Successful. Let your thoughts turn toward improving your education. Consider taking on a new course of study. Getting a certificate or degree could be in your future. Check out options regarding schools, financing, and other details. Consider taking Internet classes as a potentially more convenient way. Conversations involving subjects such as religion or politics can leave you emotionally drained. Guard against a compulsion to try to convert other people. Certain events that happen now may be surprisingly lucky for you, so pay attention. Taking a fearless look into the future may open up exciting new possibilities far from your current base of operations.

26. THURSDAY. Helpful. Public issues take on new meaning. You might find yourself speaking out. You could get your picture in the newspaper if around when a big news event happens. Personal growth is enhanced. You can get good insights if you trust your Virgo intuition. Dreams can be very powerful. Even if they do not seem to mean anything, they at least show where you are at emotionally. Draw on your religious or spiritual beliefs for comfort and guidance. Your reputation will grow as you earn more attention thanks to your recent efforts and accomplishments. Have compassion for a particular family member who is going through some tough times. Saying I told you so is never helpful.

27. FRIDAY. Fruitful. The past is over, so let it go. You are finally ready, once and for all, to leave behind an old resentment that you have been carrying on your shoulders for far too long. You will feel much lighter after you forgive. You may never be able to forget, but at least the emotion will no longer be attached. The work you have done behind the scenes during the past few months is about to get noticed. Now is the time to bring your ideas and concepts to the attention of higher-ups. Do not be afraid to take that risk, which might lead to significant improvements in your life. Just do not let overconfidence cause you to gamble what you have. Play on the safe side.

28. SATURDAY. Beneficial. Prepare yourself. The next few days begin a new cycle in which you should focus on your future hopes and dreams. Consider how groups can assist you in getting where you want to go. Check the newspaper and other resources for professional meetings as well as those that might fulfill your personal desires. Then rearrange your schedule so that you are free to attend. A rather unusual course of action could be needed in order to get ahead of the competition. Do not worry about what people will think about it, just move ahead with confidence. You will enjoy a conversation with an older person, and you may learn something. Listen with an open mind.

29. SUNDAY. Challenging. This is a starred day for outlining your goals and future course of action. Do not let anyone discourage you from following your dreams. People less intelligent and with fewer resources than you have risen above their circumstances to create a fulfilling lifestyle. If one of your friends is having a birthday, do not let it go by without a little fanfare. Arrange a surprise party, or have a potluck meal in honor of the birthday. If you feel you have not received much help lately, consider what some others have to go through on a daily basis. Accept your problems as challenges to rise above. You have the talent and temperament to achieve even your wildest dream.

30. MONDAY. Stimulating. You are likely to feel somewhat nervous and excited, although the source may be unclear. You may be dissatisfied with some aspects of life, most likely your work. You may be ready to make a new start as far as health and fitness matters are concerned. Speaking with a friend could inspire you to break out of your old mold and make some significant changes in your life. Just keep in mind that if you jump into a major change without preparing yourself, you could be asking for trouble. This is an excellent time for self-improvement, but be realistic about it so that you do not burn yourself out. A support group can be especially helpful, as members encourage you by sharing their experiences.

JULY

1. TUESDAY. Rewarding. If you go out of your way to come to the aid of a stranger, you will be paid back in many ways. You may become frustrated if your path is blocked by those who do not understand your goals. If you can keep your cool you should make great strides. You are more likely than usual to be spontaneous and take risks. You may also be accident-prone. Balancing assertive action with caution is the winning formula for making an important change in your life. You might want to spend some time with a friend but have to run errands or chauffeur children around instead. Bring the friend along if you can. Keep evening plans simple. Watching television and going to bed early is recommended.

2. WEDNESDAY. Easygoing. You can probably coast through the day. Ongoing business and personal matters are concluding, to your benefit and perhaps to your surprise. A newcomer in your life should be very helpful, although there is one in particular you should not trust too much. You might enjoy a not-too-subtle flirtation. The effort you have been putting into your appearance is starting to pay off. Do not be timid when it comes to love; you only live once. Quit wondering so much about what other people think about you. Get some exercise during lunch or after work. Run around the block a few times, or do some good stretching exercises.

3. THURSDAY. Serene. This day may be mildly dull all around, but that should not bother you. Enjoy the opportunity to be alone with your thoughts. You may have to hit the snooze button on your alarm clock more than once before you are willing to get out of bed. Start the day with a little early-morning yoga or a walk around the neighborhood. The fresh air and rising sun will do you good. Try to avoid activities which consume too much energy or require complicated thought processes. You will be much better off if you work in peace and quiet. Reading historical fiction can be a wonderful escape, especially if you are also learning about the period.

4. FRIDAY. Helpful. You are apt to be the center of attention, which may cause you to feel insecure about your looks, manners, or overall ability. Do not worry, however; most people are so wrapped up in their own thoughts and concerns that you will not even invade their consciousness. If you feel you need a lift, head to the beauty parlor or barbershop. This is also a fine day to shop for some fashionable new fall clothing, although you will probably tend toward utilitarian wear. As a Virgo you can sometimes be so practical. Do not buy anything unless you absolutely want it. Talking about your feelings with someone you trust can help if you are moody and moping. You deserve to enjoy life.

5. SATURDAY. Spirited. You are likely to be invited to a party or other gathering, where you could be taken by surprise. Be warned: there could be some strange or unusual guests in attendance. Although you may be uncomfortable at first, you will warm up and enjoy yourself. The secret is to remain cool and unruffled. A love affair could begin for you. Have fun while it lasts; it will probably put you on cloud nine for a short time, then bring some gloom. This is another good day to go shopping. Take a trusted friend with you to get a second opinion before parting with your money. Your taste will probably be a bit wild and you could end up with something completely out of character as well as out of fashion.

6. SUNDAY. Happy. Luxury, beauty, and harmony appeal to you. You could spend a good part of the day in pursuit of what makes you happy. You are likely to feel positive about yourself and the direction your life is taking. Financial worries should be clearing up, or at least you are putting them into better perspective. Get some flowers, art, or gourmet food to enjoy. Resist an urge to be a couch potato. Forcing yourself to get up and leave the house will do you a world of good. A visit to a beautiful part of your state will feed your soul. Have supper tonight at a favorite restaurant if you do not feel like cooking. Opt for good service rather than ordering at a counter.

7. MONDAY. Good. You should be unusually perceptive. If someone is trying to give you the hard sell, you will notice immediately. Back away even if the person is quite slick. This is one of those days when you could end up opening your wallet when you least expect it, and be sorry for it later. You may want to make a major purchase on impulse, but promise yourself to wait overnight. Nothing is so important that it cannot be put off that long. In that time you might change your mind entirely or be able to bargain for a better price. This evening is excellent for romance. Play your favorite romantic music while enjoying a gourmet meal by candlelight with your mate or steady date.

8. TUESDAY. Worrisome. You might feel that luck has not been on your side. If lonely, it may be because you are not transmitting the kind of warmth that attracts people to you. As a Virgo you can get so caught up in your worries that you seem quite a cold fish. People are able to sense negative emotions a mile away. If this is part of your current life, do not feel helpless. Talk matters out with the one friend who can always cheer you up. Repeat some powerful affirming words to yourself. Listen to upbeat music. Then get busy cleaning your home or office. Focus on the extras that really make a difference, such as washing walls and rearranging furniture. Proving that you can be in control will restore your good feelings.

9. WEDNESDAY. Problematic. It is not yet time to sign a certain contract. Weigh your options. You may not feel comfortable talking with strangers or even going to work. You would probably prefer to stay home and do your own thing. Call in sick if you are entitled to leave and it will not jeopardize your position. Everyone needs to take a day off for mental health now and again. You might have to go to a new place where the environment is dirty or the people are rude and uncaring. You will have to be patient and put up with it whether you like it or not. Just do not remain any longer than absolutely necessary.

10. THURSDAY. Pressured. Unexpected changes at home or within your family can shock your entire system, although you may have seen them coming. Take a day-by-day approach; there is not much else you can do. You are apt to be a bit nervous but not able to identify any reason for it. Take comfort in your loved ones. Deals that involve real estate, property, or leasing probably cannot be concluded quite yet. If you are still a long way from getting the price you want, you need to decide whether to just turn and walk away. Sometimes playing hardball is the only way to get what you want. Business between the sexes should be on an equal footing.

11. FRIDAY. Fortunate. This is a good day to plant the seeds of suggestion to that special someone in your life or just transforming from friend to lover. Do not expect a full-blown affair to materialize immediately. You will just get a hint of what is to come. Sports, games, and other types of recreation are featured. You could decide to go on a picnic to the beach or park. If around children, take the time to really answer their numerous questions in a way they can understand. If you snap at someone due to frustration, a quick and sincere apology will be all that is needed to set things right. Your mate or partner wants to hear you whisper sweet nothings. Evening hours favor allowing yourself to be pampered.

12. SATURDAY. Fair. Emotions can run high due to a solemn outlook that is at odds with your inner urge to have fun. You may even take entertainment quite seriously. Follow the old formula of taking care of business first and then relaxing. Impatience with people who are not as particular as you could lead to offering unsolicited and unwelcome advice. You might not be pleased with the kids that your child is associating with, but there probably is not a lot you can do about it. Just try to get the youngster involved in an extracurricular activity of your choice. If you cannot afford an expensive summertime program, you may be able to form a sports team or arrange some educational day trips.

13. SUNDAY. Satisfying. This is one of those days when you get a chance to be creative. Get involved in an art project, writing poetry, playing music, or gourmet cooking. Do not try to be an expert; the idea is to have fun. If you feel romantic, get moving. However, try not to have great expectations. Commitment is not a word that should even be discussed today. Married Virgos may want to arrange a special date to spend quality time at home. Your mate or partner may be feeling somewhat left out because you have been busy doing your own thing lately. It would be good to make a gesture of love through poetry, flowers, or candy, which can say all that is in your heart.

14. MONDAY. Complicated. A situation at work could really annoy you. Although you may feel like telling someone off, doing so could start a scandal or get you into serious trouble. You may be ready to push forward with a certain project or goal, but you are not likely to get cooperation from other people at this time. Frustration and grumpy feelings are part of this day. Taking your mood out on other people will not make you popular and, in fact, could harm your reputation. If you are the type who never gets upset, a display of emotion can motivate you to stand up for yourself. Other people are sure to take notice. Be resourceful. Try to find new ways to approach or sidestep the obstacles that are currently blocking your way.

15. TUESDAY. Unsettling. A strange dream in the early morning hours could wake you with a start. Do not even try to analyze it. Just take it as a sign that you are under a lot of stress or overloaded with work. Job-related matters may not turn out to your satisfaction, perhaps due to an employee who is acting out of jealousy or spite. Be mature and set your mind on other goals. It is more important now than ever to take good care of your physical condition. Body, mind, and spirit have to work together in harmony. If one is out of kilter, they all go out of balance. Keeping yourself centered and detaching from outcomes you cannot control will take away a lot of stress. Focus on what is within your power.

16. WEDNESDAY. Sensitive. Emotional pressure at work is foreseen when a co-worker pushes some sensitive buttons. This will set off a touchy mood that can last all day if you do not consciously keep it in check. You may have a hard time making decisions since your desires do not seem very clear. Unsure of what you want, you can miss out on good opportunities and foolishly opt for bad ones. It can be difficult to avoid being impulsive, but that is just what you need to do. You may feel very frustrated with a family member who has been ignoring your repeated requests. If you nag you are likely to get into an argument. Try to relax quietly at home tonight with a good book as company.

17. THURSDAY. Choppy. Jumpy is one way to describe your behavior. You may realize that you recently made a major commitment without really understanding what you were getting yourself into. If you have a change of heart you may be able to rescind the deal if you act fast. If at odds with a business partner, you need to discuss the matter in greater depth. Misunderstanding is most likely. Little unexpected obstacles could arise repeatedly, but they are likely to be more of an irritant than anything serious. This is another day when you should not make any decisions based on impulse or emotion. Talk over your choices with other people, but in the end make up your own mind since you will have to live with the consequences.

18. FRIDAY. Productive. Tidy up loose ends. Other people will be more than happy to assist you in handling minor details. Someone may offer you the moon and stars, but whether this person will come through is another matter. Past experience is likely to reveal how reliable they are. You can earn points with your mate or partner if you keep your word regarding a promise made some weeks ago. Decide whether it is more important to pursue a personal project right now or to help your partner. You may get upset if someone does not agree about a certain move you made. If you insist that it is just business and not personal, they are likely to calm down and accept the outcome.

19. SATURDAY. Eventful. You may have received a financial gift recently from a relative, but such good fortune rarely comes without strings attached. You might have to contend with family members who are not pleased with the way decisions are being made. Or it could be that the government wants extra taxes. Try to be as fair as possible. Consult a lawyer or mediator if not comfortable with what has been going on. That applies if you are dealing with an insurance company that wants to pay you as little as possible for an accident or illness. An everyday encounter with a neighbor or someone from your community might leave you with a renewed belief in humanity and more optimism.

20. SUNDAY. Lively. You may have to reschedule an outing with a friend in order to keep peace at home. Friends who are in a committed relationship themselves will certainly understand. Nonetheless, friction can occur between you and your mate or partner if you do not see eye-to-eye on important manners. This may just be an underlying concern, but today of all days you can expect to be chastised. Working on a project in which you are teamed with another person is a good idea. You should be able to get it completed soon. Some frustrations could arise, but if you think of them as learning opportunities you will be one step ahead of the game. Evening hours can be intensely romantic. Be willing to forgive and forget.

21. MONDAY. Comforting. Take this day as slow and easy as you can. While good conversation with a co-worker or friend is possible, you will probably prefer being alone with your thoughts. If you are on vacation, you will enjoy meeting new people. Be assertive and start up conversations with cab drivers, waitresses, or other interesting people. You might meet someone with whom you form a long-term friendship. Take time to look around your environment. You have a special ability for noticing beauty in all shapes, sizes, and forms. If you have a garden, go outside and commune with nature. Whether you enjoy sitting in the sun or the shade being outside with a good book is pleasurable on this quiet day.

22. TUESDAY. Stimulating. Consider giving some serious thought to future educational plans, since the choices you make now will affect you for the years to come. Some Virgos may decide that going to a foreign school might be a good idea. Others may be able to take classes through correspondence. Whatever your plans, you should start working on them as soon as possible. No one is too old to learn more. Today might be a very good time to consider making vacation plans. If you are already traveling expect minor irritations. If you are thinking about a trip to a faraway country, you might experience culture shock. Enjoy the differences and count your blessings for some of the benefits you have living in the western world.

23. WEDNESDAY. Diverse. An activity involving the public, such as attending a show, summer festival, or other event, may not come off as planned. Keep your schedule open since a better offer could come up. You might hear of a great deal on a tropical vacation or get invited to go along on an overseas trip. Do not pack your bag just yet, however, since there may be some strings attached. An old friend or lover could be eager to come back into your life, against your better judgment and instincts. Instruct your friends not to give your phone number out to anyone. A new romantic partner may not be available at this time, but do not give up completely on love. Try not to be too demanding this evening.

24. THURSDAY. Challenging. Getting ahead in the world can be an uphill climb in the best of times. Right now you could find it especially stressful. Old-timers who are threatened by your enthusiasm could try to put a damper on your ambitions. Be sure to show them the respect they deserve, even if you do not feel like doing so. You are apt to be impatient with a parent or other older relative who seems to be going against your every wish. Here again, however, you should bow to the wisdom of experience and age. If you are harassed by someone with seniority, or otherwise are being discriminated against, file an official complaint or at least make it known what is happening. If you do nothing it will seem that you do not care.

25. FRIDAY. Bumpy. You may feel like you are on a roller-coaster ride during this period of transition. Expectancy is in the air. While some obstacles seem to be easing up, others are pressing forward. You should get the go-ahead when it comes to your long-range plans. Someone having authority over you could exert a powerful influence on some of the decisions you must make. Although you may be hesitant to listen to anyone who appears to be too conservative, their words do have value. Business matters should proceed right on schedule, with only a few minor hitches. If you are thinking of getting romantically involved with someone from work, think about it carefully first, then think about it again!

26. SATURDAY. Promising. Although you feel good about yourself, spend some quiet time on personal reflection. A conversation with a good friend can help you piece together a fantastic idea. Write it down immediately, since it can be profitable in many different ways. Today is one of those days when you are able to count on your friends and family members alike. Everything should run very smoothly, partly due to the wonderful spirit of cooperation and teamwork. Someone who looks up to you may be very eager to take on more responsibility. If you feel comfortable, go ahead and allow this person to do a little more. This will give you extra free time to do as you please. If driving, follow all traffic laws or you could get pulled over and ticketed.

27. SUNDAY. Slow. This day is likely to be somewhat slow after yesterday's revelations. Routine activities will probably bore you since you would rather be out socializing. Finding a friend willing to go out can be a chore in itself, although you will have no trouble locating one who will want to talk on the phone for an hour. A new acquaintance may have you feeling somewhat uneasy. Avoid making a rash judgment in case you are wrong. Good friends are hard to find, so try to figure out what has motivated a pal to make a bad decision in your opinion. You do not know how it feels to be in the other person's shoes. Daydreaming about your desires for a perfect future could be more powerful than you realize.

28. MONDAY. Enjoyable. Friends could be more than willing to lend an ear if you want to discuss a personal matter. However, you may not be too pleased if all you wanted was to talk. They may offer unwanted advice, answers to your problem, or a list of your imperfections. Even though you may not want to hear what they have to say, listen anyway. You did ask after all, and you just might get some good insight into your situation. Add some spice to your love life. Your partner is likely to be very enthusiastic toward your attempts to get the sparks flying again. If you really do not have a clue what to do next, visit your local bookstore or library. You will find several books that offer all kinds of romantic ideas. You may get as much as you give, or more.

29. TUESDAY. Fruitful. Today starts a month-long cycle where you should pay close attention to your inner voice. Intuition is likely to be very powerful, although you will probably have a hard time believing in yourself. Recognize and try to understand your feelings. Decide whether they are reliable or not, then act upon them. This will give you an awareness that allows you to develop your sixth sense. Try to not make any major decisions now, such as changing jobs or moving unless you have to. On this day in particular, you will feel happier being alone to sort out your thoughts and feelings. Spiritual and religious activities can restore your faith if you have misplaced it.

30. WEDNESDAY. Positive. Your enthusiasm and sense of optimism makes this day very pleasant. If you are able to take a break and enjoy the gorgeous summer weather, all the better. You have to keep your eagerness in check, as you are likely to be into everything today. If you get into trouble, you will finally be able to see how you are a victim of your own faults. This awareness will enable you to be an adult, take responsibility for your actions, and make sure it never happens again. Recognizing that you are a student of life gives you new freedom. Such a philosophy allows you to ease up on yourself. Avoid judging other people. Live and let live is the best approach to follow.

31. THURSDAY. Changeable. You are likely to feel emotionally unstable occasionally. Unexpected news might really shake you up, causing some anxiety. If you take everything too literally, you could overreact and not be able to keep control of your emotions. This does not have to happen as long as you know how to keep cool under pressure. If you are feeling good about yourself because of some great things that have happened in your life lately, try to remain humble. Being cocky and tooting your own horn too loudly will draw unwanted attention. Your independent Virgo spirit can be considered extreme when you refuse to cooperate. Acknowledge other people's input, even though their ideas may seem odd to you.

AUGUST

1. FRIDAY. Demanding. It may seem like there is not enough energy to go around. People at work and those at home are apt to be noncommittal and downright lazy. You could have a bad case of the blahs. Acting tough is probably not a good idea. Just go about your business, taking good care of everyday affairs and not worrying too much about the future. You will have to light a fire under yourself if you want to get moving on a self-improvement project. Actually, it might be better left to another day. Being overly critical with yourself and your loved ones is not going to help matters. Do not make any hasty decisions about personal issues since you are likely to change your mind before the end of summer.

2. SATURDAY. Variable. A new financial opportunity requires careful scrutiny. Even if it comes highly recommended, check it out fully before investing even a dime of your hard-earned cash. Your tired feeling may be due to the fact that you have been working harder than usual lately or have been experiencing stress due to money worries. If your bank balance has reached rock bottom, there is always something you can do about it; but excessive worrying is not going to make much of a difference. Enjoy playing with some of your favorite possessions. Polish your antiques, catalog your music collection, or play with electronic equipment. Later in the day go window-shopping with a friend.

3. SUNDAY. Cautious. People who are around you on a daily basis can seem quite dramatic. Be careful or you could be drawn into an argument or an ongoing disagreement between colleagues or two family members. Be ultrasensitive, quick to come to the aid of those who really need you. Just watch that you do not get depressed over other people's problems. Self-esteem issues may come up now, but someone you really love and admire knows just what to say to restore your confidence. Sales pitches that seem too good to be true are probably exactly that. You could end up with an expensive and useless gizmo if you fall for an infomercial on television.

4. MONDAY. Troublesome. Watch your back. Someone you know quite well is out to get you. Do not be too trusting. Usually you are not gullible, but at this time some people see you as being fair game for their fast talk. Hold on tight to your wallet; it might not be a bad idea to also leave your credit cards at home. Do not sign any contract or other legal document. You could be kept waiting as someone arrives late for a scheduled appointment, or they may cancel altogether. It is all too easy to be disappointed by the actions of other people. Try to be realistic about a community project you became involved with recently. Do not believe big corporations when they tell you they have your best interests in mind. What they say right after that could be an attempt to fool you.

5. TUESDAY. Reassuring. With the way the past few days have been, your faith has probably been battered quite a bit. Fortunately things should start to turn around today. You can help improve life if you use the power of positive thinking. Your mind is an extremely powerful tool, as any world-class athlete can tell you since athletes use affirmations and visualizations to hype themselves up before a competition. Check out some of the many books on the subject or sign up for a class. Spend some quality time with a family member, but avoid bringing up old business. Instead, practice forgiveness and benefit from the power that comes with such an act.

6. WEDNESDAY. Pressured. A mountain of paperwork could be causing you some unnecessary anxiety as it keeps getting bigger and bigger. As a Virgo you are good at organizing and keeping track of other people's stuff, but not necessarily your own. Team up with someone who enjoys helping with that sort of thing, and sort one paper at a time. You will feel very free when it is all taken care of. Competition between you and those in your immediate environment could surface, but do not let it get out of hand. A little extra effort will help your self-esteem as you prove what you are capable of doing. Running errands can take you all over town. If your car is making a new noise, get it checked by a mechanic.

7. THURSDAY. Unsettling. When you first wake up it may seem like everything is just fine. You may think about bringing friends and your family members together, perhaps by having a friend stay with you while looking for a job. People you know well can be demanding of your time and hospitality, but not directly. Undercurrents may suggest there is something unsettling going on beneath the surface. A loved one could be taken in by a glam-

orous ideal that involves treachery or dishonesty. If you both encourage each other's negative traits as part of your relationship,
this is likely to come up as an issue that can no longer be ignored.
Consider joining a support group or obtaining some help from a
trained counselor. You will be proud of yourself for doing so.

8. FRIDAY. Favorable. Energy should be excellent. A do-it-
yourself project around the house is likely to be completed well
and quickly. Get down to work in order to really accomplish your
goal. Settle for nothing but your best effort. Involving older children will help build good character and work habits. Problems
that usually plague you can now be viewed as exciting personal
challenges, and you will rise to the occasion surprisingly easily.
There is a possibility that single-minded ambition, however, can
antagonize people who are not as motivated as you are. Do not
expect anyone to be at the same level as you. Instead, go out of
your way to be compassionate toward their particular circumstances and as helpful as possible.

9. SATURDAY. Fulfilling. Aim for pleasant, mellow activities
that bring a sense of creative satisfaction. Arrange to be alone or
to spend some quiet time only with your romantic partner. If
someone has been trying to interest you in a new idea, step outside your comfort zone and give it a try. A visit to a beach would
be perfect, especially if you take the time to leisurely build a castle
in the sand. If there is a fair or carnival going on in town, you will
enjoy being among kids and watching the crowd. Control your
spending; you have a tendency to fritter dollars away by gambling
despite wild odds. Spiritual pursuits are very profitable and should
lead to greater understanding of yourself and your ingrained habits. This can help you break free of negative patterns.

10. SUNDAY. Promising. At work you could be forming a long-
lasting friendship with a co-worker. If you have already done so,
you can now enjoy all of the benefits from the relationship. A
friend could get you a job. You tend to be deeply involved with
the people with whom you spend time, and you should feel good
about your loyalty to them. Go ahead and ask for a big favor if
you are sure you need it and can pay it back. An emotional crisis
involving a friend of the family gives you a chance to be of service.
Be grateful you have people to care about and who care about
you. Because you are highly susceptible to emotions at this time,
pay close attention to your physical and mental state, which are
very closely intertwined.

11. MONDAY. Tricky. The future could seem uncomfortably unclear on the job. Your company may be in the process of being

absorbed by a large corporation or be madly downsizing. Even if you are sure your position is safe, it may not keep a feeling of anxiety from ruining your day. On the calmer side, you might be bothered by missing files, an equipment breakdown, or unreliable employees. Consider your words carefully before speaking; your listeners will have their own versions of what you said. If you can work alone you should be able to get a lot accomplished. Shut your door and put all calls on hold for a few hours.

12. TUESDAY. Volatile. A certain work-related problem involving managing people is not likely to be solved today. You may make some headway, but do not expect the whole situation to blow over just yet. You may begin to obsessively go over it again and again in your mind, but force yourself to do what you can and then let it go. This is the sort of thing that can cause nervous disorders and continual bouts of anxiety. If secretly plotting a plan in which you have great hope and faith, watch that you do not tell too many people. One of them could cause your dream to come crashing down in an unfortunate manner. A competitor may be waiting for you to slip up and reveal your next move or grand scheme.

13. WEDNESDAY. Eventful. If you have been putting off making an announcement that involves another person, such as an engagement, separation, or formation of a business partnership, you may now be forced to reveal your plans. Unforeseen changes require an immediate shift of attitude or strategy. Your main relationship occupies a prominent part of your life, for better or for worse. Alliances are being tested. If yours are healthy and strong, you may feel the stress but will be able to work through the upset. If one or more are not meant to be, you are apt to find out today or very soon. You may have to stay up late this evening in order to make sure a certain job is done correctly and on time.

14. THURSDAY. Disquieting. Do not blame anyone or anything if you find yourself in an unfortunate situation. Consider how the choices you made led you to where you are right now. Review your role in all that occurred and you will be one step closer to obtaining peace of mind. You could have the feeling that something is not quite right. This is one of those days when you need to check twice whether you turned off the iron or the oven or whether you have the keys when you go out. You are unusually sensitive around other people. You might feel like going to a party or going out with a group of friends, but you will be better off in the company of just one person who you know supports your goals and your dreams.

15. FRIDAY. Intense. A romantic attraction could become quite intense, especially if the object of your affection is not currently available for a relationship. Working yourself into an obsessive state is not very healthy emotionally. You are likely to be let down in the end by this person. However, you might enjoy some fantasizing about the possibilities that never will be. Do not get involved with someone you know is into anything illegal or is otherwise dangerous. You may be attracted to the shadow side but do not act it out. Although you can try to kid yourself into believing that you are able to handle any situation, in the end you may get burned, caught, or just confused.

16. SATURDAY. Stimulating. This is an excellent day to work within your home and yard to spruce it up. Your car, too, can be cleaned out, washed, and polished. Painting, decorating, and other beautifying will give an incredible lift to your life. You will benefit if you involve your mate or partner, or do the work as a surprise. Artistic and creative pursuits can also give you a sense of joy and happiness. While you work away, listen to glorious music such as classical, jazz, choral, and gospel. This is a starred time to work out joint finances and plan your fiscal future together. You may receive a special gift from an older family member.

17. SUNDAY. Good. Spend part of the day thinking of all the good times you once had with a special family member. Enjoy reliving those days by talking about them with a younger person. You can keep the relationship alive by reminiscing. Go ahead and talk out loud to someone who is not present, although not when others are around. There is a wisp of romance in the air; chase after it with your heart and soul. Connecting with someone special on a deep level can be intense, meaningful, and transformative. Passion, whether toward a person or a field of study, contains strong magic as long as you apply it in a positive manner. Put an element of excitement into all of your activities by focusing totally on one at a time.

18. MONDAY. Enjoyable. Your world may seem much larger than it actually is. Having a philosophical or spiritual viewpoint, and applying it to your daily life, gives you pleasure. You may see symbolism everywhere as routine occurrences take on new meaning. For instance, a flower might speak to you of the various stages of life, from seed to sprout to plant to flower and then all over again. Outdoor activities will be particularly enjoyable. Participating in a team sport or going for a solitary walk in the woods can be good ways to connect with nature. You could remember a dream or have a psychic flash that is helpful in decision-making. Give generously to those who are less fortunate than you.

19. TUESDAY. Helpful. Your travel plans may have to change. Although you are apt to be disappointed at first, it may actually be quite lucky as your new plans turn out even better in time. Unseen forces are working to assist you, helping you to be in the best place at an opportune time. Faith in your own personal beliefs can be very empowering. You may well be motivated to share this excitement with other people. Be warned, however, that some listeners will not be open to your more outlandish views. Virgo students should enjoy the last days before school goes back in session. You might find some really good deals on school supplies if you check the advertised sales.

20. WEDNESDAY. Diverse. You may feel in a frenzy as many people pull you in all directions. Unless you keep your focus, you might lose out on an important contract or career opportunity. On the other hand, now is a good time to gather information rather than making any specific moves. Do not let anyone move you around like a pawn on the chessboard of life. Remember that everyone starts at or near the bottom and has to work way up the ladder of success. Do not chat a lot when supposed to be working. A colleague who does not know you may accuse you of being a disruptive influence, but soon you will be the best of friends. Your ship will come in soon, so be patient but persistent.

21. THURSDAY. Comforting. An attitude of gratitude will get you far at this time. Be thankful for all that you have. Whatever your income, you should feel rich. Due to favors you have done and kindness you have shown in the past, certain people could now be secretly working behind the scenes on your behalf. They may even be planning to throw you a surprise party or otherwise put you in the spotlight. You could find money or a lost check when looking under a pile of papers or in an old coat pocket. Charity work brings you much good karma. Do all that you can to support a worthy local cause. This is the day to get a new hairstyle or go shopping for designer clothes.

22. FRIDAY. Lucky. You should wake up with a smile on your face, looking forward to the day. A good deed that you did in the past is likely to be remembered by someone now in high places. You may hear through the grapevine that your name is next in line for a promotion or pay raise. A deadline may be extended, leaving you more time to successfully negotiate an important contract. Any new responsibilities that fall on you at this time are likely to be agreeable and potentially profitable. Being in the right place at the right time is easy today. Romance can be like a dream come true, but do not start planning too far into the future yet. Just enjoy all that is happening right now.

23. SATURDAY. Uneasy. A friend may let you down because your mutual hopes and expectations are too high. Have other plans ready in case a social outing is canceled at the last minute. You are more sensitive to group mentality and politics than usual, perhaps even wondering why you do not find a new bunch of friends. You may be disgusted now, but do not let one or two bad apples spoil the whole bunch. There is no reason to stand for a loved one being dishonest or unreliable. Today, however, that is exactly what may become apparent. Stand up for yourself when you have been wronged. Overall, however, if you can relax and take it easy, life will be much happier than if you let yourself get uptight over it.

24. SUNDAY. Unpredictable. A strange, unusual mood could overtake you. On the one hand you will probably be quite sensitive and self-protective, if not actually moody. On the other hand, a relaxed, rebellious, devil-may-care feeling could overcome you if restricted by your current circumstances. If you feel at all threatened by a family member or friend who is not letting you do your own thing, clam up. Giving the silent treatment is sure to get your whole household upset. If you insist on using this, be prepared to wind up apologizing. An infatuation that comes on rather quickly can leave you in the lurch just as fast. A newcomer you meet at this time is apt to be interesting, exciting, eccentric, and brilliant, all in one personality.

25. MONDAY. Quiet. What starts out as a routine day may not be quite so routine by nightfall. Minor disruptions can shake you up, but they should not be a big deal. Cultivate a tendency to daydream, which can be very creative and relaxing. Doing intense physical labor is not recommended unless you absolutely cannot avoid it. Even so, use good form such as bending your legs rather than using your back muscles when lifting. You may sense that your subconscious mind is trying to tell you something, but do not act too impetuously. Trusting your own judgment can be tricky, so get additional facts and opinions if you are about to make a big decision. Someone or something in your life can be deceptive after dark, trying to lull you to sleep.

26. TUESDAY. Sensitive. You may be obligated to take part in an event involving your own or your partner's work. If you do not feel like attending, back out by offering a good excuse. To do so is okay; it probably will not be the end of the world or of the job if you fail to show up, as long as you can handle the Virgo guilt factor. Throughout the day be pleasant and turn on the charm, no matter how negative you may feel or how much you dislike the company in which you find yourself. Love can be disappointing. A date may be canceled or events outside your control conspire against your best-laid plans. If you need to release some tension, hard physical exercise, a good cry, or a pillow fight should be effective.

27. WEDNESDAY. Opportune. Use this day to look at both your public and personal image to see if it measures up with how you want people to view you. A good, honest look in the mirror shows you are not getting any younger. Although you may feel young and hip, your hairstyle and choice of clothing may say otherwise. If you are like the typical Virgo, you probably have a closet full of clothing in every shade of brown, black, and gray. Go out and splurge on some colorful new outfits and accessories. There is no good reason to spend a lot of money. Consignment stores offer bargains. This is also a great day to start on a personal project you have been planning for a while.

28. THURSDAY. Mixed. Today's events and circumstances may not be to your liking, probably due in large measure to your own hypercritical attitude. It is nice to know it all, but you cannot expect everyone you come in contact with to be as sharp as you. Actually you are more powerful than you may realize, so be careful where you aim your angry words; some of them may be like weapons. The energy you feel is a great boon when it comes to working with numbers or precision-detailed tasks. Starting a new or enhanced program of self-improvement can be worthwhile, but take it easy on yourself. Your tendency is to go overboard so that you wind up with sore muscles or become discouraged.

29. FRIDAY. Favorable. If intentionally going out on a limb, have faith in your ability to succeed. An unusual opportunity can have a great effect on your bank account. As always, however, check it out thoroughly before investing. This particular possibility should be a better than ever chance to earn some extra cash. Make sure your mate or partner is behind you all the way. Optimism can get you far. If you are enthusiastic about a certain product or idea, selling it should be no problem. Sudden gains in business can be very exciting but may be short-lived, so bank the cash and consider it a bonus. Figure out all that you are doing right, then try to do it more on a regular basis.

30. SATURDAY. Promising. You might feel that you have had a reversal in fortunes lately, or that you are just on the verge of a major shift when everything will start going your way. You may be right, but do not become overconfident or you might fall down on the job. Longing for more excitement in your relationships can leave you with an empty feeling, but the grass always seems greener on the other side. Be contented with those who care about you. Safety and reliability in a relationship are far more important than having a thrill, which is likely to come and go in an instant. Try to create a pleasanter environment for you and your loved ones by focusing on little niceties of speech, especially more thank you's and I-love-you's.

31. SUNDAY. Auspicious. Getting new neighbors can be kind of worrisome because you never know whether you will turn out to be friend, foe, or neutral. It is likely that the people who are moving in now will be wonderful additions to the neighborhood. They may be especially nervous about meeting you, since they are on your home turf. Be old-fashioned and take over some cookies or flowers to welcome them. Attending a community function such as a festival, parade, or other event can make you nostalgic with childhood memories. A tear may come to your eye when you realize just how important such rituals are in the lives of local residents of all ages.

SEPTEMBER

1. MONDAY. Lively. An unexpected invitation to lunch or to a business-related social event later in the week offers an excellent opportunity to network. You might find that someone who lives near to you is involved in your line of work in some way, giving you an instant in. Stick with formalities when dealing with people you never met before. In your immediate work environment, you may notice that something is not quite right. Files or boxes that were moved without your knowledge can be a bit confusing. Sophisticated new electronic equipment probably seems more glamorous than it really is. Try to catch up with the times if you have been working with yesterday's technology.

2. TUESDAY. Choppy. Keep up with your schedule or things may have a way of getting out of hand. You could be procrastinating unconsciously, adopting an out-of-sight, out-of-mind attitude. Try to manage your time by setting some realistic goals. First thing each morning, make a list of four important tasks, one of which absolutely positively must get done. You might also consider getting up half an hour earlier each day in order to have some quiet time to reflect and contemplate. Judging a situation too optimistically may mean details have not been well thought out. You probably have to personally take stock and make some adjustments even if you are not actually in charge.

3. WEDNESDAY. Productive. Handle family responsibilities with patience. Staying calm can turn a stressful situation into a smooth transition. When it comes to any type of home improvement, try to be as efficient as possible even if the job then takes a little longer to complete. Sort through closets, drawers, and other storage areas to clean out junk that you no longer want or use. Being organized will make you feel more comfortable. Be prepared to take on more of an administrative or managerial role. Extra effort can impress your superiors. Although you may feel overwhelmed with all that there is to do, just keep plugging away in a controlled and persistent manner. Everything will work out thanks to your can-do approach.

4. THURSDAY. Challenging. You will not be very pleased if one of your young family members has a new friend with a checkered past. Or it may be you who has a new mysterious love interest and your family is not too happy about it. Whatever the particular, expect challenges involving love. Obstacles may involve friends as well. People in general are not likely to be cooperative, which you will find disheartening. It may be necessary for you to compromise more than you prefer. Issuing an ultimatum can arouse angry feelings. A project designed to improve your living situation should go very well, especially if it involves art or music. Enjoy a takeout meal tonight instead of cooking.

5. FRIDAY. Demanding. Loved ones can be very demanding, wanting a lot of your time and energy. You will probably have to spread yourself quite thin in order to tackle everything on your to-do list. Plunge into a creative project with enthusiasm; the momentum will keep you going through some tedious moments. A child's temper tantrum could interfere with your plans. Exercising is a great way for you to let off steam, either individually or by playing sports. Games and other fun activities can take your mind off things you cannot change right now. You might have to cancel plans to attend a friend's party because your mate or partner does not get along with other guests who will be there.

6. SATURDAY. Beneficial. In the past you may have felt somewhat insecure about your creative potential and about expressing your talents. Now, however, you should feel inspired to finally share your abilities in a very positive way. You might even decide to make a business out of it; this is a good time to do so. Because Virgos tend to be very serious about parenting, you may not agree with your mate or partner on issues of nutrition, discipline, or education for children or even for a pet. The important thing is to work out these matters in private, not in front of other family members. Children sense any undertone of negativity, and it can be harmful to their sense of security. Once you arrive at a decision, stick to it.

7. SUNDAY. Inspiring. Your friendly, trusting attitude will be very helpful if you try to sell something or need to ask a favor. A feeling of well-being sets the tone for the next few days. However, it could also create a false sense of security or idealism, particularly when it comes to your physical and emotional health. You may crave sweets, but try to resist. Do not kid yourself when it comes to diet and exercise. Come up with a be-fit plan and stick to it. A tense issue between you and a loved one may not be solvable at this time, but if you can at least talk it out you will feel better. This is a good day to bring the disagreement out in the open to see where you may not differ.

8. MONDAY. Favorable. Being sympathetic with all of your co-workers puts you in a favorable light. You know just what to say to make them feel better. Your cooperative spirit makes you a good team player, and in turn colleagues will help you with a difficult job. Your good Virgo intuition should be right on the money. If you are looking for a new job, get creative. Do not rely solely on newspaper ads or an employment agency. Check the Internet and do some calling around yourself. Females make the most congenial company today. A certain woman may have excellent news regarding a work matter. A minor health problem should be improving, but if not make an appointment with your family doctor.

9. TUESDAY. Volatile. Your number-one relationship could be going through a major transition, which is not likely to be completely pain-free. Compromise may no longer be an option for you on certain issues, and your mate or partner may be equally unwilling to give an inch. As a Virgo you are usually quite reserved and mature, but you could get a little rude unless you keep your emotions in check. Do not force any issue. Some time alone to gather your thoughts would help the situation, although this could be impossible if your mate is badgering you. Try to eliminate what no longer works in your life anymore, like bad habits and relationships that keep you down. Once you break free you can make some necessary adjustments.

10. WEDNESDAY. Eventful. You will probably have to let go of some negative factors in your life if you want to be successful and happy. A strong felling of empowerment can rush over you today, so that you are not likely to put up with any putdowns or the usual upsets that people in superior positions try to blame on you. A business partnership could break up if you are unable to reach an agreement on important issues. Be forthright in expressing your opinions and choices rather than resorting to vague words. Try not to judge those who disagree with you. As a Virgo you have a tendency to believe that you are superior to some people in morals or values, but such an attitude could eventually come back to haunt you.

11. THURSDAY. Mixed. A feeling of isolation is likely if you have to spend time with someone with whom you cannot have an intelligent or interesting conversation. Your definite opinions about other people's version of the truth should be kept to yourself, frustrating though it may be. Do not take your anger out on others. This is one day when it is better to hold back the truth in order to avoid hurting someone's feelings. Discussions with people who know you well are likely to be very intense but meaningful. Arguing with your mate or partner over money probably will not be fruitful. However, if you can come up with a plan you can make excellent headway in budgeting. Avoid being vengeful or plotting against a supposed enemy.

12. FRIDAY. Good. Today's assertive mood could lead to finally standing up for yourself with someone who usually makes you back down. One of your colleagues in particular will be shocked when you go face to face with the office bully. Compromise is just not in the cards, but impulsive behavior is foreseen and may surprise even you. If you made plans to go out but are thinking about staying home instead, be aware that you could change your mind again. You are likely to be increasingly enthusiastic as the evening draws nearer. A member of your household might decide to throw a party at home. That way you will know they are home safe and sound, and they will appreciate your unseen but present support.

13. SATURDAY. Variable. Financial or property matters that involve a friend or family member require close scrutiny. You may have different ideas regarding how to deal with the financial arrangements. Be patient, give your views, then wait for the final decision to be made. You will probably get a chance later to make an adjustment. Enjoy spending quality time with a friend who shares your values and ethics. It can be fun sharing some juicy gossip about someone you do not like, although you are apt to feel a bit guilty doing so. Do not worry about such things; it is human nature to be concerned with the details of other people's lives. Just avoid trying to figure out why certain people keep doing foolish things.

14. SUNDAY. Easy. Stay late in bed if you can. Slowly come awake from a wild dream of distant shores, larger-than-life adventure, and fascinating newcomers. Your benevolent mood leads you to help other people as well as yourself. Self-development programs such as seminars, classes, or books on tape might interest you at this time. You can learn a lot if you participate in such activities. An engaging discussion with a minister or teacher could set you on a new intellectual journey. Enjoy attending a cultural event featuring foreign food, music, and dance. Science fiction and mystery books and films can get you thinking about all sorts of possibilities.

15. MONDAY. Encouraging. You should be pleased with the result of a recent test but that is no reason to rest on your laurels. Training for a certain skill or subject will intensify as new details are added. Without a good basic understanding of mathematics, you could find some tasks difficult. Your energy level is apt to fluctuate, up one minute and down the next. Avoid stimulants such as caffeine and sugar so that you do not crash emotionally. If planning a trip, check with more than one ticket or travel agent; there are likely to be more options than you are aware of. A local strike could make it difficult to do certain things. You may even have to make a tough choice about crossing a picket line.

16. TUESDAY. Diverse. This is a day of mixed blessings. You might experience some general good luck stemming from a telephone call or visit informing you of some wonderful news. This may be in regard to work, travel, or education. However, the problem comes in the form of frustrations as you go about the day. Expect to change your plans quickly and frequently. A meeting that has been scheduled for weeks may not happen because of circumstances beyond your control. Or you may not be present because traffic can slow you down and make you late. People can be unreliable. If you are able to detach yourself from having control over all aspects of life, you will be much happier and much less frustrated.

17. WEDNESDAY. Confusing. Certain decisions can be hard to make because you have so many options. Talk to different people and you will get as many different opinions. The correct answer may seem to be anyone's guess, but it is up to you to make a choice that hopefully will be a good one. Write down all the pros and cons, then spend time analyzing them. Chatting on the bus or in a checkout line could be quite enlightening as you learn something about your company or your competition. All the same, that kind of casual information may not be reliable. Do not embarrass yourself in front of other people by discussing any rumor before you check it out with sources you trust.

18. THURSDAY. Sensitive. You have to watch what you say so that you do not let privileged information slip out in general conversation. If you think quickly, you might be able to save yourself with a witty comeback. Ideas can come and go like butterflies, so if you get a good one, write it down before you have a chance to forget it. Brains rather than brawn are your virtue, but do not use words to intimidate someone who works for you. Remember, what goes around comes around. Eventually you will get what you deserve, so make it good. An older relative may discover a secret you have been trying to keep for months or even years. Do not worry about it too much, for it is not likely to cause as much discussion as you fear.

19. FRIDAY. Varied. This is definitely not a day to go shopping if you can avoid it. You could make a purchase and immediately want to return it for a refund. You may feel both social and solitary, making your day topsy-turvy. Your best bet is to be flexible and just let events unfold as they may. Spend relaxing time with friends, having lunch together or enjoying a movie. You might decide to sign up for a seminar or workshop on a spiritual or creative subject. You could make a new friend as a result. A quiet evening at home is your best bet, although someone you know well may have other ideas.

20. SATURDAY. Surprising. You might wake up in the middle of the night for no apparent reason. Probably you are working out some problem in your subconscious mind, and could arrive at the answer by morning. Keep a dream journal near your bed for such an occasion. If one of your friends needs some nurturing, you are just the person to help. As a Virgo you are protective of those you love. Their upsets become yours, and woe to the person who is mean or hurtful. You have ample energy and motivation to get involved with a favorite charity. Just watch that you do not overdo or you may get behind with some of your other responsibilities.

21. SUNDAY. Serene. You may not feel like going anywhere or doing anything, which is okay. Everyone needs a break now and then. An opportunity to set the record straight with a person you no longer speak with is yours if you just make a phone call. Apologize sincerely for your part in the disagreement, giving you a clear conscience. However, if you intend to insist that you were right all along, you may as well not even bother getting in touch. Spiritual services and events can be moving and inspirational; you will be glad you made the effort to attend. Realizing how you have been standing in your own way will leave you free to pursue new opportunities.

22. MONDAY. Disconcerting. You are apt to get up on the wrong side of the bed this morning. If so, jump back in, sleep an extra few minutes, and start all over again. Being a little bit late to work happens to everyone now and again, even a Virgo, so do not berate yourself if it happens to you. Do not be timid when it comes to asking favors, especially from friends. If you feel pessimistic about your working conditions or your day-to-day routine, stop and count your blessings. Some people are not half as fortunate. Besides, being discontented can spur you to action when you are finally ready to make a change. Focus on the boring everyday tasks that need to be done, then use your time this evening for creative work.

23. TUESDAY. Pressured. Obstacles remain in the way of getting a certain personal wish fulfilled. You are being challenged to get it together in a more organized fashion. Do not be discouraged by one particular person who is acting like more of an enemy than a friend. Simply forge on despite opposition. Someone in your life will restore your faith in humanity. You may receive flowers or a surprise visit. Although excited, you might sense that something is not quite right. Probably it is just your own worrying nature that is causing you to question your good fortune. Root for the underdog, and have compassion for those who are weak, but do not bet based on such emotion.

24. WEDNESDAY. Excellent. Your confidence should be really high. You are in your element and can succeed at just about anything you decide to do. Acting the role of peacemaker is a distinct possibility. You will be able to relate while being sensitive to all sides. Involvement in a community art, music, fashion, or charity group is a positive way to express thanks for all that has been given to you. You may be somewhat idealistic when it comes to love, but most of the time Virgo folks are a bit too discriminating. Just relax and enjoy yourself with no restrictions. This is an excellent time for making a very special dream come true.

25. THURSDAY. Fair. A selfish tendency could annoy certain people, but you probably will not care since you cannot rely on them anyway. You may be disappointed if your mate or a good friend lets you down first thing this morning. Sometimes it seems you are the only one who has the stamina and the force of character to face up to reality. Romance will have to be put off until another day since you feel quite cold about matters of the heart. A past relationship in which you were hurt may have led you to preconceived notions of independent action as the best policy. Plug ahead with your work; you are very capable, so avoid procrastinating. Be sure to meet or beat a deadline.

26. FRIDAY. Positive. Today begins a powerful time in which you can get your act together in many ways, including financially. If you start a new savings account and are determined to add to it on a regular basis, you will be surprised how quickly it grows. Just about anything done formally, such as starting a new project designed to increase your cash flow or making a symbolic contract with yourself, should be lucky for you. You should be feeling good about yourself. Do not turn down an offer to go out and socialize tonight. Not only can you make good contacts, you might find romance as well. Dress to impress the opposite sex.

27. SATURDAY. Auspicious. Reread yesterday's horoscope. If you ignored any of those suggestions, go for it today since the forces are just as powerful. Try to break out of a self-imposed rut. You have a flair for fashion and decorating. Shopping can be both fun and therapeutic, especially if you take your best friend along. If buying clothes, stick with classic lines, spending a few extra dollars in order to get the best quality you can afford. Do not buy something just because it is on sale, and avoid anything that could be considered trendy. Be prepared to give a big smile to everyone you meet. Your attitude can make the day.

28. SUNDAY. Suspenseful. An overnight shift all of a sudden makes you quite serious and introverted. You may not trust what some people say; they may seem to be hiding something. People will not easily admit that you have all the answers, and you may not feel like trying to convince them. Nor should you have to do so. Your personal power and magnetism are extraordinary; if you really use them, you will get the respect you deserve. Action you take now could be more productive than you imagine. Like dropping a pebble into water, the effects will ripple out in an ever-widening circle. A neighborhood issue can have you on edge, and you are not likely to get along with one particular person who is actively fomenting unrest.

29. MONDAY. Dynamic. Today you have an opportunity to speak your mind in a very powerful way, but you must avoid words that express anger and resentment. Hidden emotions could come through and make you seem dictatorial or like an old sourpuss. However, if you can stay with your honorable intentions, you can make great headway. Working to better your town or community can be very effective. Do not hesitate to stand up for what you believe in. Some of the people you see on a regular basis may scurry out of your way because they are not used to seeing you act this way. All you need is one staunch supporter and you can make a significant impact.

30. TUESDAY. Varied. Your nervous energy can be put to good use doing filing, cleaning, or handcrafts. Refuse a second cup of coffee; you do not need it, and the caffeine will probably make you very jittery. You might have to leave work early to attend to a family matter. Frustration with a colleague is possible. Some people just do not do their jobs properly. Watch that you do not develop a know-it-all attitude. You may even have to admit making a mistake. By the time night comes, you will be pleased to stay at home with loved ones. Be willing to pitch in and help if they have not finished their chores rather than berating them.

OCTOBER

1. WEDNESDAY. Bumpy. Having a bad attitude toward a family member will not benefit anyone. A family feud could result in a major outburst. Try to treat all of your relatives with the same love and respect you show to your friends. You may be tired of the same old work situation, but taking impulsive action is not a good idea. Continue with current plans and finish ongoing projects before moving on. Relentless pursuit of money or power is not likely to bring you the happiness you seek. Get in touch with what is really important in your life, like good relationships, peace of mind, and joy. Do not do anything that might lead you to lose what you already have.

2. THURSDAY. Demanding. In order to get a child to listen, you may have to exercise your authority. It is necessary to show some youngsters who is in charge. Do not expect a toddler to think like an adult; try distraction if you are dealing with a temper tantrum. Creative energies may be somewhat dampened by a tendency to take matters too seriously. However, once you get in the right mood you can create something absolutely outstanding. Maintaining a sense of humor can help you get through the most tense and tedious situation at work. People will appreciate your wry, sarcastic, and goofy jokes. Take some time out for activities that are strictly fun, such as walking through the falling leaves or playing a game with youngsters.

3. FRIDAY. Steady. Take it easy if you can. A sense that everything is going to be all right should keep your optimism high. If romance is on the agenda it should live up to your expectations. You will be pleased when someone special starts glancing your way. Do not hesitate to show that you have noticed and are interested. Children can be little angels, enjoying art projects or anything requiring creativity and positive energy. Ask a colleague for a favor and you are likely to get it with no strings attached. An older gentleman should give you some very wise career or health advice. You probably will not have to engage in any fight today, but if you do, roll with the punches.

4. SATURDAY. Eventful. A major purchase you are about to make, although expensive, is worth the money. You have a choice of attending a variety of enjoyable functions, the more entertaining the better. Going out dancing, to the theater, or to hear some live music should suit you perfectly. You might feel a little indecisive if you attempt a decorating scheme. If so, look at a design book or magazines to get the advice of professionals. Large stores may also have employees who are also designers or design interns. Working well as part of a team should come easily. Old ideas and experiences will synthesize to create new concepts that work out just as you envision. Be bold with colors and patterns.

5. SUNDAY. Fair. Keeping on a straight and narrow path probably will not be difficult. You are apt to be your own worst critic and therefore not inclined to take any major risks. You will be frustrated if you look at all the clothes in your closet and still feel you have nothing to wear. This is not the day to go shopping, however, as you are in too frugal a mood. Only a secondhand or consignment store will suit you, and there you probably find some great bargains. You will have to juggle multiple responsibilities, including working from home, caring for a child or a pet, and arranging dinner. React to any conflict with a calm, thoughtful manner and it should not last long. Refuse to be goaded into arguing.

6. MONDAY. Worrisome. If your workload seems overwhelming, you could experience quite a bit of anxiety unless you are able to keep on top of it. Your health could even be affected. Since Virgos are the type to get headaches, stomachaches, or nervous indigestion, you need to prioritize. If concerned about money, it is probably a waste of time asking a friend to help you with a loan. Some things you just have to take care of yourself. Phone your creditors and tell them you need a break on your payment terms. They are likely to appreciate your good-faith effort and be willing to work with you. If you can get out jogging, you will release pent-up tension and those extra worries.

7. TUESDAY. Variable. Get up a little earlier than usual. Changes in your working life can range from getting a new desk to being transferred. Whatever the circumstances, you are apt to need time to adjust. You could feel quite dissatisfied with your boss or with a colleague, but hold your tongue. Right now, peace is more important than saying what is on your mind. No matter what you are doing, focus on efficiency while also being creative. You can be inspired if you relax long enough to look past all the things on your to-do list. Try to work on a day-to-day basis. Your relationships, too, need constant nurturing rather than occasional bursts of attention.

8. WEDNESDAY. Sensitive. You are especially vulnerable to cutting remarks. Sensitivity in both your personal life and your dealings on the job could be heightened by a remark you take the wrong way early in the morning. It is wise to opt for peace at any price rather than cause upsets among loved ones or your colleagues. If you run into difficulties communicating crucial directions or instructions, you probably need to slow down a bit. Going through a job at breakneck speed could cause you to make irritating mistakes. You would be better off taking your time and doing it right the first time. Be very considerate of a loved one who is going through some rough times.

9. THURSDAY. Exciting. You may meet someone very exciting, if not eccentric, who will soon be having a strong effect on your life. Pursue a friendship. This is a great time to assert your independence within a committed relationship or marriage, but do so in a manner that does not threaten the other person. If your partner is not willing to support you having a life of your own, you probably will not stick around much longer. In fact, this could be the day to make such a break. If you recently separated you should not be alone for long. Just make sure to go out meeting people rather than just staying home. You have good taste, which can lead to interesting shopping at a mall or on the Internet.

10. FRIDAY. Stressful. During these very intense times your main relationship is likely to be going through some significant changes. If you are unable to agree on basic matters such as sex and money, two of the main things people argue about, they are now apt to become a sore subject. Your tendency to want to run and hide is likely to make things worse. Instead, try to discuss your differences in an adult fashion. Wishing will not make a bad thing good, but effort might turn it around at least to some degree. Deal with situations as they are, not as how you want them to be. A project you are doing in cooperation with a partner may not produce the financial gain that you are hoping for, but the experience will be invaluable.

11. SATURDAY. Helpful. Getting along well with the opposite sex should be easy today, since you appreciate the differences. You could take on a new glow as you think about making a trip. Do not be limited by a lack of funding. Instead, be creative. You might win a trip or get your employer to want to send you. You may discover a new way to display your true passion. Taking a course would be a good idea. If you are sure of your abilities, be confident and promote yourself. Family members should be very supportive, even though you may be venturing into untested waters. Take it to the limit. You only live once so go after that elusive brass ring.

12. SUNDAY. Positive. Pay attention to the exceptional opportunities that exist all around you. Although you may not always notice them, they are there. Swift action will let you grab onto a chance to put your best foot forward. Siblings and friends are likely to stand by you as you chase after your dreams, but parents may not understand. Your life gets more and more adventurous and exciting. Taking a trip overseas could open your mind to a whole new world. This is one time when running away can resolve some personal issues, taking you outside your present circumstances and showing you that there are other options available. You do not have to limit yourself in any way.

13. MONDAY. Fortunate. You are ready to proceed with big plans and will resent anyone or anything that stands in your way. When things do not go as you hope, consider it to be luck of the best kind. Forces are at work to help you, but not exactly in the way you might think. Go with the flow. Be flexible and ready to be surprised in a very positive way. Cooperate with friends and loved ones and they will repay you in kind when you need a helping hand. Be sure you ask for what you need; people probably will not know unless you tell them specifically. Your secret might not be safe with a colleague, although his or her intention is probably not to hurt you. To be on the safe side, do not say a word about it.

14. TUESDAY. Challenging. Being in the public eye could get the best of you, as you open your mouth and stick your foot straight into it. You have great ideas and concepts but probably will not be able to communicate them in a way that is clear and easily understandable. Your supervisor may be asking too much of you. Try to complete one project before moving on to the next one. This is not a good day to ask for a pay raise or a promotion. Some big changes are coming up in your career, but they are not going to happen today. Just proceed one step at a time and eventually you will be where you want to be. Do not let rainy weather get you down. Keep in mind that every cloud has a silver lining.

15. WEDNESDAY. Opportune. Unusual new ideas are brewing, causing you to be somewhat restless. Changing the status quo may not be easy, however, so just relax. Get ready to celebrate an important turn of events as far as a certain relative is concerned. You have a chance to contact a particular group of people you have been trying to meet. They can become important figures in your life for a long time, so be open and friendly when you finally get connected. It may be hard to curb your enthusiasm when you are around older, conservative people, but that is probably the best way to relate to them. Take the time necessary to get to know a senior citizen who holds the reins of power, or knows who does.

16. THURSDAY. Fruitful. New ideas can bear fruit if you let go of a deep-seated desire to have everything turn out perfectly or not at all. You can get venture capital or other financing for a project if you are sufficiently resourceful. You want to speed right along, but try to be patient. Things will fall into place if you allow them to do so. Arrange to get together with people who may be more than willing to help you. You are right to feel alive and excited about the future, which is in your control. A period of freedom and new choices is about to begin, so focus on your innermost desires and hopes for a happy life. Visualize events happening just as you would like, seeing yourself creating an aura of good fortune.

17. FRIDAY. Rewarding. The security in your life may seem threatened by forces outside your control. In fact, however, you are just preparing for some big new changes. A deeper sense of duty and responsibility means you will have to deal with fears and anxieties that usually do not bother you much. You may feel somewhat restricted by your job, relationship, or children, but just because you cannot hop on a plane and go wherever you want does not mean you have no freedom. Attending a counseling or support session can be very helpful as you meet other people who go through the same things and come out fine. A new friend can stimulate you to make positive changes in your everyday life.

18. SATURDAY. Promising. Focusing on your social life can be profitable. You will reap many benefits from friends, especially a group of people. Attending meetings offers many rewards. You will meet new people, and one or two may have some even better contacts for you. Know your own power, and value what you have to give. Volunteer for your favorite charity organization if you have the time. You will feel wonderful knowing that you are making a difference. If hosting a party this evening, be sure to add your own special touch. You may want to buy and distribute some disposable cameras or pass around a video cam so your guests have something they can take home with them.

19. SUNDAY. Uneasy. Your Virgo taste for drama can cause you to make mountains out of molehills. Try not to blow little things out of proportion, or you might end up with a major problem. Excitement about a new opportunity could lead you to be overly extravagant. Spending too much on clothes or possessions designed to impress other people can be a real waste. Your true value does not need to be put on public display. Consider the needs of your colleagues as well as your own when you decide whether to accept additional responsibility. You could harm your health if you overindulge in food and drink that you know is bad for you. Overeating due to anger or upset begins a vicious cycle that is hard to break.

20. MONDAY. Good. Someone who is leaving your life right now is probably a person who needs to move on anyway for the good of you both. Rather than becoming upset, calm yourself by cleaning out a closet, decorating the house, or just puttering around. Extend a helping hand to friends and loved ones who will probably respond in a supportive manner when you need assistance. Buying utilitarian clothes for work or sports can be useful, and you are likely to get some great deals. Be discreet if having a relationship that you are trying to keep secret. One wrong move and the word could get out all over town. If considering having an affair, reject the idea before even taking the first step.

21. TUESDAY. Pressured. Additional pressures come along with a promotion or new responsibility you recently volunteered for. Stress can get to you today if you have few or no good coping techniques. You are apt to be interrupted by a constantly ringing phone and people bursting into your office. Setting up boundaries can be as easy as closing the door or letting the answering machine respond to your calls. You may decide to get a personal trainer or take on a harder physical training schedule. Just be aware that in your enthusiasm you could do too much too soon and wind up with an injury or soreness. You may be very hard on yourself if you are not making the kind of progress you want, but take it slow.

22. WEDNESDAY. Stimulating. Going into new places and situations where you have never been before can open you up to a lot of new experiences. You are likely to meet some new acquaintances who inspire you as far as your personal goals are concerned. You could feel bored with tradition and therefore reject old ways of doing things. Your attraction to futuristic ideas can lead to looking at the latest models of computers and electronics. You will probably be more energetic than usual. Try to operate instinctively. Aim to do what is fair and right for all the people in your life. It may seem that some folks are practically waiting in line to help you overcome a temporary impediment.

23. THURSDAY. Relaxing. As a Virgo you tend to withdraw into your work. It is okay not to be social if you do not feel like it. Just make sure that you are not robbing yourself of a chance for friendship or even romance. You might be ready to pop because of the tension. Immerse yourself in activities that keep you busy as well as giving you a sense of accomplishment. This is not a good time to be stubborn and inflexible. You are apt to be quite disturbed by changes you cannot do anything about. An interest in science, math, or medicine can provide lots of pleasure, so study away for work or as a hobby. Sign up for a CPR or First Aid class.

24. FRIDAY. Slow. You may be in line for an increase in pay, but you have to be patient. Some things may not happen as quickly as you would like, but you probably will not mind. An attraction to beautiful objects could lead you to take money from your piggy bank or from a special savings account in order to take home a shiny new object. Treat yourself if it is not too expensive. If you need to use a credit card, think twice about the potential purchase. Instead of reading a romantic novel during your lunch hour, go outside for some fresh air. If you think you have no time to exercise, try going for a walk during a work break or before breakfast or by taking the stairs instead of the elevator.

25. SATURDAY. Upbeat. As you enjoy the success of your recent efforts, you will become increasingly self-confident and probably ready to start something new. People you have been trying to convince to help you are now about to come through for you. Try to be humble about the fact that you are finally getting exactly what you want. You may feel somewhat guilty about receiving a certain gift, but you deserve it. Just because other people have less than you does not mean you must feel sorry for them. You may be expecting some funds to come through soon, but do not spend the money yet. Avoid incurring any bills that you might have trouble paying when the grace period is over.

26. SUNDAY. Fulfilling. Your social life is gearing up. You will probably discover that you can actually get along with someone you thought you did not like. Whatever caused the shift, just be grateful that the bad feelings have disappeared. Rely on your own ideas rather than those of other people. Your mental faculties are at their best. You are particularly good at research, especially getting to the bottom of a matter involving your entire community. Attending a town meeting can be very interesting. You are not likely to take any abuse from people who do not care about your neighborhood. Speak up in a meeting; you can make a difference personally and by empowering others in attendance.

27. MONDAY. Manageable. A fear of failure could be holding you back from making an important move. If you do not give it a try, you will never know. Your favorite relative may put in a good word for you or could have some excellent advice. Like most Virgos, you occasionally suffer from the paralysis of analysis. Just relax; you do not have to be perfect and probably will not be. A minor run of bad luck is not necessarily an indication of how things will go in the future. Do what is necessary to get motivated and you will feel a lot better about yourself. A certain family member needs your undivided attention this evening. Beware of loaning money to a friend for any reason.

28. TUESDAY. Problematic. You might be preoccupied with domestic matters, but while at work try to keep your mind on the task at hand. Focus on one thing at a time to avoid scattering your energy. If doing a big project, enlist help as soon as you need it. When surprising news comes, you will be cool and collected while other people overreact. The answer to a vital question is already known to you. Once you learn how to recognize the difference between intuition and mind chatter you will be ahead of the game. Do not be reckless while operating machinery or any appliance. Remember, safety first. Think back to a certain scene from your youth this evening.

29. WEDNESDAY. Favorable. You could overflow with creativity as a virtual wellspring of ideas and projects flows from your active mind. Preoccupation with romance can have you feeling a bit lonely. Make plans to be with that special person if at all possible; do something fun together. Your relationship is likely to be quite satisfactory at this time, and you do not need excitement when you have simple pleasure. Your personal magnetism is amplified. With only a smile, you can melt a heart. Enjoy this time of contentment and joy. Playing sports with children can be fun as well as quite important to their development. Consider volunteering to coach a team or to referee.

30. THURSDAY. Important. The key to your next promotion relies on being up to date on the newest technology. Investigate training programs to see which one is most respected. Do not limit yourself to schools within your immediate area. You might enjoy going to another country or region to study. You may be shocked to witness rude behavior, but it will not help if you get into the middle of it. Stay on the sidelines if possible, but be alert. A foreigner may teach you a valuable lesson. Someone with a completely different philosophy of life could come into your sphere. Virgo students can have a breakthrough that leads to more clarity with career choices. Be open to all possibilities.

31. FRIDAY. Enjoyable. You can expect business as usual at work, although you could get an opportunity to enjoy the company of a higher-up. You may have lunch together or talk on the phone. This person can help you, so go ahead and ask for a favor or for some advice. If your request is within reason, your contact should be ready and willing to assist. You have the necessary energy to do some reorganizing at work. If your desk is a mess, this is the time to clean it up. Take care of filing and paying bills, especially if you have been putting off such chores. You will not enjoy having to field phone calls from creditors.

NOVEMBER

1. SATURDAY. Fair. Changes in your daily routine are likely to be rather chaotic. All the same, they can give a real sense of freedom. If you have just quit one job or have just gotten a new one, the weight of the world has lifted from your shoulders. You may still have some leftover feelings of anxiety, however, which should fade quickly. Artistic, musical, decorating, and crafting activities can be done with amazing originality and flair. You have a real eye for beauty and glamour. Finances could be a little unstable if you recently overspent your budget, but you should get back on track with little trouble. A taste for sweets could leave you with a stomachache tonight.

2. SUNDAY. Uneasy. Overall dissatisfaction might be the best way to describe the feeling that you wake up with this morning. Your goals may not have been sweeping enough to encompass all that you truly want and deserve out of life. Rather than feeling sorry for yourself, spend the day meditating on what you basically want. Think of people you admire and would like to emulate. Such imitation is the sincerest form of flattery, but that must not lead you to just go out and copy someone. You are apt to probably feel like running away from your problems. It is okay to do so, but only for a day or two while you gather your courage.

3. MONDAY. Volatile. You might remember a disturbing dream when you get up this morning. Discussing it with a good friend or with your mate could help you understand it. If that does not work, bear in mind that some experts believe dreams are nothing more than endless, meaningless waste material that the mind creates and tosses out at night. If you approach the day with such a philosophy, you will be much happier. Overanalyzing can sometimes lead to utter frustration. Having and maintaining a sense of humor makes all the difference. You can often turn a bad time into a good one by simply making up your mind to do so. Reach out to someone in kindness and see what you get back in return.

4. TUESDAY. Variable. Expect some extremes in your life. Partnership versus individuality can be a big one. Although you feel driven to be involved, supported, and loved by one particular person, you are stronger and more self-assured than ever before. Being in a relationship that allows you the freedom to pursue your own goal can be ideal. However, you might feel unfairly held back by the current circumstances in your life. You would be wise to take a cautious, steady, conservative route, aiming at preservation rather than growth. Throwing yourself into work can be a great coping mechanism; in addition, you can be very productive now.

5. WEDNESDAY. Reassuring. Your relationship with your mate or partner could be a little tense. One of you may not be up front about your real feelings. Bottle those feelings up for too long and you could wind up angry, resentful, or even physically ill. Do not be afraid to reveal how you feel, although you might not be able to put your feelings into definite words. Sometimes it helps to ask the other person if there is a problem, and start the conversation from there. You will feel much better once you get your concerns out in the open, and you are likely to find out they were not so serious after all. This evening you should have the opportunity to kiss and make up without either of you having to apologize.

6. THURSDAY. Promising. This day is excellent for building and advancing. Whatever your project, put all your energy into it and you are likely to make excellent progress. Handle adversity with tolerance and understanding. Believe that nothing can rattle you and it will be true. This is a great time to invest joint funds or work out an agreement for borrowing or lending money. Funds for a big dream such as a mortgage or business loan could come through. This can also be a very effective day to start planning how to reduce your taxes. A friend might know of a helpful financial adviser. If you have not made a will, do so now and reduce that nagging worry.

7. FRIDAY. Favorable. Someone you know may be rather secretive, or perhaps you are being a little too suspicious. Try as you might, you may not be able to drag the truth out of some people, and what they are keeping from you is probably no big deal anyway. Be patient if you want them to eventually let you in on a secret. Patience, however, is not one of your strong points now. Chalk up your intensity to Virgo curiosity and imagination, and try to avoid being jealous or envious. Romance promises the kind of passion you read about in novels. If you have someone you love a lot, plan a special evening just for the two of you. Show how much you really care with action instead of words.

8. SATURDAY. Encouraging. Some of the changes happening in your life at this time can be uncomfortable, but they are for the best. You should have no problems speaking up and asking for what you want. Virgo students should be pleased with test results and grades on papers and exams. Being quite passionate about studies increases the chance of doing well in class. Virgo writers are likely to be very productive; publishing is featured. A long-distance romance could start all of a sudden. You will benefit from involvement with an overseas project or with someone from a distance. Your world seems bigger through connections you make outside your own limited area.

9. SUNDAY. Erratic. This day promises to be somewhat unusual. Events may not turn out as planned. Erratic behavior from someone you can ordinarily count on could thwart your ambitions. Do not worry about it, however, for it is not likely to interfere for too long. Rather than staying home and doing nothing, get out and create an adventure. A journey across town for shopping, lunch, and entertainment could be real fun. Take home an ethnic cookbook and some foreign spices and get creative. If going to the airport or train station, phone ahead to make sure arrival and departure times are as scheduled. Otherwise you could have to endure a frustrating wait.

10. MONDAY. Choppy. In the early morning you might feel a little tired, and perhaps even concerned about it. By lunchtime, however, you should be reenergized and ready to take on whatever life has to offer. Inequalities could affect your life. You may feel that you are not earning the same as your counterpart of the opposite sex or of another age, or that you have been passed over for a promotion because of your gender. Consider discussing the matter with a lawyer; not only is such action unfair and unethical, but you could have a good case. If you have a well-tuned sense of where you are going in life, this is the time to move ahead. Make an important phone call late in the day.

11. TUESDAY. Expansive. Focus on the new ideas simmering away in your mind; one of them might actually be brilliant. Write down any lightning-flash concepts that come to mind, since they are likely to be pure genius. Even if you do not know what to do with your thought, you can always come back to it later when you are more grounded. A business trip may be required all of a sudden, or you could be called to work in another location. Unexpected news means that you have to be adaptable to a change of plans. You could be somewhat nervous or anxious for no reason that you can clearly understand. If sleep interruptions persist, relaxation exercises may be necessary.

12. WEDNESDAY. Frustrating. This can be a frustrating day when it comes to communications. Try as you might, someone near you may not get your message clearly enough to respond. The problem is not likely to be interpretation, more likely the way you speak. Expressing complex emotions or even simple directions can be quite difficult. If you have any doubts after speaking, have your listeners repeat back to you what you said or write it down. Socializing can be enjoyable but you will be better off in a group rather than one-on-one. Matters of the heart are not likely to run smoothly. A date can be disappointing. Platonic relationships will fare better than a romantic one.

13. THURSDAY. Opportune. A great business opportunity could come your way following a meeting you attend. Your company may ask you to put in some overtime or take on more responsibility. Devoting extra hours to work should not be that hard on you at this time. In fact, you are probably the person who can do the job best with the least effort. You can handle stress, hardship, or obstacles without too much difficulty. Your mate or partner could give you a suggestion that you can take to the bank. This is a great night for you and your loved one to go out to eat or play cards with another couple. Plan a joint trip or other social event with your best friends.

14. FRIDAY. Good. Consider how and why some of your wishes and hopes have not been fulfilled. Do not blame anyone. Take full responsibility for all of your circumstances. Even if it seems you were a complete victim, perhaps you needed to have the experience; try to think what good it could actually do you in the future. Discussing such matters with a friend can lead to some amazing personal revelations. Love can be somewhat disappointing if you look at it in terms of sheer romance. Instead, you will find that friendship can grow. Flirting with an old pal could be fun, but you will be happier if you just remain friends.

15. SATURDAY. Eventful. You are likely to awaken with a feeling of gratitude. If you want to buy someone a gift in order to give thanks, choose something affordable. Your taste can be on the expensive side. Even though you want to impress the other person or try to make up for an insensitive mood on your part, that does not mean you should go overboard. An old pal or acquaintance you have not seen in years could appear out of the blue. You could enjoy getting together informally, but think twice before letting this person back into your life. Take good care of your health. Your body is quite sensitive. Do not overindulge in alcoholic beverages or take nonprescription pills.

16. SUNDAY. Easygoing. If left on your own you should enjoy a fairly relaxed day. Take care of the little things that will help ground you after the intensity of the past week. Catch up on paperwork and filing. Pay bills. Do your laundry and other household chores, or better yet, hire someone to do them for you. Do not feel guilty about spending money for help; just think of it as a way to spread the wealth. It is perfectly fine to be a couch potato or, the weather is nice, go out for a walk to enjoy the crisp, cool air. If you feel a little run-down or have a virus, it is crucial that you get some extra rest now since you are likely to be quite busy or even stressed out over the next week.

17. MONDAY. Demanding. Power struggles are likely. Your Virgo qualities are magnified, so you feel stronger than usual. You can be more critical than necessary with both yourself and other people. Of course, there may be one or two cases where this show of strength is necessary, since you cannot put up with certain behavior much longer. This is likely to include family members or others with whom you live. In order to have peace you will probably have to compromise, at least somewhat. Long-buried feelings from childhood could come to mind out of the blue. This is a starred time to examine any old resentments you have toward loved ones. In this way you can get over them and restart the relationship with a clean slate.

18. TUESDAY. Sensitive. You could get too upset over a situation involving someone who is not pulling his or her own weight. Emotions can run away with you unless you keep a lid on them. One more lame excuse could be the straw that broke the camel's back. If you start to lose your temper, excuse yourself from the room to pull yourself back together. Take a good look at what else is going on in your personal life. Try not to take a joshing comment personally. Situations out of your control could place a damper on your evening plans as well. You might be better off spending the hours after dark alone with your own thoughts. Exercise will help smooth out your emotions.

19. WEDNESDAY. Challenging. Demands on your time and energy can be almost overwhelming. However, it is likely that you must extend yourself to your maximum capacity in order to get certain jobs done and deadlines met. Guard your health by eating properly and getting at least a little physical exercise at some point today. Even a walk around the block or a few calisthenics might be enough to keep your blood flowing and your stress level at a reasonable point. Your love life could be a bit frustrating, as your mate or steady date becomes overbearing or asks too much of you. Later in the day you will enjoy a challenge, even though you are not usually competitive.

20. THURSDAY. Changeable. With little or notice you could hear the bad news that money you were counting on is not going to come through or will be delayed. Some Virgos might be the victim of a company's downsizing or might be beat out for a high-paying job. Try not to worry too much; think of it as one of those tests you sometimes must endure. You could just as suddenly find something better or make other arrangements. Make sure you take advantage of new opportunity right away, however. Good intentions will not amount to much. Assess how burglarproof your home, car, and possessions are, and do something about adding more deterrents to crime. Smart thinking could deter a thief.

21. FRIDAY. Suspenseful. Watch out for your own economic interests. Rely on your good Virgo instincts and research rather than solely on what other people tell you. You might gather up your courage and ask the boss for a raise. Before doing so, however, you need a plan. You will want to explain how you have gone above and beyond what is expected of you, and how valuable you are and entitled to higher pay. Just be sure you do not threaten, or you could start a power struggle. Have patience; if you do not get your rewards now, you are likely to get them soon. A high-spirited newcomer could have a major effect on your life right now. You should be able to trust this person, unless a past history indicates otherwise.

22. SATURDAY. Positive. Sticking close to home is probably your best bet, unless you have to work or attend a big event. Although the weather can be harsh, bundle up and go for a long walk. Meet and greet neighbors. If you are considering decorating the outside of your home for the upcoming holidays, come up with an original plan. Invite a friend or neighbor to comment on your tentative ideas. A family member could really anger you or bait you into an argument. It is not worth your while to fight over minor matters, which is likely to be what the disagreement is all about. Accept an invitation to socialize tonight even if it comes at the last minute.

23. SUNDAY. Tricky. An idea that suddenly comes to mind to make changes to your home can be either very good or equally bad. An impulse to paint or otherwise decorate a room can give fabulous results. If it does not please you or your family, you can always go back to the way it was. In order to save yourself a headache, check with an honest friend or relative before going out and spending money. If you are thinking of making structural changes, like knocking down a wall or doing major remodeling, wait until tomorrow to get started. Try not to become upset with a thoughtless young relative. An engrossing novel might be your best companion this evening.

24. MONDAY. Upbeat. If you have something special you have wanted to do for a long time, this is the day to get to it. Do not procrastinate or you might lose your initial momentum. Even if you are not sure of yourself, at least try. You may experience almost instant success or only see slight improvement. Making any type of change can be a gamble. Sometimes, however, you only gain by risking. Be as direct as possible with other people, especially loved ones. If you do not come right out and say what you mean, you could be accused of having a hidden agenda or being sneaky. Your passion for a certain hobby or subject of study is apt to intensify almost to the point of becoming an obsession.

25. TUESDAY. Bumpy. Dealing with a younger family member can be tough if you cannot share information or feelings. It is not smart to trust anyone who you think is hiding something. A sneaking suspicion that a certain young person is involved in harmful behavior could be right. This is a powerful time to attempt to open the lines of communication. You might even be able to transform a difficult relationship through fearless examination. This energy makes counseling and therapy groups especially effective right now. You could experience some telepathic moments. Try to guess what other people are thinking, then see if you are right.

26. WEDNESDAY. Difficult. Concentrating on tasks and completing your work is easier said than done, particularly if you have to work as a team or in a partnership. People in general may not be cooperative, in fact trying to undermine your plans. You could be dragged into a disagreement at home between relatives, one of whom is probably using underhanded or manipulative techniques in order to get an advantage. Angry people may use the silent treatment, plead ignorance, or issue ultimatums. If you can work and be alone at this time, all the better. Face up to your own worries and anxiety; discuss concerns with those who give you grief. Being brutally honest may be the only way to resolve the situation.

27. THURSDAY. Comforting. The heavy weight that has seemed to blanket your life for the past few days is slowly lifting, leaving behind good humor in its place. Having a playful attitude will allow you to get through any remaining challenges easier than you imagined. A personal battle may now come to an end. Let your happy memories be a comfort, knowing that things work out eventually. By evening you could be ready to have some real fun. Dinner out followed by a leisurely walk through the city or dancing cheek-to-cheek can put a perfect end to this long day. Allow yourself to really enjoy all of the love in your life.

28. FRIDAY. Diverse. A certain degree of satisfaction will come from finally completing a long, arduous job. Getting better organized is a requirement. If you already have a place for everything and everything in its place, you can go about your day easily and get a lot accomplished. If you are one of the messy Virgo types who can never seem to get it all together, you could be causing your own downfall due to lost papers, missed appointments, or general confusion. Get all your ducks in a row and a miraculous shift will occur. Fitness is of utmost importance at this time. If you have any destructive personal habits, start there. This is a great time to change your ways, thanks to your extra surge of willpower.

29. SATURDAY. Hectic. Your physical energy could run the gamut from quiet daydreaming to anxious enthusiasm. Complex matters may be difficult to understand. You could make mistakes even when doing usual tasks due to a certain uncaring feeling. If you have a lot to do, enlist the help of a family member or your best friend. Jobs will go much quicker and more smoothly with two or more participating. You might even find time to take a break in order to enjoy each other's company. Mistakes you made recently that let other people down should be repaired or at least explained now. You can rely on an apology or explanation being accepted.

30. SUNDAY. Pressured. Unrequited or lost love can be hard to bear in the best of times, and on this day you could feel it acutely. You are likely to have an undercurrent of worries, which for the most part are probably unfounded. Sit with pen and paper and write down all of your concerns. Then consider what would happen to you if they were true. You are likely to discover that you are wasting your time dwelling on such things. Envy or guilt does not justify unethical or dishonorable behavior, although your mind may try to convince you otherwise. A so-called hot tip or a bet placed on a long shot probably will not turn out to be to your advantage.

DECEMBER

1. MONDAY. Volatile. Keep tight control on your emotions since you are more sensitive than normal today. Loved ones, in particular, can make you feel vulnerable because they have a way of finding your weaknesses. Self-esteem issues may come up if you have gained weight or let yourself get out of shape. Not following up on a promise made a few weeks ago can give you nagging guilt along with regrets. You might feel that someone has betrayed you, withdrawn support, or otherwise turned away from you. Actually, however, it may be your own stubborn viewpoint that has caused a separation. Exert the necessary effort and you can heal the situation.

2. TUESDAY. Exciting. An exciting and perhaps even glamorous opportunity is coming your way. The window of opportunity is likely to close rather quickly, so take advantage of it right away or you could lose out. You should not have any trouble convincing a potential partner about the worth of your ideas. Do not be wishy-washy about them. Just tell it straight. A one-on-one relationship can provide the financial and emotional stability you need in order to feel secure enough to embark on a totally different path. A lighthearted romance can turn into a committed relationship very soon. An important document could arrive, signaling the end of worry for you and for a certain member of your family.

3. WEDNESDAY. Spirited. Take an honest, critical look at your finances. Talk to a banker, investment counselor, or friend if you do not feel certain about how much you are saving toward your eventual retirement. If insurance is one area that is a mystery to you, change that by talking to an agent. You might benefit from having property insurance whether or not you own your home. You may be able to find a better rate on your home or car policy. The differences between the quotes you get may surprise you. A compelling romantic attraction might be leading you to do things you ordinarily would not even consider. Try to keep your head on straight or you might embarrass yourself this evening.

4. THURSDAY. Favorable. An objective viewpoint is necessary so that you see some people and events clearly. An interest in the deeper meaning of life can lead you to look above and beyond what some people are telling you. Finding beauty and meaning in ordinary life can be spiritually comforting. Just being in the same room with someone who shares your beliefs is beneficial, helping you remember your faith and vows. Virgo students preparing for final exams, writing papers, or giving an oral presentation need to relax in the midst of all the hustle and bustle. Do what it takes to get passionate about your subject and you should be able to pass with flying colors.

5. FRIDAY. Fair. You might find yourself being held responsible this morning for chores or other duties that you were not counting on doing. Try to get someone to help so that you can be finished as soon as possible. If thinking of starting a romance with someone from the office, think again. This may not be the wisest thing to do; there may even be a company policy forbidding it. A party or get-together you attend this evening may be great fun, much to your surprise. Do not forget to bring the camera so you can get shots of friends and fellow workers. Be poised to meet someone who has important contacts. Do not enter into a discussion about politics or religion. Keep conversation neutral so that you do not antagonize a potential backer.

6. SATURDAY. Sensitive. It is likely that people are expecting more from you than you feel like giving. You may have made a promise recently that you now do not want to keep. Perhaps you volunteered to help someone and no longer feel like doing so. If you back out now, however, you will not only feel guilty but will be sending a message that says you are unreliable. Just get it over with. Force yourself to do something outside your normal, every-day lifestyle. If you are a bookworm, attend a professional sports game, or whatever is unusual for you. A last-minute vacation deal might be available if you get on the Internet and also check the travel section of your local newspaper.

7. SUNDAY. Demanding. A parent or other older relative may make some demands of you. If you have the right attitude, you can take it in stride. Virgos who feel respect and even awe for older people are likely to enjoy meeting with them. Consider that you are speaking to living history. Take charge of a situation that you care about but is lacking leadership. You have what it takes to accomplish a lot. A healthy dose of determination will help you overcome almost everything, and your clever wit will not hurt either. Be prepared for a competitor to notice what you are doing. Recognition that you are waiting for might take longer than you were hoping, but do not lose faith in yourself and your ideas.

8. MONDAY. Satisfactory. This is a very good day to ask for a favor. Before doing so, however, consider how the other person will benefit from helping you. Although sad but true, people will be more helpful if they think there is something in it for them. Take advantage of an opportunity to get better known by upper management. Bring to the office homebaked cookies or a holiday floral arrangement. Try to get your holiday shopping done early. Steer clear of crowded malls, however. You are more likely to find unique gifts at small boutiques and gift stores, plus you will be supporting the local economy. A store that will even wrap pur-chases for you deserves most of your business.

9. TUESDAY. Tiring. Routine tasks are apt to take more time than you want to give. You are likely to be quite resentful of anyone who is not doing their fair share. Try not to boss your co-workers around or act like the big shot in a group. A serious mood can lead you to clean closets and drawers and sweep away junk that is lying around. Invite a friend to help you go through boxes that you have not opened since you moved. You can make a dif-ference by donating clothing and other usable items to a charity thrift store, women's shelter, or children's center. Not only that, but you will then have room for all the new stuff you will be getting this month.

10. WEDNESDAY. Tricky. Unless you have done the prepara-tion and research on an important project scheduled to begin to-day, you might put a lot of effort into nothing. You cannot expect to start at the top; you must take the first step at the bottom and work your way up, just like everyone else. Of course, knowing the right people does not hurt, and you could get a chance to meet someone influential today. Do not turn down any chances to socialize. Although you may feel timid or unsure of yourself, people are not likely to notice. Keep conversational topics neutral, and do not pretend to be an authority on anything, even if you actually are. Just listen to other people and seem to agree with them.

11. THURSDAY. Disconcerting. An unexpected phone call can be somewhat disconcerting, but in the end you will see how perfect the situation really can be. A friend could make good on a promise from months ago, thereby saving the friendship from resentment and guilt. Conversation about the realities of life can lead you to some negative thoughts based on your childhood, but talking them out can be very beneficial. Being around a group can seem like therapy even if that is not the intention. The world is unlikely to come to an end if you do not make your bed or wash dishes for a day or two. Romantic love promises intensity, meaning, and a fantasy world of great happiness.

12. FRIDAY. Difficult. You could be too sensitive both physically and emotionally. An inconsiderate colleague can get on your nerves. It is sometimes hard to tell what might be on a person's mind, so try not to take negative comments the wrong way. A loved one may say one thing and do another, or keep you in the dark about important matters. You need to be gentle if you want to get to the heart of a problem. Pry too deeply and you may be viewed as a real threat. Just back off and do your own thing. If developing a runny nose or a cough, take the usual precautionary measures by making sure you get extra rest and plenty of vitamins. Frequently washing your hands can ward off a cold or the flu.

13. SATURDAY. Challenging. Communicating in a clear manner requires absolute concentration. Your own mental state may be quite abstract, leading you to think that other people can read your mind, which of course they cannot do. Organize your thinking, and write out your thoughts if necessary. You probably will not feel like going out, but attending a party or other get-together could turn out to be real fun. Just be careful that you do not overindulge in food or alcohol. You may feel sorry for the host and volunteer for cleanup duty. A member of the opposite sex who has been extra friendly may have ulterior motives. Put a stop to the flirting right away if your feelings are not along the same lines.

14. SUNDAY. Positive. A difficult situation with your mate or partner is about to undergo a positive change. Be the one to make the first moves toward resolving the situation. A friend you broke away from over a year ago may phone. Although you may dread returning the call, you will probably find it is not as hard as you thought it might be. You may even resume the relationship right where you left off, probably not even needing to discuss the reasons for your alienation. Virgo parents might want to offer advice to married kids, but you might be better off staying out of it. You could interfere and wind up wishing you had never done so.

15. MONDAY. Beneficial. Your intuition is very strong. If you feel you know about something or somebody, it is probably accurate. Pay close attention to the voices in your head and the feelings in your body. Learn to recognize when your body reacts to people and situations that are not boding well for you. A headache could be warning you to get away from a certain person or situation. Cultivate this ability and you will find it very beneficial. Personal matters and unfinished business from a long time ago can be resolved and put to rest now, to your great relief. This will lighten your spirit and give you added self-assurance. Try to have more faith in your own abilities.

16. TUESDAY. Diverse. Inspire yourself, if necessary, to start taking care of your holiday duties. You may have to take on extra hours or duties at work, in which case you need to prepare yourself by getting better organized. Attend to personal grooming matters while you still have time. Get a haircut or coloring now, so it has time to grow in and look natural before photos are taken with all of your relatives. Take care of all the laundry and put it away neatly so you have plenty of clothing choices available in these busy times. It can be very easy to procrastinate during the next few days, but if you do so you will just cause stress for yourself and for those around you who are depending on you.

17. WEDNESDAY. Complicated. If currently involved in negotiations of some kind, do not settle for less than you know you deserve. Keep a poker face. You could get a bit impatient about your desires, but this will only put your opponents at an advantage. Compassion for the suffering in the world can well up in you at this most commercial time of the year. All the same, it can be hard to part with money you know should be donated to charity. If you cannot loosen up your purse strings for those less fortunate than you, or if there is not any extra cash to go around, then volunteer your time. A food bank or homeless shelter will welcome an extra pair of willing hands.

18. THURSDAY. Mixed. With money on your mind at this time, making a budget can be a great help. Before you see how much you can actually spend, however, get a realistic picture of what your living and entertainment expenses are going to be over the next month. You might be surprised to discover that you forgot about a yearly insurance bill or some other drain on your finances. Shopping for gifts or clothing can be a good idea today, when your taste is likely to be exquisite and you are also extra thrifty. If anyone can unearth incredible bargains, it will be you. Make sure your purchases are returnable, however. Clearance items that are sold as-is should be very carefully examined.

19. FRIDAY. Troublesome. A run of bad luck may seem to have come your way. Some matters are taking longer than usual to work out, and you may feel you have made some bad decisions. Do not be too hard on yourself, however. Communications in any shape or form can be delayed or confused, not due to any fault of yours. Letters can be lost, phone messages not received, and instructions misconstrued. Computers, cars, and electronic equipment are likely to break down. Because this trend continues through the end of the year, be sure to follow up on critical business and personal activities. Check the return policy before purchasing anything for yourself or as a gift.

20. SATURDAY. Satisfying. Although an aura of strange energy surrounds communications at this time, at least you are more likely to finish up projects already started rather than beginning any new ones. Set important business aside until after the New Year, if you can. Now you need to start winding down, at least mentally. This can be a wonderful weekend to talk to old friends and relatives who do not live nearby. Spending most of the day on the telephone is not a bad idea. A warm feeling will fill your heart as you catch up on the latest news, and you wonder why you do not call more often. You may realize how much you miss a relative who moved out of town.

21. SUNDAY. Harmonious. A local news story is likely to bring together the whole community working for a common purpose. Although it may involve unfortunate circumstances, you will enjoy the fact that everyone is connected. Whether or not you regularly participate as a volunteer, you will feel connected to the group and proud to be a member of it. Avoid driving too much at this time, especially during rush hour when there are likely to be a lot of stressed-out drivers on the roads. Road conditions also make driving hazardous. Public transportation offers a good alternative. Keep the home fires burning. Arrange some time alone with your mate or partner, away from kids, pets, relatives, and neighbors.

22. MONDAY. Frustrating. Minor irritations caused by the people you live with can seem worse than they actually are. The usual annoyances you put up with may be magnified. Although you are tired of it, do not jump all over someone for the same behavior that usually does not evoke comment from you. An intense relationship with a parent or dependent child can seem overwhelming, but if you can relax everything will be okay. You are soaking up the stress of other people at this time, taking it on as your own. Hiding a secret from a loved one could be very difficult. Everyone will be suspicious, so do not even offer a little hint about a special gift or outing.

23. TUESDAY. Helpful. Amidst all the hustle and bustle of the day, try to find time to participate in activities that bring you joy. You may derive special pleasure from a creative hobby, perhaps even making a few last-minute gifts or doing some holiday baking. Virgos with young children at home do not have to take time out to play with them, but try to do things together that you would be doing anyway. Allow them to help. You cook, clean, or wrap gifts. You can get real joy out of some of the cute things kids say, so get them talking. You will enjoy chatting with whoever is nearby. Tonight orchestrate some quiet time for you and your sweetheart. Just holding hands and listening to favorite music sets the mood for the rest of the month.

24. WEDNESDAY. Varied. Virgos who work in retail should prepare for the rush. Treat each customer as a special individual who you are glad to help. You may feel like playing rather than working, but do not let that ruin your attitude. Keep a smile on your face and people will smile back at you. Although you may be rushing around constantly taking care of last-minute details, do not forget to stop for some fruitcake. With any luck you should be able to get together with friends and family members this evening, sharing a meal and some pleasant reminiscing. Do not worry over the details; as a Virgo you have a way of making a get-together absolutely perfect. Enjoy a relative's sarcastic sense of humor but do not try to match wits.

25. THURSDAY. Merry Christmas! This is one of those days when everything is perfect. You will have plenty of energy and enthusiasm. Include any friends or neighbors who are alone on this day, and even their friends. Everyone is certain to have a wonderful time. Make sure you get some of the good times on videotape. All of your personal relationships, and especially romance, should go extremely well. Hopefully you can get a few minutes away from the rest of the guests to be alone with your mate or partner. Spend the evening playing board games or cards. Children will be especially pleased to have you help put together a new toy or read a new book.

26. FRIDAY. Unpredictable. A day of rest is in order for most people, but probably not for you. You will either be on top of everything, cleaning up after all the festivities, or will be feeling overwhelmed by the mess. Try to find a happy medium. If parents or in-laws are visiting from out of own, you could be ready for them to leave. Watch what you say and how you act. Bad vibes will be felt, almost as if they could read your mind. Do not even think anything negative when you are around them or you may never hear the end of it. Dealing with a pet could be a challenge at this time; you may have to make an emergency visit to the vet or give a bath to an unhappy animal. Tempting though it may be, do not gorge yourself on leftovers.

27. SATURDAY. Interesting. Your relationship with your mate or steady date may not be going exactly as you would like, but you can make it better if you follow your heart. Consider whether you trust your intuition enough to follow it blindly. If so, you could reach a higher level of trust as a mutual partnership. Virgo singles who are making wedding plans can enlist the help of a friend to shoulder some of the burden of all the details. You might find that you have more in common with a business associate than you thought at first, leading to a new friendship developing. It might seem that your world is consumed with concerns about people. Teammates can be as demanding as any boss.

28. SUNDAY. Eventful. Be flexible so that you are available for whatever comes up. You will enjoy stepping out at the last minute and can adapt well to whatever situation or environment you find yourself in. Your mate or partner may take you on a mini-adventure, or you may be traveling to a faraway destination. Whether you are leaving for a few days or a few weeks, you will find warm people and wonderful hospitality once you arrive. If a quiet day at home is the only activity on your agenda, you will enjoy the camaraderie of a good friend or loved one. A reconciliation is in the works, or at least you should be giving it some thought.

29. MONDAY. Complicated. The next couple of days could be challenging, as you seem to take two steps forward and one step back. You are apt to be disappointed when a friend backs out of an offer to help you with a project that is important to you. Your mate or partner may not give you the support you want either, due to being busy with other things. You could be caught in a jealous triangle and see no way out. A few angry words may be exchanged before you are able to get out or get over this one. In the future avoid letting some people know about your personal life because they always come back to haunt you. Lingering doubt between couples can make for an exciting evening.

30. TUESDAY. Rewarding. If you are able to focus your energy you can make some meaningful progress. You are a force to be reckoned with in business matters and negotiations. Be tough; you are up against some staunch opposition. A family member or close friend could ask you to loan money or a favored possession. If you do so, make sure you first have an understanding that both of you comprehend and agree to. Write down all the details; do not just make a verbal agreement. If this situation involves a teenager or young adult, show that you mean business; this is a great opportunity to teach some important values. Include a reasonable payment plan, and ask for collateral if you will be loaning a large sum.

31. WEDNESDAY. Pleasant. Spending time with friends and acquaintances can be pleasant, but you might wonder if they are really all that you want for your life. If you do not think so, you will feel better not making such a big effort to please them. Clear this up and you will have more time to spend with the people who really count in your life. You could mix business and pleasure this evening by going out with a group of clients or co-workers. You might be in for a surprise when a friend admits a secret attraction to you. Of course, this is more likely to happen if alcohol is flowing freely. Staying home tonight and just thinking about your future plans might be a better option if you are currently far from your loved one.

VIRGO
NOVEMBER–DECEMBER 2002

November 2002

1. FRIDAY. Tense. Today you will want to do what you want, but other people will be trying to dissuade you or actually stop you. As a result you could end up in some serious conflict. The most likely sources of opposition will be a superior at work who has been giving you some difficulty recently as well as from family members with whom you often do not see eye to eye. You are going through some displacement and dislocation in regard to your home these days, and the current sense of disharmony will not help. You have to deal with any roadblocks put up by other people by stating your case patiently, clearly, and forcefully.

2. SATURDAY. Sensitive. There is increased potential for conflict regarding money matters. You could be envisioning a clear course ahead for improving your financial situation. However, there are some impediments in the way that will make you impatient to push them aside. Do not become too preoccupied with fighting your way through problems; most of them will sort themselves out soon enough. You may find some refuge in spiritual goals and aspirations. These provide a way of raising your head above the clouds and seeing everything in broader perspective. Focus on long-term plans that will help you achieve your special goals. Your current love is giving you a secure base for the future.

3. SUNDAY. Favorable. You should find it easy to tie together many different strands. The focus of your attention may still be on money. However, other facets of your life will also be involved, especially family, work, and even spirituality. Particularly striking about the current situation is that the forces in your favor are very powerful. You should have the sense that people in the background of your affairs are working to help release you from obstacles you have encountered. You will probably have a strong sense that someone in a position of authority is not only being helpful in general but takes a personal interest in you. Do not let childish skepticism cloud your vision.

4. MONDAY. Happy. You will probably find that close family members are very much on your mind. There could be some important matters between you that need to be sorted out. Your contact is likely to be intense and mostly agreeable. You will be reminded of just how much you have in common. If you do not live near any relatives, at least make some effort to get in touch by phone, letter, or e-mail. Today is an excellent opportunity for putting your relationships on solid new ground. Do not let old baggage get in the way of a reconciliation if that is what you want. Forgiveness is the healer. Work will be more interesting if you take a creative approach.

5. TUESDAY. Deceptive. Deception, deceit, and illusion play a strong role today. This is especially true of any messages, phone calls, or letters you receive. Greet anything that comes your way with a large dose of healthy skepticism. It may also be that you were far too gullible in a business matter early in the year and the harsh truth is only now coming to light. This is not a good day to enter into any business contract or other commitments. Whatever you arrange will probably have to be renegotiated at some later point, or will simply fall apart. Wait and see what new developments arise before signing anything. Look around the house for a bill you have forgotten to pay.

6. WEDNESDAY. Inspiring. You will probably feel the urge to do something unusual and refreshing. You might have noticed that there has been something missing in your life. This could be in connection with your home. There may be some small tasks around the house that have been nagging at you for some time. Do them today without fail. This is a good time to give away or throw away some old junk that you have been meaning to get rid of, to weed the garden, or simply straighten up a little. If you are in a more ambitious frame of mind, consider adding some striking new decorative touches. Your intuition about what to do is working well. Put your creativity into improving your surroundings.

7. THURSDAY. Manageable. Continue to focus your attention on the home front. Issues of personal control could come to the fore. You may have some conflict with a person you live with, or a neighbor may not be very cooperative. This could create some anxiety and fear on your part. Fortunately you have the resources to deal successfully with the situation. The key is a clever mix of aggressiveness and kindness. You might have to play good cop-bad cop all on your own. You will also find a touch of the unusual and unorthodox helpful. This offers a good opportunity to develop your versatility and flexibility without too much worry.

8. FRIDAY. Pressured. Early in the day you may be weighed down with burdens and chores. It may seem you do not have enough time to accomplish everything that is on your schedule at the moment. The best way to tackle this is by doing one thing at a time. Do not let the pressure of everything else that awaits you throw you off. Fortunately you can accomplish your tasks in less time than you thought. By evening the mood will lighten considerably. You can then set aside concerns and have some fun. Artistic entertainment could be particularly rewarding, such as a play or a concert. Opt for the best seats available.

9. SATURDAY. Suspenseful. Today you are facing a major issue that involves getting to the truth of a situation as opposed to pretending everything is all right and letting it slide. It may not be all that easy to figure out what to do. You have the right to know what is going on in this situation. It may involve a brother or sister. On the other hand, your desire to get to the bottom of things could have the unintended effect of making the situation worse. If you feel you must know the truth, act like a detective: gather your evidence on the sly and do not necessarily broadcast what you have discovered. If the truth is unpleasant, remember that to understand all is to forgive all.

10. SUNDAY. Diverse. You should be unusually sharp today. You can turn this to your advantage if you know where to look. The key is balancing a large range of options and being willing as well as able to take some major risks. You will have to put a large amount of effort into your decision making. The main obstacle in your way is your dreaminess that makes you less concerned with ordinary reality. If you feel somewhat indifferent about a situation, it is probably a sign that there are some hidden drawbacks that you recognize but have not consciously admitted to yourself. You may need some extra time to sort out what is really going on and what you intend to do about it.

11. MONDAY. Lively. The day will have an unusually rapid pace. There may be some financial opportunity that you have been hesitant about investing in. You may have been going back and forth about it, but today you can come to a rapid decision. It might seem impulsive, but examine it closely and you will recognize a situation that has been on your mind. All of your thoughts, anxieties, and worries about this prospect have gone into making today's decision. Your supposedly impulsive move now is just the answer stemming from this process. You should have confidence in what you decide. Act and do not look back.

12. TUESDAY. Reassuring. Early in the day you could receive some welcome and unexpected news about a health matter. A doctor could be reassuring and also give you some good advice. You will probably sense that a large load has been taken off your mind. Later in the day you may want to spend some extra time with your mate or partner. A little flurry of romance is sure to be pleasant. You can go to elaborate lengths, making plans to go out for a nice dinner, bringing flowers or adding some welcome touch around the house, but it may not be necessary. Just do something, however small, to make sure that special person in your life knows how much you care even though you do not always show it.

13. WEDNESDAY. Quiet. Not a lot out of the ordinary is likely to happen. You are sure to welcome the quiet. You may even have some extra time to yourself. Give a little thought to what you really want to do. You may want to use your spare hours to solidify a relationship that is growing more and more important to you. If so, give the other person a call and arrange to get together. It can be difficult to get to know someone well when both of you are rushing around in the frantic pace of modern life. If some of the bustle subsides for a brief time now, you have a superb chance for genuine human contact. If someone calls you out of the blue, consider the possibility that it may be important.

14. THURSDAY. Stimulating. Your perceptions and reasoning are unusually sharp. No sooner will you be confronted with a situation than you will immediately be able to form a very clear and generally accurate picture of what is going on. You should be able to take advantage of this insight in a different way than usual. Sensory impressions can be food for the soul; test the truth of this by exposing yourself to some new impressions. Go someplace that is fresh for you, such as a neighborhood park you have not visited in a while. Just walk around and keep your eyes wide open to all that is around you. The effect this has on you may be a very pleasant surprise.

15. FRIDAY. Mixed. Do not become too concerned if your partnership in life or in business seems a bit oppressive early in the day. You will probably discover that you have some forgotten or overlooked obligations to another person that are not as easy to discharge as you would hope. Just take your time and be patient. You can get through everything if you go at a steady pace. Later in the day things should ease up a bit. You will probably be in the mood for some entertainment by the time evening comes. A movie may be the answer if you can find one that is both entertaining and inspiring. This will seem like the perfect way to end the workweek and get in relax mode for the weekend ahead.

16. SATURDAY. Unsettling. It will be harder than usual to keep your life on an even keel. You may encounter a family member who insists on having his or her own way and seems willing to be deceitful. Do not allow yourself to be emotionally blackmailed. Nor should you imagine that you can simply talk with this person and set things straight. You may have to loosen the reins, possibly even pretending that you do not see all that is going on. You have to strike a balance between allowing someone to run a little wild and maintaining a straight-and-narrow path. There is also the possibility that this situation is none of your business. If so, you can wash your hands of it and turn away with a clear conscience.

17. SUNDAY. Discomforting. You may have some serious questions about life for which you have never found any good answers. You might think about long-term goals and realize you do not have much of an idea of what you really hope to achieve. Under most circumstances you might take this as the normal course of events, but today you could find it strangely irritating. You may feel that you have the right to a plan. The fact that you do not have one may seem to be someone else's fault. Rather than focusing on blame, you may find it helpful to open yourself to all sorts of possibilities. This may not be comfortable, and it may not even seem to make sense. However, it is a way to find answers that will serve you well for a long time.

18. MONDAY. Confusing. You may have to deal with a small legal matter that leaves you confused. It will probably be something simple such as a summons to jury duty or a communication from a lawyer about some past item of business. It will probably not seem entirely clear at first. You may even wonder if there is a deliberate attempt at confusing you. This does not really matter, because either way you will have to figure out what is going on. If you have to deal with a bureaucrat, you may find it hard to make yourself understood or to understand what is being said to you. Keep asking questions until you have no more doubts.

19. TUESDAY. Uneasy. Expect some disturbance or unrest. A legal issue that upset you yesterday may continue to be vexing, but do not trouble yourself too much about it. In all likelihood the situation will sort itself out in a few days. In the meantime you need to employ some especially skillful tactics to negotiate present circumstances. There is someone who can help you, but this person is temporarily unavailable. If you are tempted to try to solve the situation in a clever but unorthodox manner, be warned that it will probably have to be taken care of more than once. You can deal with the issue, which is not as big as it may seem right now. However, it will test your patience and good humor while you are in the process.

20. WEDNESDAY. Disconcerting. There is likely to be a strange buzz in the atmosphere. You may notice that you have more energy than usual, and as a result could be somewhat restless and ill at ease. Do not become too anxious; it will pass soon enough. Later in the day focus your attention on your long-term ambitions. You will not be able to advance them just by being quick-witted at the present. If you try this approach, you will probably only hit upon obvious schemes that have little chance of succeeding with the situation. An intuitive approach is more favorable. You may even have a dream tonight that puts some unexpected light on the matter. Be open to new possibilities.

21. THURSDAY. Fair. A long-standing issue involving career matters and family concerns is likely to reappear. You may have the sense that loved ones are trying to control or manipulate you, but this is not necessarily true. They may have some legitimate needs and concerns that they do not think you care about very much. If you turn to a mentor for advice, you may get some valuable insights. Romance could pick up its pace once again. Your love life may not have progressed very much in recent weeks. You may even have given up hope regarding a particular relationship, but do not stop hoping quite yet. Instead, pick up the phone and call the person you are thinking about with such affection.

22. FRIDAY. Constructive. This is one of those days when you have a strong sense of responsibility and personal integrity. You have a number of important duties to carry out. Even if you are apprehensive about some or all of them, you will discover that you can perform them perfectly. You can even get into the swing of work so that you are dealing effectively with a number of different duties all at once. This should be both productive and enjoyable. Evening hours favor socializing. You may want to call up some friends and get together with them. If you can combine friends with romance, so much the better. Your mate or partner will enjoy your social crowd as much as you do.

23. SATURDAY. Profitable. You may be focusing on money matters. This is not necessarily a matter of fear or anxiety; you might just be feeling the urge to earn a substantial sum for a change. Your enterprise and creativity can really pay off now. One option is to introduce some innovations at your workplace. There should be considerable willingness to try a novel approach right now. In fact, you may have trouble keeping up with all the changes that are taking place. If you can navigate these rapid twists and turns, you stand to benefit. It is probably time to upgrade the company's computer system or your own, or to learn a new program for tracking money or job progress.

24. SUNDAY. Unpredictable. It is impossible to say exactly what might happen right now. The most likely eventuality is that your rational mind and the dreamy, mystical side of your nature will be in great harmony. This may be a good time to start a dream journal or simply write down some of the most striking thoughts that have been occurring to you. You do not need to show this to anybody, and you do not need to follow any rigid rules about when and how much you write. Just keep it handy, and write when you are moved to do so. This can be a valuable record to refer to in the future. Another advantage is that it will encourage you to clarify what may be only vague ideas. Just writing them down can help you see additional possibilities.

25. MONDAY. Slow. You will not be in a very outgoing mood. Romance is not likely to go especially well. Your mate or partner may want to do something active and outgoing, such as shopping or taking a drive. This probably will not appeal to you. Do not feel obliged to go along for the other person's sake. You will benefit most if you adopt an attitude of enlightened selfishness, doing what you feel is best for you without causing any difficulties for anyone else. This can be tricky if someone insists that you are necessary to fulfill a plan. However, as a Virgo you know perfectly well how to get out of situations you want to avoid. Make up an excuse if what you really want is to be left alone.

26. TUESDAY. Rewarding. Today favors any act of generosity you are moved to make. You will find it most rewarding if you do it in secret, and that will be best for the recipient, too. Even if you give to an organization, consider making it an anonymous donation. Also be aware that charity often begins at home. There is someone in your family who could really use some support and assistance right now. Be as open-handed as possible. There is a slight chance that you will be dissuaded from your charitable impulses by a fear that people may think you are being a show-off. This feeling is not justified; in fact, it is irrational. Do what you think is appropriate and do not be concerned about the opinions of other people.

27. WEDNESDAY. Fruitful. Some important issue involving your self-discipline, probably in the area of finance, is coming to a head. You have the chance to resolve it favorably, but first you need to clearly understand why you must discipline yourself. You also need to understand what is realistic in the circumstances. You might have to put yourself on a tight budget. However, if it is too tight you probably will not stick to it for more than a few days. What you need is not to limit your expenses but to increase your income. You have some wonderful opportunities waiting for you if you check the help-wanted ads not only in the newspaper but on the Internet.

28. THURSDAY. Erratic. You may find yourself acting head-strong. You will not be inclined to stay home. Your place of residence may seem more like a prison than a refuge. If you want to venture out into the wide world, go ahead. However, if some domestic duties that you have to fulfill are nagging at you, do your best to take care of them before leaving. If you are unable to do so, make the conscious effort to set them aside for the duration of your expedition, not thinking about them till you come home and actually have to handle them. Family members may not support what you want to do. You may need to reassure them that you still care and will not be gone very long.

29. FRIDAY. Good. Early in the day focus on a few tasks you do not like doing. You may also have to turn your attention back to the financial picture, which will probably not be enjoyable. You may also have to slog through a load of paperwork in order to sort out bills, payments, and expenses that you thought you had already dealt with. You can get it all done by the time the evening comes. Then you may be in the mood for nothing more than a quiet evening relaxing at home. By all means indulge yourself. Play a favorite game with your family or rent a video that everyone will enjoy. The present circumstances foster a sense of togetherness that makes you appreciate loved ones all the more.

30. SATURDAY. Eventful. It may be time for a family discussion not only with your immediate relatives but also with your extended family. Together you will be able to decide what to do about a major problem involving the health of an elderly relative, common property, or how to resolve a feud that has been going on for too long. The situation could bring up an unusual confession or revelation. Even if nothing really surprises you, people will be revealing their true feelings whether they are aware of it or not. You will know your relatives much better after this takes place. Whether you will still love them is really up to you. It takes a bighearted person to forgive some act of the past that caused embarrassment, heartache, or loss.

December 2002

1. SUNDAY. Excellent. Today is a great time to enjoy yourself at home, with friends and family. Your dealings with loved ones, family members, and just about everyone should be harmonious. Past roadblocks to understanding should be gone, making all forms of communication favored. Try picking up the phone and calling someone you have not spoken to for a while, especially a sister or brother. This is a good day for a trip to visit a museum or to go shopping for a surprise gift for a loved one. A visit with older relatives may well be in the planning stage. You will have energy to accomplish a lot. Some of your relationships may have an unexpectedly beneficial effect on your work.

2. MONDAY. Demanding. After a wonderful weekend, your workplace may feel tense. Poor communications can lead to further misunderstandings rather than straightening them out. Superiors may be making unreasonable demands based on a faulty grasp of your current workload. Be careful about making promises that may not be fulfilled. Do not trust any gossip you may hear around work, or at home for that matter. Someone may give you unrealistic advice about a health concern. Be sure to verify anything you are told before attempting to put it into practice. Someone's generosity toward you may have a hidden objective. Guard against going in anyone's debt.

3. TUESDAY. Frustrating. You may feel stymied at every turn by unexpected events or responses, especially at work. Plans for business or for a short personal trip may be blocked or delayed. Communications with your own siblings and children could be confusing. There continues to be a trend toward unconventional changes at work. In addition, you may experience unusual shifts in your overall health. Do not get too excited by the unexpected today. Try to keep your balance, roll with the punches, and see where it all ends up. Double-check any arrangements or contracts signed recently. Do not be too surprised if they need to be modified quite soon. Avoid being seen with someone who is acting outrageously, even if they have not been drinking.

4. WEDNESDAY. Positive. Today offers an excellent opportunity to begin new projects and get a fresh start. This is especially important on the home front, where needed changes can finally be made. This can range from a simple housecleaning to an overhaul of the whole place. It is also a great day to call family members in order to reminisce or plan a get-together. You could be inspired to take care of a certain situation that has remained a stumbling block to your relationship for a long time. This will be beneficial to all involved. At the workplace you may come up with refreshing new ideas that are of real benefit. Now is the time to present them to those with the power to make decisions.

5. THURSDAY. Favorable. Conditions favor having a heart-to-heart talk with loved ones, or even just discussing day-to-day activities and plans for a holiday trip. If you do not have a romantic partner, the chances are good of meeting someone interesting through casual conversation or on a short jaunt. Relationships between men and women in general should flow smoothly. Home life is favored. You may want to investigate an unusual new diet to try at home. Career worries could put a damper on your day, but an idea such as working at home may offer an unexpected solution to your basic concerns.

6. FRIDAY. Sensitive. Today may be a bit unfulfilling romantically. While your thoughts may turn to fun and pleasure, the reality is that you have a lot of responsibilities. You may feel a pull between your home responsibilities and wanting to pay attention to home matters, such as getting ready for the holidays, sending out cards and gifts, or planning a get-together. Buckling down and taking care of business should be your priority despite your wishes. File away plans for celebration and recreation and keep your attention focused on work. You will have time during the weekend to be sociable.

7. SATURDAY. Enjoyable. With the weekend here, you will find this a low-key time to prepare for the rest of the month. It is a good day to spend time with children and to enjoy yourself with leisure activities or entertainment, especially during the daytime hours. Your thoughts may turn to health concerns, work, or how to be of service to other people. Investigate various volunteer opportunities available during the holiday season and beyond. Or think about how you could help your community in the coming months. All in all, this is a day without too much disruption, so make plans and begin to implement them.

8. SUNDAY. Variable. While this Sunday should be fairly quiet, be alert for any misunderstanding or conflict with loved ones. Relationships with the opposite sex could be confusing. You may have difficulty explaining exactly what you mean, even though it may be quite clear to you. You may feel an urge to retreat into daydreams and fantasies. You may also decide that it is time to volunteer some of your time or resources to people who are less fortunate. Communicating with children is favored. You are sure to take renewed delight in their company. This is a starred time to attend a matinee performance.

9. MONDAY. Challenging. Today you may be challenged both at home and at work. Things happening behind the scenes will have a major impact on you at your workplace. They will continue to remain hidden while still exerting an influence in surprising ways. Your home life and family are in the midst of quite a major shift. Although it probably seems somewhat unsettling and even frightening, you will find that the changes being made are necessary and beneficial in the long run. Be supportive and reassuring in your contacts with other family members. The strains and challenges on the job will be resolved as new ideas are instituted.

10. TUESDAY. Successful. Communication improves today and the big picture brightens both at home and at work. Your thoughts may revolve around partnerships, both business and romantic. This is an excellent time to communicate your thoughts and feelings to important people in your life. You may receive unexpected support at home from a distant or hidden source, even from someone in as unusual a situation as a convent or prison. Something valuable to you that was lost, whether a treasured keepsake or an inherited piece of jewelry, may show up today, much to your relief. Short trips are favored. Calling a sibling or a new acquaintance is likely to result in a friendly and uplifting conversation.

11. WEDNESDAY. Tricky. You may be distracted by concerns about changes taking place within your family. There could be a power struggle at home as everyone in your household reacts to changes. Partnerships, whether romantic or business, can be very tricky, so it is best not to rock the boat too much. Instead, try to keep your focus on what is best for other people. Actively pursue the fine art of compromise, which is often the best way to ensure that all turns out well. Be on guard against impulsive actions based on emotional reactions. These are likely to have less than agreeable consequences, especially with loved ones at home.

12. THURSDAY. Pressured. You may feel that your actions on the job are being blocked at every turn. Frustration can quickly set in. Pressing deadlines, last-minute changes, and an increased workload could add to your stress. Try to keep a balanced outlook and not let work demands overwhelm you. Eventually the pressure will ease off and you will be grateful you did not lose your cool. Teamwork and all cooperative efforts will be helpful. However, take care not to associate with dubious people or organizations who may have counterproductive goals. Your hard work will eventually bring you increased public recognition and respect if you persist in sticking to your principles.

13. FRIDAY. Fair. Even though it is Friday the 13th, the day is not totally unlucky. You may find it difficult communicating with other people at this point. However, you are apt to be filled with inspirational thoughts and ideas for helping others. You may even be able to turn these ideas into concrete steps that will help provide money or other basic necessities for the needy. Misunderstandings with children are foreseen. Your evening plans for fun and relaxation could end up being interrupted or changed as a result. It may be best to plan a quiet evening at home tonight, resting up for the hectic social weekend ahead.

14. SATURDAY. Eventful. With so much going on, you may find your head spinning at times. The day is likely to be very busy as you prepare for the coming holidays. Unexpected help could come from surprising sources. Your home life will be dynamic and energized by all the activity. Communication is emphasized. You will probably be in contact with family members, acquaintances, even neighbors. This is a good day for getting together with them. Just be cautious about overspending; you can all too easily be swept away by inspiration while shopping, so that you make inappropriate purchases. Do not be lured by glitter and gold. Be sure to check the guarantee on all purchases.

15. SUNDAY. Lively. Your thoughts may be on distant places and people, but you will find plenty of distractions at home as you juggle multiple priorities and concerns. Although communications should flow well with friends and family, you may become frustrated because you are unable to see certain situations clearly. Be sure to take a deep breath and relax when things begin to feel overwhelming. This is a good day to take some time to spend with children or to do something that brings you personal enjoyment. An outing to the theater or a walk in the park could be ideal. Finding time to relax may also ease any tension that might emerge in your romantic partnership.

16. MONDAY. Rewarding. Your efforts at work are likely to pay off in unexpected ways. Public recognition of your contributions could result from the focus and discipline you have brought to the workplace. Do not be surprised by this well-deserved attention, but be cautious about being too self-congratulatory. Any ungracious behavior on your part will reflect badly on you and negatively on your public image. Today you may find it difficult to contact people far away for reasons that are not immediately clear. However, someone from your past may unexpectedly appear in person or on the phone. This is a day to practice tact and diplomacy in all your endeavors.

17. TUESDAY. Mixed. With all the mixed signals in the air, you may be wondering which end is up. Tension between your responsibilities at home and on the job will pull you in totally different directions. Fortunately, an inventive co-worker may help you come up with a novel solution to ease your concerns. Unpredictable or unconventional insights into your job may help advance your career, but take care not to become too wrapped up in the changes going on right now in your workplace. Do not forget to consider what is most important to you personally. An unexpected health concern could crop up, especially one related to diet and nutrition. Eat sensibly, and do not skip any meal.

18. WEDNESDAY. Auspicious. This is a starred day to make your dreams come true in your professional life. You have the vision to achieve greater public recognition and overall appreciation. Take care, however, to balance your Virgo idealism with concrete, down-to-earth plans and goals. In general you will find much inspiration in your work. On the home front, needed changes will be positively influenced by unexpected sources. There is an abundance of surprises in store as the end of the year draws near. A necessary transformation is likely to create new opportunities for you and your loved ones, although it may not be immediately clear how, when, where, or even why.

19. THURSDAY. Changeable. The ups and downs of the holiday season may affect you a great deal today. Be sure not to overtax yourself with busy preparations either at home or when you are out and about. Energy and emotions are running high at this point. You may find yourself pulled between your public and private responsibilities. This is a good day to make some last-minute secret purchases for loved ones, but be careful not to spend too much. Your recent work has garnered you much respect at your workplace, and this may have unexpected benefits in the new year.

20. FRIDAY. Buoyant. You are likely to be full of energy and enthusiasm. There is little to stand in your way or block your progress at this time. Once you make up your mind, you can accomplish a great deal. Interactions with friends and family members will give you much satisfaction. This is also a good day to spend some time with friends or with a social group or organization to which you belong. Neighbors and siblings are featured as well. Your relationships with them should prove harmonious as long as there is no serious disagreement brewing among them. A short trip could bring you much pleasure at this time; communications with your loved ones and family visits are favored.

21. SATURDAY. Stimulating. Today offers an opportunity to enjoy yourself with friends and family members. If the weather cooperates, outdoor activity could be enjoyably invigorating. A day trip into the countryside or in a city park will provide a refreshing change of scenery and an opportunity to spend time with people you do not see very often. You may well meet new friends as well. There could be some tension in your communications, especially if children are involved or are the subject. If you can keep the focus on the joy and pleasure of companionship, all should be well. Taking time to write or phone friends or loved ones will brighten your day and theirs.

22. SUNDAY. Uncertain. Turn your thoughts toward people who are less fortunate than you. You may dream of ways in which you can be of service to the needy. However, do not allow these concerns to bring you guilt or self-doubt. It is best to act on your generous impulses with simple, practical actions such as contributing to a canned-food drive or to a toy collection campaign. Indecision may trouble you, but try to move past old habits and approaches that are no longer useful to you. This is a good day to focus on celebrating and enjoying life with your loved ones, especially children in the family circle.

23. MONDAY. Good. As the year draws nearer its close, you may find your attention turning to finishing up old business, completing minor matters, and discarding papers and projects that are no longer useful or of interest to you. This is a good day to focus on such tasks and to clear the clutter in order to make way for positive new influences in your life. You may want to begin to formulate your own private goals and plans for the New Year, but keep these to yourself for the time being. Communications with the opposite sex may not flow well today, especially with a romantic partner or a potential date. Misunderstandings in everyday matters are possible, so be forgiving and understanding.

24. TUESDAY. Pleasurable. While unexpected news regarding your professional life could cause some disruption today, keep your focus on celebrating with family and friends. You may feel as if you have returned to center stage in your life. People will recognize you as a vibrant, important part of any social event. You will be at ease socially and will find other guests cooperative and friendly. Try to let work concerns take a backseat for a while so that you can totally enjoy yourself. Recreation and romance are favored. You may be inspired to put your creative talents and artistic abilities to use at home or even in the workplace. Do not let worries about your health or diet distract you.

25. WEDNESDAY. Merry Christmas! Today is a wonderful opportunity for you to relax and enjoy the company of other people. You may well be in the spotlight as family members and friends appreciate your unique Virgo qualities. Your physical energy should be high. This is a wonderful day to call absent friends and loved ones to wish them the happiest of holidays. Keep your cool if any conflict appears at home. It is best to smooth ruffled feathers, ensuring that the stresses that accompany any holiday do not cause too much disruption. An unexpected phone call or visit from someone out of your distant past may surprise you. Arrange a romantic evening as a wonderful way to end the day.

26. THURSDAY. Easy. Take it easy after the excitement and good cheer of the past few days. Spending time at home putting the house in order or going out to see a movie are favored activities today. If you have the time and the weather is suitable, spending time outdoors playing a sport or enjoying other forms of recreation is recommended. You may be inspired to try a new hobby or artistic endeavor. Your natural Virgo curiosity will draw you to learning more. Worries about work and career matters may put a damper on the evening, but try to keep your concerns balanced. There will be time enough to focus on professional matters. Go out of your way to pamper a pet.

27. FRIDAY. Fruitful. You may notice the forces working in your favor, particularly in your work life. Your finances are strongly favored. This could mean a year-end bonus or an unexpected legacy from a long-lost relative. Or it could simply mean that you have survived the holiday season with your budget still on the plus side. Changes at home could positively affect your earning ability. The biggest challenge today comes from the lure of amusements and entertainment, which are apt to distract you from your work. It will be best to avoid gambling or any other speculative venture. You are not likely to meet with success if you risk your cash or your reputation. Stick with what has worked in the past.

246 / VIRGO—DECEMBER 2002

28. SATURDAY. Deceptive. Broken promises by overly enthusiastic friends or neighbors may mar your day. It is best not to place too much trust in people who seem overconfident or extravagant, especially if they have recently reappeared from your past. Also make sure you do not repeat mistakes you made in the past. Today it is vital to avoid any sort of behind-the-scenes dealings. It may seem that other people are not playing fair, deliberately trying to conceal facts or figures. Be cautious with any new business venture. By keeping to a disciplined course of action you are likely to meet with success. Do not be tempted by what seems too good to be true; it probably is. Prove that you can let your mind rule your heart.

29. SUNDAY. Slow. Today favors lying low and recuperating from the excitement and celebrations of the past few weeks. Your thoughts may turn toward simple enjoyment. It will be pleasant to spend time with family members, especially children. Your judgment may not be too good when it comes to work and money, so postpone making any business or financial decision. Unsound propositions or unrealistic proposals may be put forward by unusual sources. Examine them closely, but do not allow yourself to make any judgments at this time. Communications are likely to be confusing and exaggerated, especially in dealing with someone at or from a distance.

30. MONDAY. Beneficial. Your ability to communicate is likely to shine. This is a favorable time to make important phone calls and write letters. Strive to keep all avenues of communication open in your business and professional life. Try not to drop any impulsive or unconventional ideas into your conversations today; they are only likely to confuse and confound other people. Drastic changes are likely to have unexpected negative results, so try to keep everything on an even keel. Focus on the exchange of beneficial information, whether with family members or co-workers. Teamwork is favored for the very best results.

31. TUESDAY. Exciting. The end of the year brings you dreams and visions of how you can best be of service in the coming year. Try to figure out ways to achieve your goals in a well-grounded manner. For example, you could decide to help deliver meals to senior citizens, coach a sports team, or lead a Scout troop. Your focus right now should be on your friends, neighbors, and family in your immediate community. New friends and contacts you recently made will prove useful in the year to come and may inspire you to become more involved with community affairs. This is a good day to focus on all your blessings at home and elsewhere, then renew your hopes and wishes for an even better future.

WHAT DOES YOUR FUTURE HOLD...?

DISCOVER IT IN *ASTROANALYSIS*—

COMPLETELY REVISED TO THE YEAR 2015, THESE GUIDES INCLUDE COLOR-CODED CHARTS FOR TOTAL ASTROLOGICAL EVALUATION, PLANET TABLES AND CUSP CHARTS, AND STREAMLINED INFORMATION FOR ANYONE WHO HAS EVER LOOKED TO THE STARS AND WONDERED....

__ARIES	0-425-17558-8/$12.95
__TAURUS	0-425-17559-6/$12.95
__GEMINI	0-425-17560-X/$12.95
__CANCER	0-425-17561-8/$12.95
__LEO	0-425-17562-6/$12.95
__VIRGO	0-425-17563-4/$12.95
__LIBRA	0-425-17564-2/$12.95
__SCORPIO	0-425-17565-0/$12.95
__SAGITTARIUS	0-425-17566-9/$12.95
__CAPRICORN	0-425-17567-7/$12.95
__AQUARIUS	0-425-17568-5/$12.95
__PISCES	0-425-17569-3/$12.95

Prices slightly higher in Canada

Payable by Visa, MC or AMEX only ($10.00 min.), No cash, checks or COD. Shipping & handling: US/Can. $2.75 for one book, $1.00 for each add'l book; Int'l $5.00 for one book, $1.00 for each add'l. Call (800) 788-6262 or (201) 933-9292, fax (201) 896-8569 or mail your orders to:

Penguin Putnam Inc.
P.O. Box 12289, Dept. B
Newark, NJ 07101-5289
Please allow 4-6 weeks for delivery.
Foreign and Canadian delivery 6-8 weeks.

Bill my: ❏ Visa ❏ MasterCard ❏ Amex _____(expires)

Card# _____

Signature _____

Bill to:

Name _____

Address _____ City _____

State/ZIP _____ Daytime Phone # _____

Ship to:

Name _____ Book Total $ _____

Address _____ Applicable Sales Tax $ _____

City _____ Postage & Handling $ _____

State/ZIP _____ Total Amount Due $ _____

This offer subject to change without notice.   Ad # 893 (3/00)